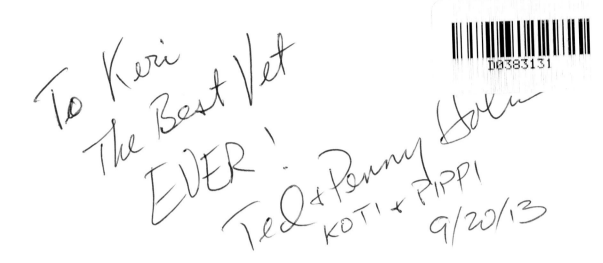

To Keri
The Best Vet
EVER!
Ted + Penny Holm
KOTI + PIPPI
9/20/13

VERSATILE
VIZSLA

VERSATILE VIZSLA

MARION I. COFFMAN

P.O. Box 7027 • Loveland, CO 80537
Alpine Publications Inc.

Printed in the United States of America
First Edition
      4   5   6   7   8   9
ISBN: 0-931866-54-5

Library of Congress Cataloging-in-Publication Data

Coffman, Marion I., 1928-
    Versatile vizsla / Marion I. Coffman. -- 1st ed.
        p.   cm.
    Includes bibliographical references and index.
    ISBN 0-931866-54-5 : $34.95
    1. Vizla. I. Title.
SF429.V5C64   1992
636.7'52--dc20

                                         91-40141
                                            CIP

Contents

There is a special place in life,
A goal I must attain.
A dream that I must follow,
For I won't be back again.
There is a mark that I must leave,
However small it be.
A legacy of love for those,
Who follow after me.

— *Author unknown*

Foreword

AS a breeder, dog fancier, AKC Sporting Dog judge, and a friend, I thoroughly enjoyed reading *Your Versatile Vizsla*. The history of the Vizsla breed is also a history of the Magyar people and, in this book, the evolution of one is intertwined with the other, giving a better understanding of values and lifestyles. Marion covered the development of each in an interesting approach.

Marion Coffman loves all dogs, but she is intensely involved with the Vizsla. Her dogs have been her companions and friends in a loving and civilized way for many years. Some people have an instant rapport with their dogs, and Marion is a prime example. In her book she clearly, patiently, and lovingly shares her knowledge with the reader. If you heed her advice on puppy raising, you will be well on your way to developing a strong, lifelong bond with your new Vizsla.

While many books deal with diseases, ailments, and whelping problems that confront a dog and his owner throughout the former's life, Marion's book is practical, complete, and succinct as it relates to the Vizsla. Her background in nursing uniquely qualifies her in this area. The chapters on breeding and whelping are excellent and should be easily understood and followed by the first-time breeder.

Marion, and her Cariad Vizslas, have greatly influenced the development of the breed. From her line of breeding have come not only the top-winning show records, but the first Triple Champion in AKC history. In her book she demonstrates the knowledge, understanding, and empathy for Vizslas which will enable them and their owners to reach the heights of distinction.

— *Howard Falberg*

To Loki and Bear,
those wonderful, once-in-a-lifetime Vizslas.
They lit up my life.
And to Kutya — you did us proud.

Preface

I came upon the Vizsla scene a little later than most of the early importers and developers of the breed in this country. Actually, I did not even see my first Vizsla until 1965. At that time I had been active for several years with Golden Retrievers, training and showing in both conformation and obedience. I was thinking of taking on a new breed when I met Joe Cunningham and his Glen Cottage Vizslas. It took me another two years of watching Vizslas before I was convinced that it was the breed for me. Glen Cottage Loki Barat became the turning point in my life. From that lovely, dark "runt of the litter" came thirty-two champions, including the first Triple Champion in AKC history. Loki was a grandson of Ripp Barat, and a great-grandson of Broc Olca, both Vizsla Club of America (VCOA) Hall of Fame members. In 1986 Loki himself was elected to the Hall of Fame for his outstanding contribution to the breed.

The history of today's Vizsla is a composite of fact and fiction, legend and conjecture, that often lacks specific dates and descriptions. However, by closely studying the history of Hungary and its people one is able to combine both the development of the country with the use and type of dog desired for specific conditions. What we do know is that in feudal times, hunting was the exclusive privilege of wealthy landowners, and they demanded high standards in everything associated with hunting. We owe them much for developing the wonderful Vizsla.

In twenty-four years of breeding, raising, training and exhibiting innumerable Vizslas, I have accumulated a wealth of practical experience and knowledge which I hope, by putting into book form, will interest all Vizsla owners, whether first-time buyer or experienced breeders or exhibitors.

All puppies are appealing; it is how they grow up that makes the difference. Hopefully, the photographs of young puppies will help the beginner to the extent that he will be able to make a wise choice when selecting his first Vizsla. I hope I have emphasized often enough that the Vizsla has to be a close family member and live in the home to be truly appreciated. His intelligence, affection, and wonderful personality put him on a level far above most breeds.

My treatment of genetics and its application to the breeding of Vizslas may seem beyond the understanding of the beginner (although I have tried to keep it simplified), but it is only through some knowledge of how the genes function that we can have control over the results of any breeding program. My main advice to each breeder is never to compromise — aim for quality from the first litter to the last, and do not settle for anything less than the best.

Most authors offer thanks to their spouses for loving support, and I am going to do the same. My husband, Rodger, has supported my love for the Vizsla both financially and physically these many years. He has shared the joy of new puppies, new champions, and new records won, and he has shared the sorrow of the loss of so many aged ones. He has encouraged me to write this book and share the love, rewards, and understanding my Vizslas have given me.

My thanks and appreciation to Pat Boelte for her encouragement, advice, and ideas. My most sincere thanks go to the many owners around the country who responded to my need for special photographs, especially Mark and Bonnie Goodwein who did many of the detailed shots. Thanks also to Brent Aronson for my first quail hunt, and to him and Ron Hershberger for help with my field chapter.

I hope readers enjoy the book as much as I enjoyed putting it together.

— *Marion I. Coffman*

Introduction to the Vizsla

OWNING a Vizsla will change your life forever. The Vizsla Standard calls for the breed to be "demonstratively affectionate," and whether they are jumping up to lick your face, grabbing your wrist in their mouths, sharing your bed, chair, or lap, or just bringing a favorite toy, they are impossible to ignore.

The Hungarian Vizslas represent the best in both sporting dog and loving, loyal companion. They are the smallest of the all-around pointer-retriever breeds and size is undoubtably one of their most attractive characteristics.

Vizslas hold a unique position for sporting dogs — that of both house companion and family dog. They do not make good kennel dogs and only reach full capacity as enjoyable companions when they are members of the family. Bred and owned originally by wealthy Hungarian landowners, Vizslas were a very privileged canine, holding a high place in the Hungarian sporting circles but not expected to sleep outside at the end of a day in the field. The Vizsla always lived and traveled with his family and was as much a family member as a child.

Vizslas are striking in appearance. Their beautiful golden-rust color never fails to attract attention. They are a joy to watch in motion and they are just as enthusiastic about chasing a ball as a butterfly, leaf, or squirrel. Still, they can freeze to a perfect pointing statue when they have quartered a bird field and found game.

Vizslas are highly intelligent — do not ever underestimate the learning potential of a 10-week-old puppy. They are obedient and ever striving to please, but they are bored without a challenge. Because of their highly developed sense of humor and intelligence they cannot only be taught easily, but can think up things to do on their own. For example, a Vizsla can use his front feet or mouth to figure out how to turn doorknobs or open re-frigerators, or even get out of his crate. They have been known to climb ladders and sit on roofs. They can ring bells, collect shoes, empty wastebaskets, be official greeters, and guar-dians.

A comfort seeker, the Vizsla would rather sleep on your bed than on the floor. They think sofas were made especially for them and, if allowed, will remain lap dogs for life. They will follow you around the house from room to room rather than be left alone for even a minute. If you put a Vizsla outside, he will sit on the doorstep begging for you to come out with him.

In the field Vizslas combine all the attributes of the Pointer, Setter and Retriever. They point by instinct, and are very close-working dogs (no more than 150 yards from their owners), making them the ideal weekend companion gundog. They are fast, extremely birdy, en-thusiastic, and with a good nose. They have soft mouths, retrieving game without damag-ing or marring, and are diligent workers on upland game, with discriminating bird sense. Their striking color in the field and quick, graceful movements make for an enjoyable combination.

The Vizsla has become more popular in the show ring as his aristocratic appearance, dig-nified and balanced bearing, intelligence, ani-mation, and graceful carriage have attracted new enthusiasts. Once you own a Vizsla, you are hooked for life. Each new owner finds a new and different way to incorporate this dog into his life.

Vizslas can cheerfully go backpacking, hik-ing, and camping, or accompany their owners to the office. They enjoy tobogganing in snow and they love water. A perfect companion on a boat ride or in the swimming pool at home, a Vizsla will be happy to swim or retrieve balls all day. He will even be content just to stand for hours in a shallow stream and silently watch small fish swim around him.

As trained obedience dogs, Vizslas have been used to educate and entertain at civic events, county fairs, schools, and even nursing homes. They have been employed as drug sniffers, guide dogs for the blind, and as hearing-im-paired dogs. Their easy care and intelligence make them an ideal choice. Obedience com-petition enthusiasts will tell you that this is where the Vizsla excels. They are natural showmen, and are never happier than when they have been given something to do. They are easily bored with the repetition of the novice classes but they find their element in the jumping and retrieving exercises of the ad-vanced classes. It comes as no surprise to Vizs-la owners that the first dog in American Kennel Club history to earn the Triple Championship title for completing field, show, and obedience championships was a Vizsla. The breed is truly versatile.

For an emotionally disturbed or handicapped child the Vizsla can be sensitive and loving. In many cases a child has been able to relate closely to a dog when everything else has failed. A Vizsla will bond easily to someone who needs him in a special way.

Vizslas teach so much about love because they have so much to give. Their affection is always there for you. They are a joy to know and happiness to own. They are full of strength, vitality, elegance, and beauty. A Vizsla is a 365 days a year companion, accepting the role of protector, friend, and hunter. A Vizsla is truly a dog to be proud of owning, and he is forgiving in case you call him a dog — he is a *Vizsla*.

Star and Vic wait for the start of the Fun Run sponsored by Purina in Houston. Owned by Brent Aronson.

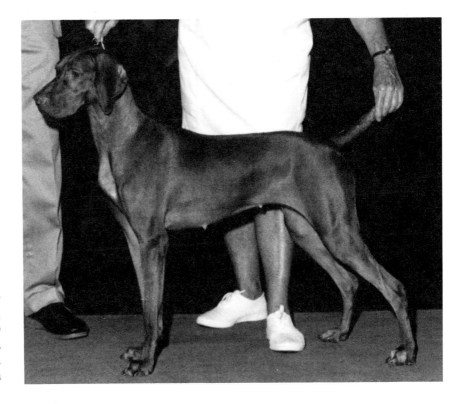

Ch. Cariad's Pride N Joy
Sire: Ch. Taunee's Loki
Santana, CD
Dam: Cariad's Cassandra
Baratam
Owner: Marion Coffman

Photo of oil painting done by Elizabeth Mihalyi of her Panni XV while a refugee in Austria in 1948.

1

Early History of the Hungarian Vizsla

THE history of Hungary, and how its Magyar nomads had hounds that may have been the ancestors of the Vizsla, first appeared in writings around 890 A.D. Before that date there is little to be found in history books that is not guesswork. Language researchers have been able to establish the nomads as descendants of Ugrians and Finns. Included in that group were people from areas ranging from Turkey to Manchuria and Mongolia. There have been many attempts through the years to find the original home of the Magyars but all without success.

While it has been established that most of the nomads raised reindeer, cattle, and horses, it is doubtful that there was any set pattern of breeding dogs for a specific use during the years of their wanderings. Their "camp dogs" were yellow–colored descendants of the Mastiff and hound-type dogs encountered along the way.

When the Great Wall of China restrained the nomads in their search for new grazing lands and diverted them to the west, out of that melee of footloose tribes the Hungarians began to emerge. Climbing the Carpathian Mountains, they crossed the Vereke Pass, and in 895 A.D. moved into the area that came to be known as Hungary. Primitive carvings in stone found in the Carpathian regions and estimated to be 1,000 years old, show the early Magyar hunter with dogs closely resembling the early Vizsla.

The Magyars elected Stephen I (969–1038 A.D.) as their first king and settled down to periods of farming between wars with invading hordes. It was during King Stephen's rule that the country was centralized. He organized Hungary into counties, each headed by a count. Conveying land titles to these major nobles assured Stephen of their aid during times of need. This form of feudalism kept its grip longer in Hungary than in almost any other country in Europe.

This organization of tillable lands then entered a peak period that would last almost three centuries. With the landowners settled down to peaceful farming, horse, cattle, and pig raising, along with the production of grain, there was time to develop a breed of dog related to these landowners' needs and the type of hunting they pursued.

A Mastiff–hound strain of dogs was originally found in the great mountain spine stretching east to west across Asia and Europe, comprised of the Himalayas and the mountains of Tibet — the very area that the Magyars had traversed in their nomadic search for farmland. The Magyar's yellow dogs, closely allied with this type of dog, were then selectively bred until the hunter had dogs with specialized abilities. The breeds they developed, despite their diversity in size and color, resembled each other in the acuteness of their sense of smell, a pronounced stop, large floppy ears, and a short muzzle.

At this point the sporting element was secondary to necessity. Bird hunting was done with these scenting dogs to search for game, and falcons to retrieve it. Thus it was that the pointer type evolved as a suitable dog. Their

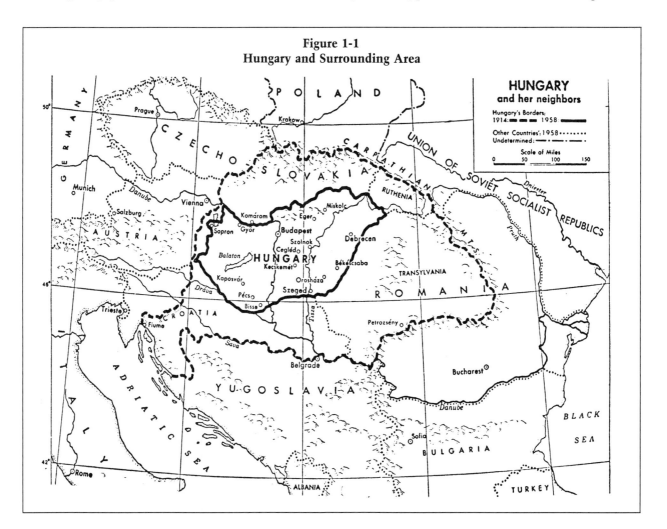

Figure 1-1
Hungary and Surrounding Area

quiet movements and deliberate action made them especially useful to the Magyars. This pointer type could also drive the pheasants and partridge they located into nets, or serve as useful retrievers of the dead birds, although at that time they probably lacked the soft mouth of the later dog.

In 1526 the Turks invaded Hungary, occupying and ruling it for the next 150 years. The Turks brought their own dogs which were subsequently bred to the Magyar's yellow pointers. Since the Magyars were supposed to have come from that part of Asia which was the land of the Turks, the crossbreeding of these dogs could be considered as a sort of "linebreeding." The name *Vizsla* in Turkish means *seek* and in Hungarian it means *point*. The Vizsla obviously did both at this stage of development.

With the end of Turkish occupation, Hungary was ruled by the German Hapsburgs and, under this new rule, the inheritance of the land was limited to the upper class and its descendants. These were the people who played an important part in the early development of the Vizsla as we know it today.

During this period in history, firearms were developed. In order to use this new weapon, the sportsman had to get it ready by seeing that the priming was right and lifting the lid of the pan holding the powder before advancing to shoot game. He needed a dog that could stand still during this procedure. Such a dog could then be found all over Eastern Europe — one developed by many German and English hunters, mainly from the early hound types brought in by the Normans.

Small shoots were organized by the aristocratic landowners, and hunters from other countries were invited to bring the pointing dogs they had developed. These dogs were eventually crossed with the yellow–colored dogs of the Hungarians, and the Vizsla began to evolve into the breed as we know it today. The Vizsla became versatile in the hunting of both birds and small game. A dog would show he had found game by freezing into position with his head held low, one forefoot raised, and his tail held straight out. As better guns developed, the use of the Vizsla grew into the

Drawing from the Viennese Illustrated Chronicle, done by Carmelite Friars in 1357 show a hunting scene with an early Vizsla. *Photo courtesy of Joan Hunt.*

pointer-retriever type that brought the game back from a distance. They were also used as tracking dogs to find the large hares and small deer prevalent in that area.

Once the Hungarian hunters had developed the Vizsla into the type of dog needed for their specific hunting areas, they kept it pure for many generations to come. As sportsmen came from other countries and saw how the yellow pointer blended into the wheat fields, making it easy to stalk game, they wanted it crossbred with their own dogs.

German hunters took male Vizslas back to their own country to improve their stock, as did sportsmen from Austria and England, where they crossbred them to their Pointers and Irish Setters. When the first field trial for Vizslas was held in 1882 near Budapest these sportsmen from Germany and England brought their dogs back to compete. However, the island where the trial was held was not felt to have the same hunting conditions as the dogs were exposed to inland, and the following year it had little support and interest.

At this point the aristocratic landowners realized that they had remaining but a few of what they had originally bred and called the Vizsla. They set about rebuilding the breed and it is believed that they may have used the Schweizhund (a solid red hound with powers of scent said to be equal to those of the Bloodhound) to bring the desired coat color back to the Vizsla. They may also have used a Pointer from Transylvania to re-establish the pointer ability. Since this Pointer had as his ancestor a black, tan, and white hound from the same area, the white markings on his chest and feet also appeared on the Vizsla.

Whatever breeds were used, once the Vizsla was re-established, dedicated owners joined forces to keep the breed from extinction.

Hubertus, an organization formed by Hungarian hunters in 1917, established a hunting dog's division which greatly helped in preserving the breed. This organization selected a dozen Vizslas which it felt represented the true breed as it was depicted in the early historic drawings, and all the registered Vizslas in Hungary descend from this foundation stock of three males and nine females.

The re-establishment of the breed was drastically affected after the end of World War I when, in 1920, the Hungarian Peace Treaty was signed at the Grand Trianon Palace in Versailles. Before the war, Hungary had 125,000 square miles of which sixty-one percent was farmland. Romania was given most of the Transylvania area; Czechoslovakia got all of Northern Hungary; Yugoslavia acquired most of the south of Hungary; and Austria was awarded part of the west. Some 3 million Hungarians were transferred to foreign soil. The kingdom that had withstood the Turks, the Hapsburg Empire, and great power jealousies, now underwent a gigantic land reform. The Vizslas, personal gundogs to the large aristo-

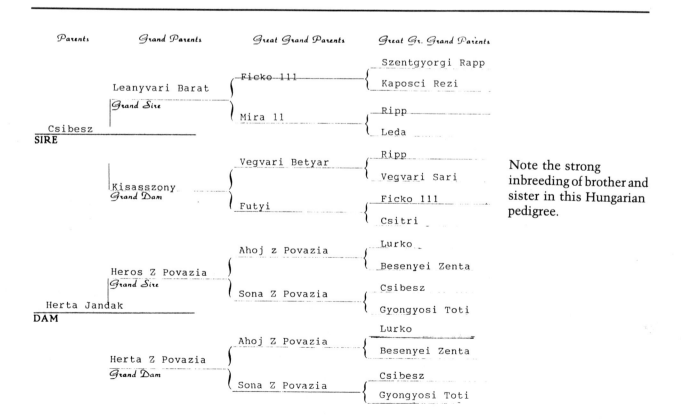

Parents	Grand Parents	Great Grand Parents	Great Gr. Grand Parents
			Szentgyorgi Rapp
		Ficko 111	Kaposci Rezi
	Leanyvari Barat		Ripp
	Grand Sire	Mira 11	Leda
Csibesz			
SIRE			Ripp
		Vegvari Betyar	Vegvari Sari
	Kisasszony		Ficko 111
	Grand Dam	Futyi	Csitri
			Lurko
		Ahoj z Povazia	Besenyei Zenta
	Heros Z Povazia		Csibesz
	Grand Sire	Sona Z Povazia	Gyongyosi Toti
Herta Jandak			
DAM			Lurko
		Ahoj Z Povazia	Besenyei Zenta
	Herta Z Povazia		Csibesz
	Grand Dam	Sona Z Povazia	Gyongyosi Toti

Note the strong inbreeding of brother and sister in this Hungarian pedigree.

cratic estate owners, were now living in parts of Hungary that had become other countries.

This, however, did not deter the dedicated owners, and late in 1920 the Magyar Vizsla Breeding Association was formed with the help of Dr. Kalman Polgar, Count Laslo Esterhazy, and Elemer Petocz. The heads of the organization were Dr. Polgar, Andre Felix, Karoly Baba, and Balazs Otvosf. When this group held their first field trial in the fall of 1922 they drew tremendous support.

The Association drew up the first Vizsla Standard at this time and kept separate stud books for both the show and field dogs. The standard was revised in 1935, at which time the Federation Cynologique International (FCI), a worldwide federation of national dog clubs, gave recognition to the breed.

Hungary had suffered political battles and armed aggression through hundreds of years of history, but the next battle fought changed the world. It also took the Vizsla out of his native land and eventually to America.

By March 1941 German troops occupied part of Hungary and World War II had started. When

Soviet planes dropped bombs on North-Hungarian towns, Hungary was forced into the war against the Allies by German pressure from within.

Before the war 5,000 Vizslas had been registered in Hungary, but with the Soviet invasion and occupation, eighty to ninety percent were destroyed or lost. The Vizsla had been the personal gun dog to the wealthy land owners and many of these owners fled the country, leaving their dogs behind. Hundreds of Vizslas were destroyed by the Communists who resented the breed as a symbol of wealth. Many emigrants were able to take their Vizslas with them when they fled, but most of the dogs had to be left behind in other countries when the owners immigrated to America.

Elizabeth Mihalyi was one of the Vizsla breeders to flee Hungary. She took with her eleven loaded farm carts, forty–four horses, two carriages, and her Vizsla, Panni XV. Panni was pregnant with her third litter but when she whelped the puppies during the flight, it was impossible to care for them, and they had to be destroyed. Elizabeth arrived in Austria

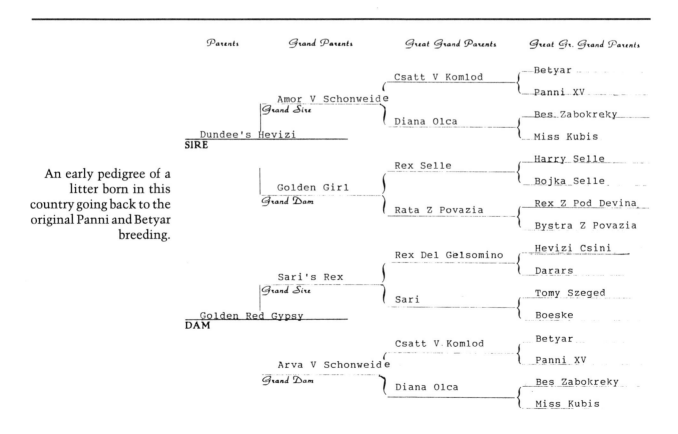

An early pedigree of a litter born in this country going back to the original Panni and Betyar breeding.

Above: Photo from the 1982 Breeder's Tour of Hungary shows that the breeders there have regained the quality in their dogs that was lost during early years of the Communist government. *Right:* 1942 photo of Hevizi Lurko at the Festetic's kennel in Toponar, Hungary.

two months later and was able to keep Panni with her; she managed to remain outside the refugee camp by doing menial jobs. An accomplished artist, she also painted portraits for American army officers in exchange for food for herself, her relatives, and Panni.

During the six years she spent in Austria awaiting passage to America, Elizabeth located a male Vizsla owned by a Mr. Hofbauer of Vienna. The dog had been born at the kennels owned by the Festetics in Hungary and rescued by their gamekeeper. The Hofbauers had named him Betyar and registered him as the first Vizsla in the Austrian International Dog Registry. Panni was registered as the second Vizsla in this book and when she gave birth to Betyar's puppies the litter was registered as the first Vizsla litter born in Austria. Born 19 January 1948, there were seven puppies which all carried a name beginning with a "C." Several of these puppies went to people living in Italy and Germany, and they were the foundation stock for Vizsla breeders in those countries.

Elizabeth Mihalyi had to leave both Panni and Panni's daughter with the Hofbauers in Austria when she finally emigrated to America. However, several years later she was able to have a bitch from Panni's line sent to her and she continued breeding Vizslas in her new country. Panni lived past 17 years of age and her contribution to the breed both in Europe and in America gave many Vizsla owners their foundation stock.

Vizslas that had been left behind in Hungary when the aristocratic landowners were forced to flee in 1944 were impossible to identify. It is probable that in future breedings brother and sister were unknowingly bred to each other. Without identifying pictures or pedigree backgrounds, new litters were finally registered as "of an unknown breeding" in the Hungarian stud books that were compiled in 1955.

During the post-war years when the Communist government was established, purebred dogs and activities related to them were discouraged, especially with a breed that had belonged to the aristocracy. Dog breeding and canine pursuits became more and more difficult as the Hungarian people struggled to survive and rebuild. In 1956, after a revolt against the regime, living became easier in Hungary, and dog activities again began to flourish. In that year Mike Kende was appointed Director of the Magyar Dog Breeders' Association, and he started to register dogs that fit the Vizsla Standard. These registered dogs were then able to be bred to those that had identifiable pedigrees, but if any questionable characteristic appeared in the litter it was culled. It was only by means of this careful culling that the breed was finally re-established in its homeland.

With the government's bare tolerance for dog shows and breeding, difficulties again surfaced in 1973 when the license tax for a dog was raised to an amount similar to what most workers earned in a month. This action did more damage to the breed than both World Wars. Dogs became too costly to own and had to be abandoned; breeding came to a standstill. It took several years before the Hungarian Kennel Club was able to persuade the government to change this luxury tax on dogs but when it was finally resolved, the hunting breeds were given a tax break.

All field training and hunting in Hungary now falls under the province of the Ministry

Elizabeth Mihalyi shown at a hunt in 1944 in Hungary with the dam of Panni XV, Csitri. *Photo courtesy of Dr. Louis Mihalyi.*

Above: In Hungary Vizslas hunt fur and feather. G.N. Toth shows one morning's catch by his Vizsla.

Below: The Vizsla in Hungary today is still used for hunting wild boar, fox, and rabbits, besides the native birds.

Waiting for the judging of the bitch class at the dog show in Budapest in 1982.

A Vizsla at rest after hunting demonstration for the Breeder's Tour of Hungary in 1982.

of Agriculture and Food. The Forestry and Wood Industrial Office regulates the hunting seasons, hunting grounds, and licenses. Field trials are held by the National Association of Hungarian Dogbreeders under the FCI regulations.

The standards for the Vizsla, like other European versatile breeds, are high, and the dogs are expected to perform superbly. They are used for hunting deer and wild boar, along with the native partridge, pheasant, fox, and rabbit. The dog has to possess a keen nose, and retrieving and tracking instincts.

In the early 1930s Hungarian foresters and gamekeepers interbred the Vizsla with the Wirehaired German Pointer to get a dog with a heavier coat, suitable for work during the colder periods. The result, known as the Wire-

Wire-haired Vizsla puppy in Hungary.

Wire-haired Vizsla adult. The course coat protects the dog from injury while hunting in heavy cover. *Photo courtesy of Judy Heiser.*

Photo taken in 1952 shows possibly the first litter of Vizsla puppies born in America. Breeder — Frank Tallman. *Photo courtesy of E. Mihalyi.*

Early import Fritz V Auskia, son of Rex Selle, is the grandsire of Dual Ch. Bobo Buck Selle.

haired Vizsla, is everything the shorthaired Vizsla is, except for a rough coat, but as they are mainly required by professional hunters, greater emphasis is laid on their hunting performance than on an elegant appearance. With this weatherproof coat they are able to lie quiet in wait on foggy, frosty autumn dawns or to fetch wild ducks out of icy water and then sit for hours in a boat. The Wirehaired Vizsla has slowly gained popularity in Canada where the Vizsla has two classifications: smooth and wire coats. However, to date, it has never created interest in the U.S.

In Hungary today Vizslas have regained their early popularity and pride held by the Hungarian people as the national dog of Hungary. From the early differences in color, size, bone and body type, and half a century of crossbreeding, the present–day Vizsla has finally evolved.

The breed's many excellent attributes are not only bringing him appreciation by the hunters but he is loved and valued as a family dog.

THE VIZSLA IN AMERICA

As Hungarian refugees fled to safety in different areas of Europe, their Vizslas attracted interest from dog lovers in the American Occupation Forces. A man stationed in Italy in October 1950 sent a dam and her two young puppies to a friend, Frank Tallman, in Kansas City. Sari and her pups Shasta and Tito were exhibited for the first time at the Heart of America Kennel Club Show in February 1951. A few months later Frank Tallman sent to Europe again, for another Vizsla, and this time Rex

Del Gelsomino, a 2–year–old male, was sent to him from Italy.

Although one of the first Vizslas known to be in the U.S. was a bitch bought from Mike Kende by Joseph Pulitzer in 1938, very little is known about her and there is an absence of records which show other Vizslas in this country in the years between that date and when Frank Tallman imported Sari.

In 1951, after Jack Hatfield and William Olsen, both from Minnesota, had seen Tallman's dogs at the Chicago International Kennel Club Show, they became interested enough

which many of the first breeders were able to start from. In 1953 a veterinarian from Minnesota, Dr. Ivan Osborn, imported Broc Olca, his first Vizsla, with a five-generation pedigree registered in the Czechoslovakian stud book. Dr. Osborn had previously imported Hess V Schloss Loosdorf and Marika Dravavolgy from breedings which had come down from the Betyar and Panni line in Austria, but neither dog was able to be registered in America. Dr. Osborn imported over forty Vizslas and, along with the other early importers, he bred extensively and campaigned widely for the breed.

Atari V Taszaltha, son of Czechoslovakian import Gingo V Schloss Loosdorf.
Dam: Tasza V Naudvar

Gingo V Schloss Loosdorf, early import owned by Vern Halmrast, is shown after a day of duck hunting. Gingo is the sire of the first AKC Vizsla champion, Miclos Schloss Loosdorf.

in the breed to arrange shipment of their first Vizslas from Austria and Germany. The first to arrive were puppies, Gelse V Schloss Loosdorf and Gemme V Schloss Loosdorf, 3½–month–old littermates, two generations down from the Betyar to Panni breeding in Austria. Jack Hatfield and William Olsen eventually imported a total of fourteen Vizslas.

Frank Tallman bred his Rex Del Gelsomino to Sari in 1952 and had the first litter of Vizslas born in America. However, without a complete pedigree, the litter could not be registered, but it was to be the foundation stock

Hungarian refugees were now coming to America in large numbers, many of them bringing their own Vizslas. In most cases, pedigrees and registrations had been lost in the flight from their homeland and there was no way to establish claims of ancestry. One of the immigrants was Jeno Dus, who had been the last director of the Vizsla Club of Hungary. Before he had fled, Dus buried the original stud books, leaving them forever unclaimed. With the loss of these documents, the only complete stud book for the Vizsla was Czechoslovakian registration. Although there were a great number of litters born in America during the early days of importing Vizslas, when Dr. Osborn bred Broc Olca to his Czechoslovakian–registered bitch from the Povazia line, the litter was the first to have a complete six-generation pedigree.

Jeno Dus settled in northern New York state soon after arriving in this country in 1952, and had one of the first litters born in the east when he bred his bitch Jutka, from the Rex Del Gelsomino to Sari breeding, to his male Pik in 1954. From that combination came Csisckas of Goncoltanya, one of the foundation stud dogs for the Hunts of Tennessee. The Hunts had also imported dogs from Czechoslovakia and they were to become a leading force in breeding and promoting the Vizsla over the next twenty years.

In June 1953, the Magyar Vizsla Club of America was organized and it held its first meeting in Des Moines, Iowa. The first elected officers were: President Jack Hatfield, Vice-

Diana Olca, owned by Alexia Manner in Austria, was the top producing bitch there in 1954. Several early imports to this country came from Diana.

An early photo of Broc Olca shows his excellent water retrieve of a duck. *Photo courtesy of Joan Hunt.*

Broc Olca, imported from Czechoslovaki by Dr. Osborn, considered to be one of the most valuable stud dogs both in Europe and the U.S. *Photo courtesy of Joan Hunt.*

Imported from Czechslovakia by the Hunts, Morho Z Povazia was the sire of Adalyn Hunt, the first American-born Vizsla imported into England by the Hunts.

Nine month old Red Ryder, son of Brilliant, an English import owned by Charles Hunt.

Left: Radar Z Povazia, early import owned by F. Verrall, shown pointing a pheasant in this 1955 photo. *Photo courtesy of Joan Hunt.*

Below: A 1955 litter born at the Hunt's kennel from Morho Z Povazia and Asta Z Povazia, both imported from Czechoslovakia by the Hunts.

President Harry Holt, Secretary Charles Hunt and Treasurer Roy Hawkinson. In 1960 the club met the requirements of the AKC by submitting 500 three-generation Vizsla pedigrees, and on 25 November 1960 the Vizsla was officially the 115th breed to be recognized by the AKC and was accepted into the Sporting Group. At that time the club dropped the Magyar from their name and became the Vizsla Club of America (VCOA). A new standard for the breed was approved in December 1961, and remained the same until it was revised again in 1983.

Vizsla breeders have always been determined to keep the true heritage of the breed in mind. The years following AKC acceptance were crucial in setting standards for the Vizsla breed. With ther first appearance at AKC dog shows and field trials their popularity grew. The first Vizsla to gain a show championship title was Miklos Schloss Loosdorf, owned by the Warholms in California in 1961. Miklos followed that with several group placings and was the top–winning Vizsla in 1962.

Csisckas of Goncoltanya, owned by the Hunts, was the second Vizsla to finish a cham-

Rakk Selle showing excellent style on point. Rakk was the winner of the Derby stakes at the first field trial held by the Magyar Vizsla Club.

Rakk Selle shown doing a water retrieve as six month old Teato of Shribob watches.

Sire: Rex Selle
Dam: Asta Olca
Owner: Dr.Osborn
Photo courtesy of Joan Hunt.

Nikki of Bayview after winning the Puppy and Derby stakes in the 1955 Magyar Vizsla Club of America field trial.
Handler: Robert Foster

Nikki of Bayview shows excellent form retrieving at only six months of age.
Sire: Broc Olca
Dam: Iskra Kubis
Owner: G. Yamamoto
Photo courtesy of Joan Hunt.

Csillan V Hunt
Sire: Ch. Csisckas of Goncoltanya
Dam: Ch. Annavolgy Arany

Csisckas of Goncoltanya shown after a day's hunting in Utah. *Photo courtesy of Joan Hunt.*

pionship title and the first to earn a Sporting Group placing. He was the top–winning Vizsla in 1961. Csisckas lived to the age of 17 years and had an impressive future as a stud dog. His son, Ch. Csopi V Hunt, was the top–winning Vizsla in 1967.

The Hunt's bitch Annavolgi Arany, imported from Hungary in 1957, was the third Vizsla to finish a bench championship and the first bitch to do so, when she earned her title in 1961. The fourth champion was also a bitch, Duchess of Shirbob, owned by Walter Campbell.

Only nine Vizslas finished their championship titles in the year following AKC acceptance, and only twelve gained titles in 1962, but the breed was rapidly attracting attention in the show ring, and more dogs were being brought into the U.S. and being bred. The next few years saw an increase in registrations and activity in obedience and field competitions.

The Vizsla enjoyed several years in the obedience trials even before AKC recognition. One of the earliest to gain a title was Georgia's Auburn Heidi, owned by Hayward Phillips in Georgia. Heidi, three generations down from the Betyar to Panni breeding, earned her Companion Dog (CD) title in August 1958. In November 1962 the AKC granted a license to the VCOA to hold their first field trial granting points towards a field championship. Open to other breeds in the Open Limited All-Age stakes, the trial drew a total of fourteen entries with Vizslas making an exceptional showing. Ripp Barat, owned by Betty Kenley of Arizona, and handled by Paul Sabo (who had also handled Ripp's sire, Broc Olca), placed first in both the Open All-Age stakes for Vizslas only, and the Open Limited All-Age stakes. Ripp Barat is considered by many to have been the best field trial Vizsla on record, having had over seventy wins and placements in all types of competition. He was voted into the VCOA Hall of Fame in 1981 for his outstanding contribution to the breed.

Vizslas had to compete in field trials against other pointing breeds in those early years of trialing and, unfortunately, it took considerable effort before judges were willing to recognize the Vizsla as being a breed apart. With

Annavilgyi Arany, imported by Joan Hunt from Hungary, became the third Vizsla to earn a championship title.
Sire: Ripp
Dam: Flora

Osborn's Starfire, winner of the Puppy Stakes in the 1961 VCOA Field trial.
Sire: Rakk Selle
Dam: Osborn's Miss Kubis

Derekas Rex Selle, son of Rex Selle, is shown winning the Derby stakes at the 1961 VCOA field trial. *Photo courtesy of Joan Hunt.*

Am. & Can. Fld. Ch. Ripp Barat
Sire: Broc Olca
Dam: Rata Z Povazia
Owner: Betty Kenly
Photo courtesy of Joan Hunt.

Vizsla Club of America Field Trial 1962 winners of Puppy Stake. 1st) Osborn's Cimmeron, 2nd) Urcsi V Hunt, 3rd) Brok V Loosdorf, 4th) Amber. *Photo courtesy of Joan Hunt.*

that acceptance, the Vizsla slowly began to build a reputation in field trial circles. All who worked with the Vizsla — handlers and owners alike — were impressed by their easy trainability, intelligence, great driving power, stamina, and tremendous desire to hunt. The breed's sensitivity and desire for praise and affection along with the close–working tendencies led to an increase in owner–handlers who enjoyed owning a companion gun dog.

In the thirty years since AKC recognition the Vizsla has gained a respected place as an all-around sporting dog: adaptable and comfortable in a variety of tasks. Vizsla owners and breeders have kept the heritage foremost. The courage and loyalty to the breed shown by displaced people from a war-torn country, makes us continuously grateful for the affection, companionship, beauty and enjoyment of our Vizslas.

Betty Kenley shown with Ripp Barat after winning the Amateur Gun dog stakes at the 1962 VCOA field trial. 2nd) Osborn's Red Rebel. 3rd) Alma Olca.

Dual Ch. Futaki Darocz, the first Vizsla to gain a Dual Championship.
Sire: Ch. Hunor
Dam: Piri
Owner: Bela Hadik

The first Vizsla Field Champion was Broc Selle, bred by Dr. Osborne, and owned by Don Anderson of Colorado. Broc earned his title in 1964.

Bela Hadik of New Hampshire was one of the strongest promoters of the Vizsla as a Dual dog. His Futaki Darocz gained a show championship in July 1965, two months after earning a field championship, thus becoming the first Dual Champion for the breed. Darocz was also the sire of two Dual Champions, Bobo Buck Selle and Szekeres Kis Szereto, (the first Vizsla bitch to earn the title).

THE VIZSLA IN CANADA

As far as can be determined, Vizslas were first brought into Canada by residents of Hamilton and St. Catherines, Ontario. Ed McCoy, a well–known Hamilton sportsman, was a strong promoter of bird dog field trials in Ontario and he had one of the first Vizslas in the area — a male by the name of Gay V Schloss Loosdorf registered in the Field Dog Stud Book in 1953. Following this purchase, several of his friends bought imported Vizslas

Kitron's Buster Bayleaf on his way to a Canadian championship at eight months of age.
Sire: Ch. Cariad's Jakab Barat
Dam: Ch. Yorsla's Cinnamon sassy, CD.
Owner: Kit Browne

Ch. Yorsla Yankie Boy, a top winning Canadian Vizssla in 1976 and 1977.
Sire: Ch. Trisha's Bogart by Loki
Dam: Charisma Trifari
Owner: Sue Bush

and the breed was firmly established in Ontario, mainly in the Niagara Peninsula. The first imports from Europe into Canada were no different than the U.S. imports in that they almost all came from Czechoslovakia and Austria.

In the fall of 1957 two Vizsla puppies — a male and a female — were imported from Czechoslovakia by A. G. Gerle of Montreal. Mr. Gerle, by his own initiative, got the Vizsla recognized as a breed in the Canadian Kennel Club, prior to such acceptance by the AKC, despite larger numbers and interest in the U.S. Mr. Gerle's dogs were shown as a recognized breed at the Ladies Kennel Club Show in Montreal in 1958.

Soon after, in his desire for a more athletic field type Vizsla, Mr. Gerle imported a bitch from Budapest — Csikcsicsi Ari-Nora. Born 27 July 1956, she was already a mature bitch at the time of import, but he enjoyed a number of field trial wins in the All-Breed competition with Ari-Nora.

Mr. Gerle had raised several litters of Vizslas with the puppies being sold fairly wide in the Montreal area, where some of their descendants are still to be found. Some were shipped to other parts of Canada (British Columbia, in particular), and they formed a nucleus of breeding units wherever they went.

In Western Canada several persons, usually with relatives in the Western U.S., imported Vizslas for their personal use and, in many cases, decided to breed litters. By the end of the 1950s more and more Vizslas were being brought into Canada, from both the U.S. and Europe. Of particular note is the founding of the Bakony Kennels in Calgary, by Elizabeth and Albert Kemenes-Kettner. They started with a bitch named Greta Selle Karpat and then later acquired Agres Z Povazia and Lyska Z Tatler from Mr. Gerle, followed by imports from Hungary — Arokparti Parazs, Approd Prucsok, Egerhegyi Tinci and Bodrogkozi Aprod. The first three named made a major contribution to the Canadian Vizsla breedings from the early 1960s on. At the same time they also exchanged puppies with the Hunts in Tennessee to broaden their breeding base. Phil Wright founded his Napkelte Kennels when he became the proud owner of "Suntan" (Janora's Pawlane Suntan), bought from John Janora in Buffalo, New York. During the next few years he was to import fifteen more dogs from both Hungary and the U.S.

In about the mid–1960s another kennel of note was founded in Winnipeg. Wes and Dorothy Basler of St. Vital became attracted to the breed and started with stock from Minnesota, mainly from the kennel of Frank Engstrom. The Baslers became significant breeders of Vizslas carrying the "Gamefinder" prefix. After importing and breeding Wirehaired Vizslas for many years, the Baslers were instrumental in getting the Canadian Kennel Club to accept the recognition of them in 1978, making the Vizsla breed further designated in their registrations as "Smooth" or "Wirehaired."

Also in Winnipeg and just slightly prior to the Baslers, Elizabeth Kubinyi started her breeding program with dogs descended in part from Mr. Gerle's early breedings and in part from U.S. sources.

On the west coast several breeders were in operation on a small scale. Of particular note were the Sullivans, with mainly Selle breeding from the U.S. The Sullivans produced some of the top–winning dogs in the area for show and field activities.

From these early beginnings came many other top breeders and kennels: Gary MacDonald and his Kutya Kennels, Mrs. Maria Sved and her Farkasmajor dogs, the Petras of Toronto, Mr. Palasty of Stratford, Sue Bush of Ontario, and Stan and Bill Robson. Many stayed with the breed for several years and made outstanding contributions and some have gone on to other activities, but they have all left an imprint on major lines in Canada today.

Winning Sporting Group Team at International Show, Chicago, 1963. Left Handler: Lucy Jane Myers Right Owner: Joan H. Hunt. Dog at left is Ch. Csisckas of Goncoltanya.

The head is lean and muscular, eyes medium in size and depth of setting.

2

The Vizsla Standard

A breed standard is a set of qualifications and detailed descriptions covering the ideal example of a breed. The purpose of the standard is to provide a blueprint with which to work in order to have uniformity. However any standard is subject to individual interpretation and variations developed within each breed, depending on the country and conditions.

The first Vizsla Standard was drawn up in 1922 by Hungarian breeders. It was revised in 1935 and again in 1956. The following Standard was translated by Nandor Szayer from the book *A Kutya* which was published in Budapest in 1970.

THE HUNGARIAN STANDARD

General Appearance

A medium–sized, dark amber pointer-retriever breed of noble appearance. The breed developed from the native Hungarian hound and the yellow Turkish hunting dog.

His characteristics are well–developed but smoothly lined muscle structure, gracefully flowing movement and an alert expression.

The height of the males ranges from 57–64cm (22½–25¼ in.) and of the females from 53–60cm (21–23 in.). Their weight ranges from 22–30kg (49–67 lb.).

His characterizing traits are: intelligence, good temperament, obedience, and learning ability. From the point of view of hunting, he possesses a good nose, excellent pointing, retrieving, and tracking ability.

and forming a well–rounded "V" shape. The nose is fairly large and rounded looking at it from the front. The nostrils are open and movable. The neck is of medium length and well proportioned. It sets in at the upper half of the body. It is muscular and arched below the back of the head. The skin is looser at the throat than elsewhere but not to the extent to form a dewlap.

Photo from the 1982 Breeder's Tour of Hungary shows the muzzle of this Vizsla to be the same length as his skull. *Photo courtesy of Judy Heiser.*

The median line starts on the top of the skull and runs down the center of the nose. The step, or stop, between the eyes is moderate on the Vizsla.

The Head

It is lean, and the top is slightly inclined forming a groove along its median line. The stop is short. Its angulation ranges between 30° and 35°. The top of the muzzle is straight. The occiput is slightly visible. The end of the muzzle forms a wide angle with its top. The lips are dry and they fully cover the opening of the mouth. The teeth are orderly and perfectly closing. The canine teeth meet in a scissors bite. The eyes are medium sized, slightly oval shaped and almost totally parallel with the top of the muzzle. The eyelids are well closing. The haws should not be visible. The ears are slightly larger than medium–size, set fairly low and hanging down. They are thin

The Body

The chest is deep and long. It should reach down to the elbows at its deepest point. The forechest is moderately wide and protruding to the front. The forechest bone (sternum) is long and strong. The cross section of the chest is oval and the ribs are moderately sprung. The back is straight and muscular and of medium length. The pelvis is sloping but without a steep drop of the croup. The rear is well muscled and its side lines are almost parallel. The high point of the top line is over the loin and it is 1–2cm (⅜–¾ in.) lower than the shoulder height. The setting of the tail is slightly low, and it should be carried horizontally. In tranquil state of mind the tail is hanging. The tail is docked one–third off. For a grown dog it should reach down to the level of the stifles.

The Legs

The front legs are like columns. They support the body in a well–balanced manner. They are muscular. The shoulder is very muscular although not rigid. The shoulder blades are sloping. The hind legs are strong boned and extremely muscular. They are perfectly proportioned. From a side view the angulation at the stifle is between 110 and 120 degrees. The thighs are long and the hocks are deeply set. The feet are short and round. The toes are short and tightly closed. The pads are large, hard, and rough. The nails are flexible and well arched. Dewclaws are to be removed.

The Coat

Coat is short, smooth, strong bodied and close lying. It is dense and shiny. The individual hair is thick and elastic. The coat has a greasy feeling to the touch. The color of the coat is solid. It is a slightly darker shade than bread crust. The whole animal is pigmented in a medium brownish amber color. The nose, eyelids, edge of the lips, eyes, pads, and the nails are a slightly darker shade of the color of the coat, never black or grey.

Movement

The characteristics of his gait are a lively trot or a ground-gaining gallop.

Body Proportions

The male and female body proportions are somewhat different. The male is slightly stockier and coarser; the female is longer and finer. The standard sizes of the individual physical parts are expressed as a percentage of the height. (The numbers given in parentheses are for the female.)

Length of body	100%	(102)
Length of head	42%	(43)
Depth of chest	44% min.	(38 min)
Width of forechest	33% min.	(32 min)
Chest circumference	117%	(114)
Length of muzzle	46% of head	(48)
Length of ear	76% of head	(75)
Length of hair	0.5cm to 1.5cm	

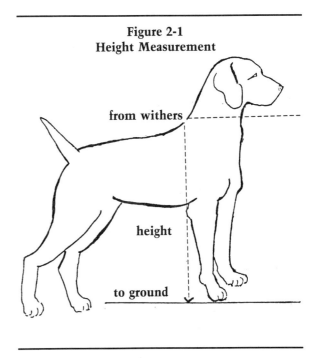

Figure 2-1
Height Measurement

Reasons for Disqualifications

The dog must be disqualified if, in general, he does not satisfy the previously affixed type description of the Hungarian Shorthaired Vizsla or his faults are of such magnitude that their occurrence in his offspring would result in the deterioration of the breed.

Dogs that are of mixed breed of a Shorthaired and a Longhaired Vizsla may not be registered in Hungary as a Shorthaired Vizsla even though their hair may be short.

Further reason for disqualifications are: parti-colored nose; black nose; loose droopy eyelids; droopy, open drooling lips; parti-colored coat; larger than 5cm (2 in.) diameter white spot on chest; light grey eyes; less than 56cm (22 in.) tall for a male or 52cm (20½ in.)

for a female, or more than 65cm (25 in.) for a male or 62cm (24½ in.) for a female; undershot or more than 2cm (⅘ in.) overshot bite.

Faults

Overly fine body structure; loose body structure; loose eyelids; loose hanging lips; weak bone structure; too small or too large; coarse head; bloodhound-like head; faulty teeth; poorly docked tail; not dense enough coat.

Minor faults include pendulous flews.

THE VIZSLA CLUB OF AMERICA, OFFICIAL STANDARD 1983

The VCOA drew up its first Breed Standard in 1960 when it was given recognition by the American Kennel Club. It was revised in 1983 with the most outstanding changes being in size, general appearance, coat and eye color and defining body descriptions.

General Appearance

That of a medium–sized, short–coated, hunting dog of distinguished appearance and bearing. Robust but rather lightly built. The coat is an attractive solid golden rust. This is a dog of power and drive in the field, yet a tractable and affectionate companion in the home. It is strongly emphasized that field–conditioned coats, as well as brawny or sinewy muscular condition and honorable scars indicating a working and hunting dog, are never to be penalized in this dog. The qualities that make a "Dual dog" are always to be appreciated, not depreciated.

Head

Lean and muscular. Skull moderately wide between the ears with a median line down the forehead. Stop between skull and foreface is moderate, not deep. Foreface, or muzzle, is of equal length or slighlty shorter than skull when viewed in profile. It should taper gradually from stop to tip of nose. Muzzle square and deep. It must not turn up as in a "dish" face nor should it turn down. Whiskers serve a functional purpose; their removal is permitted but not preferred. Nostrils slightly open. Nose brown. Any other color is faulty. A totally black nose is a disqualification. Ears thin, silky, and proportionately long, with rounded leather ends, set fairly low and hanging close to the cheeks. Jaws are strong with well–developed white teeth meeting in a scissors bite. Eyes are medium in size and depth of setting, their surrounding tissue covering the whites. Color of the iris should blend with color of coat. Yellow or any other color is faulty. Prominent pop eyes are faulty. Lower eyelids should turn neither in nor out since both conditions allow seeds and dust to irritate the eye. Lips cover the jaws completely and are not loose or pendulous.

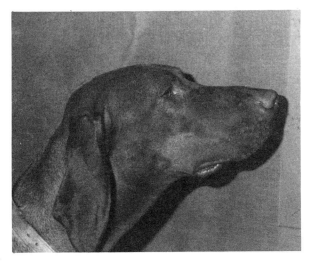

This nose is slightly longer than the head and does not end squarely but tapers slightly to a point.

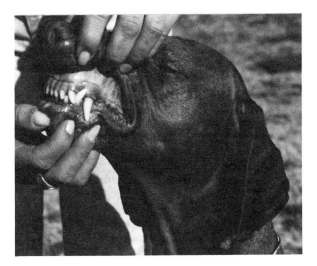

The correct bite: a scissors bite.

This muzzle ends squarely with the upper lip covering the lower lip neatly.

Neck and Body

Neck is strong, smooth, muscular, moderately long, arched, and devoid of dewlap, broadening nicely into shoulders which are moderately laid back. This is mandatory to maintain balance with the moderately angulated hindquarters. Body is strong and well proportioned. Back short, withers high and the top line slightly rounded over the loin to the set of the tail. Chest moderately broad and deep, reaching down to the elbows. Ribs well sprung; underline exhibiting a slight tuck-up beneath the loin. Tail set just below the level of the croup, thicker at the root and docked one–third off. Ideally, it should reach to the back of the stifle joint and be carried at, or near, the horizontal. A tail undocked is faulty.

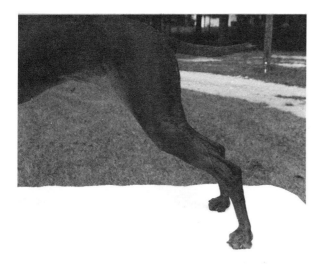

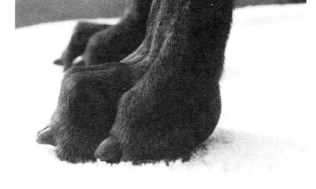

The ribs are well-sprung and the underline exhibits a slight tuck-up beneath the loin.

Feet are cat-like, round and compact with toes close. Nails are brown and short.

Shoulder blades proportionately long, sloping moderately back. Forelegs are straight and muscular.

The correct chest is moderately broad with a fairly prominent brestbone.

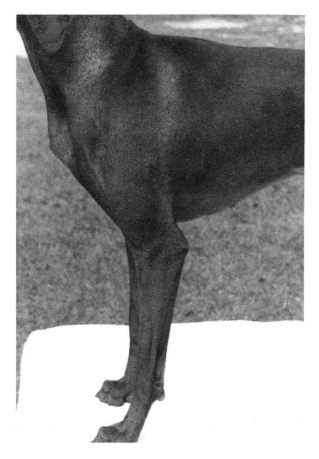

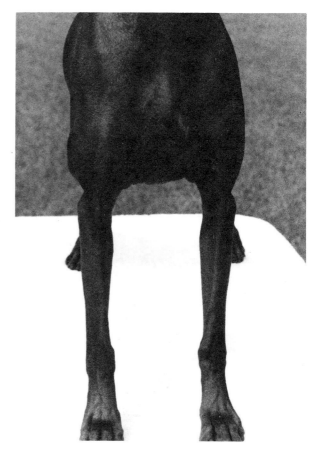

Forequarters

Shoulder blades proportionately long and wide, sloping moderately back and fairly close at the top. Forelegs straight and muscular with the elbows close. Feet are cat-like; round and compact with toes close. Nails brown and short, pads thick and tough. Dewclaws to be removed on front and rear. Hare feet are faulty.

Hindquarters

The hind legs have well–developed thighs with moderately angulated stifles and hocks in balance with the moderately laid back shoulders. They must be straight as viewed from behind. Too much angulation at the hocks is as faulty as too little. The hocks are let down and parallel to each other.

Coat

Short, smooth, dense and close lying without woolly undercoat.

Color

Solid golden rust with different shadings. Solid dark mahogany red, or pale yellow are faulty. Small white spots on chest are not faulted, but massive areas of white on the chest, or white anywhere else on the body are reason for disqualification. Occasional white

---

Hind legs have well developed thighs. They must be straight as viewed from behind.

Upper and lower thighs should be strong and well-muscled.

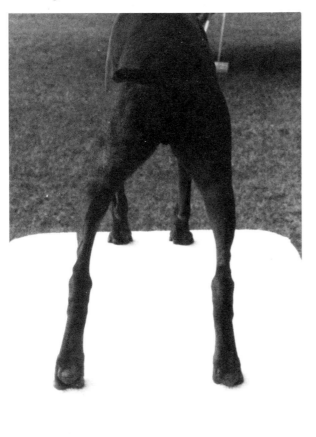

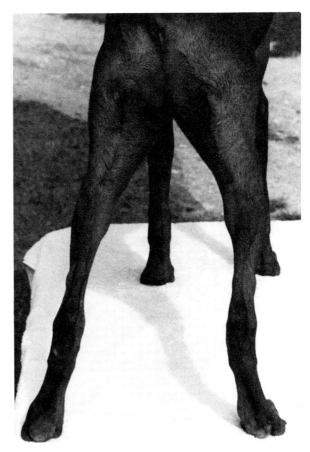

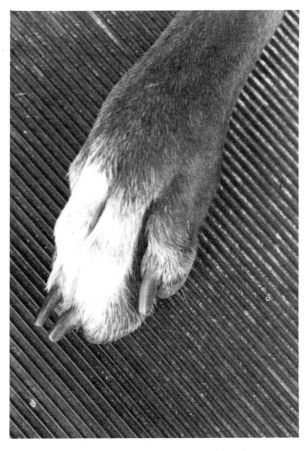

White extending above the first knuckle of the toes is a disqualification.

A massive area of white on the chest is faulty.

hairs on toes are acceptable but white extending above the toes is a disqualification. White due to aging shall not be faulted. Any noticeable area of black in the coat is a serious fault.

Gait

Far–reaching, light–footed, graceful and smooth. When moving at a fast trot a properly built dog single-tracks.

Size

The ideal male is 22–24 in. at the highest point over the shoulder blades. The ideal female is 21–23 in. Because the Vizsla is meant to be a medium–sized hunter, any dog measuring more than 1½ in. over or under these limits must be disqualified.

Temperament

A natural hunter endowed with a good nose and above-average ability to take training. Lively, gentle-mannered, demonstratively affectionate and sensitive though fearless with a well developed protective instinct. Shyness, timidity or nervousness should be penalized.

Disqualifications

Completely black nose.
Massive areas of white on chest.
White anywhere else on body.
Solid white extending above the toes.
Any male over 25½ or under 20½ in. at the highest point over the shoulder blades.
Any female over 24½ or under 19½ in. at the highest point over the shoulder blades.

ANALYTICAL DISCUSSION OF THE VIZSLA STANDARD

Extreme departures from the Breed Standard do not occur very often and newcomers to the breed should realize that even though opinions and interpretations are bound to vary somewhat among breeders, most Vizslas do fit the

1. Muzzle
2. Flews
3. Stop
4. Occiput
5. Neck
6. Withers
7. Loin
8. Croup
9. Hock
10. Pastern
11. Lower thigh
12. Stifle
13. Thigh
14. Flank
15. Chest
16. Forearm
17. Elbow
18. Upper arm
19. Shoulder
20. Back

Standard. The Standard describes, trait by trait, those features which make up type and soundness, with each minor trait considered in relation to the whole dog.

Head

A good head is essential for true type. It should be well–proportioned without being heavy or coarse; and even though both males and females have a lean, smooth look to their heads, the male head is slightly larger and wider. The skull is fairly flat on top without the occipital bone being conspicuous. The median line, formed by furrow of bone formation, should start on the top of the skull and run down the center of the nose. The step between the eyes, called the stop, should be moderate and never as abrupt as in the Cocker Spaniel or the Pointer. It should lend definition to the sculpture around the eyes without being a deep groove. Without that step between the eyes, a Vizsla has what is called, a "roman nose". The length of the nose is slightly shorter than the skull.

The muzzle ends squarely instead of tapering to a point. The flews, or upper lips, should not be pendulous but should end cleanly at the bottom of the jaw. The Breed Standard says nothing about the reverse layer of hair growing on the top of the nose, but quite a few Vizslas have what looks like velvet rubbed the wrong way. Brown pigmentation of the nose is called for in the Standard, but it is actually closer to the color of the dog's coat, as is the area around the mouth and eyes.

The eyes are medium sized and more almond shaped than round, and although the color of them should be in harmony with the coat color, a dark eye is always preferred. The eyes should have an expression of intelligence, alertness, and trustworthiness. A light eye lacks this and often appears hard instead of soft and gentle. The lower eyelids should fit tightly and not droop, allowing dust and dirt particles to irritate.

The ears are fairly large and long, set slightly lower than most sporting breeds, laying close to the side of the head. Correct ear-set contrib-

The female's head will be smaller and narrower than the male's but in correct proportion to the entire body.

An incorrect ear set ruins the expression. These are too long and set a trifle low on the head.

utes to an alert expression, and too low an ear-set ruins the look of even the prettiest dog. The ears should be thin with rounded ends, reaching no longer than the canine tooth.

The teeth should meet in a scissors bite, the front surfaces of the lower incisors touching the inside surfaces of the uppers. While an even bite, in which the teeth meet end-to-end is often allowed, this type of bite causes considerable wearing of the teeth and so the correct scissors bite is preferred.

Neck and Forequarters

The neck should be well–muscled with tight–fitting skin. There should not be any excessive dewlap, which is loose skin on the neck and throat area. The length of the neck should be in proportion to the length of the back and they should balance each other. If a dog is in balance, a longer neck and back, along with correct angulation, will give a longer reach and smoother moving gait. There is a slight arch to the neck and it should flow smoothly into the shoulder area without any obvious flatness at the withers, which are located directly behind the base of the neck, at the neck and back junction.

The Vizsla Standard calls for moderate angulation both on forequarters and hindquarters. Angulation is the angle created by two bones meeting at various joints. One of these junctures is where the shoulder blade, or scapula, meets the upper arm, or humerus. The most desirable angulation is 105°. Along with correct shoulder blade angulation, a strong muscular development in that area is also necessary or good movement will suffer.

The lower arm must also be strong with good muscles. Lack of exercise can weaken the muscles to the point of loose elbows and weak pasterns.

The chest is deep, reaching down to the elbows. The forechest bone, the prosternum, is prominent. A too narrow, or under-developed chest will restrict lung capacity, but a too broad or round rib cage will interfere with front movement and cause a dog to be out at the elbows, or toe–in.

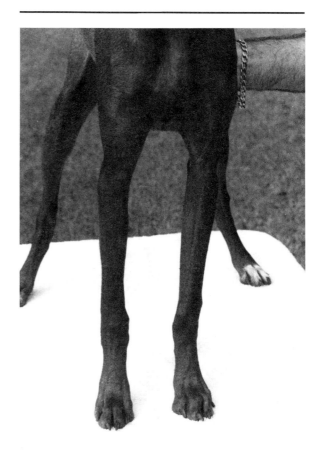

Faulty front: too narrow, with the chest not reaching to the elbows.

Back and Body

It is interesting to note that the Hungarian Standard calls for a back of medium length; in fact it defines the differences in length of back between the male and female. Our Standard calls for a short back, but balance must be the first consideration. Coupled with a short neck, it would be hard to get the long reach or the ground-gaining gallop stated in the Hungarian Standard. The total dog must be considered as height must balance length.

The back must be straight and strong without any signs of a weak, or sagging, top line, or a roached back. There is a slight rise over the croup with the tail set on slightly lower than the back.

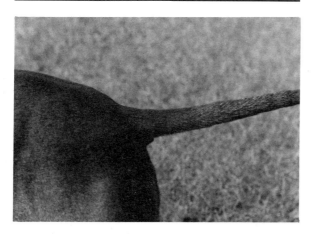

Topline slightly rounded over the loin to the set of the tail.

Tail

Since the Vizsla does not have the high tail-set that is usual in most sporting breeds, many judges in the conformation ring fault the breed incorrectly. The tail is carried outstretched above the level of the back and should not drastically bend towards the back in a curve, as in a "gay" tail. The tail is usually in motion as evidence of the happy nature of the breed. Docked to the correct length, it should reach down to just opposite the stifle joint when measured.

The abdomen should have a moderate "tuck-up" beneath the loin. Exercise keeps the area tight and strong.

Hindquarters

The pelvic bones should be strong and wide, covered with well-developed muscles. The angles at the junctures of the hip socket where the hip bone, or femur, attaches to the pelvic girdle should be equal to the angle of the shoulder blades in order to have freedom of movement and a good length of stride.

The lower thigh area should also be well muscled. When viewed from the side, a properly angulated dog will stand naturally with his rear pasterns perpendicular to the ground

on a line just behind the point of his buttocks. With a short lower thigh, the legs will be under the rear too much and if the lower thigh bone is too long, the dog will appear to be over-angulated and give the impression of standing too far behind himself.

The hocks should be strong and turning neither inward or outward. Unless it is a genetic fault, weak hocks can often be corrected and strengthened with exercise.

The hindquarter angulation should be in balance with the angulation of the forequarters.

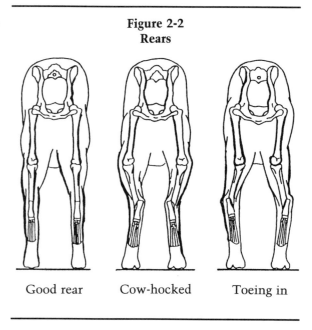

**Figure 2-2
Rears**

Good rear   Cow-hocked   Toeing in

Feet

Really good feet are genetic, although exercise can strengthen the muscles and improve poor ones. Feet are too often overlooked in the make-up of the complete Vizsla but are extremely important. The feet should have thick pads not only to protect them from injury, but to cushion effectively the impact on the forequarters. The toes should be close together and well knuckled. Flat feet are splayed, causing fatigue in an otherwise well moving dog. The nails should be cut short so they do not touch the ground. Long nails can rapidly break down the foot structure and take away the shock-absorbing effectiveness.

Balanced angulation, and balanced length of neck with length of back gives a longer reach.

Inadequate angulation will result in a poor moving dog and wasted energy.

Coat

The coat is short, smooth, and a golden-rust color. In some lines a slightly lighter or darker overall shade predominates, but all should have the lighter color shadings over the sides of the neck and shoulder. In some very dark lines this "saddle" is missing. A thicker undercoat will be present in cold weather but is easily stripped out in the spring. Good health assures a glossy sheen to the coat, making the Vizsla an attractive breed in any circumstance.

A small spot of white is permissible on the chest. There has always been a debate over what is actually considered as a "massive" area of white. Both the Canadian and the Hungarian Vizsla Standards spell it out to say no more than two inches. It is up to each breeder to interpret what could be considered "massive" but it is probably safe to say no larger than a couple of inches. White is permitted on the toes but not above the first knuckle, at which point it is considered to be on the foot.

The pigmentation of the nose, eyelids, and around the mouth is close to flesh-colored. Any black shades would be considered a sign of crossbreeding. Pads of the feet and nails are a darker shade of flesh. Eyes should harmonize with the coat color.

Gait

The Vizsla needs to have a far-reaching, smooth gait. A correct gait is dependent on correct angulation at both ends. If the front fails to match the rear, gaiting defects will show up in the form of crabbing, hackneying, and overreaching.

Crabbing occurs when the rear legs track to one side to avoid interference with the front feet. This action is usually caused by the dog having less angulation in the front than in the rear, in combination with a short back.

A hackney gait is shown in a dog that is trying to avoid the pounding his shoulders may take when a poorly angulated front restricts reach. The dog flips and extends his front feet just before they hit the ground in order to soften the thrust from the rear legs. The shorter steps mean that more of them will be needed

Figure 2-3
Rear Movement

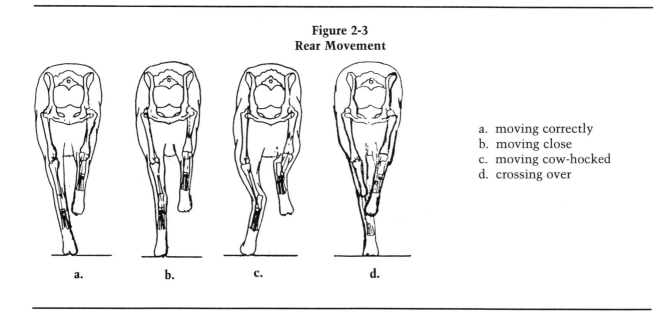

a. moving correctly
b. moving close
c. moving cow-hocked
d. crossing over

a.   b.   c.   d.

to get the dog where he is going. This is a terrible waste of energy for the dog in the field.

The trot is always the easiest gait in which to judge correct angulation. The diagonally opposite legs move back and forth at the same time, each taking equal portions of the stress on the joints, with the front feet leaving the ground just ahead of the hind feet. When viewed from the front or the rear, the dog's legs should tend to angle in toward a central line beneath his body, seeming to converge on one track as the speed increases. When this action, called single-tracking, is correct the rear legs travel on the same planes as the front without any extra twisting or turning out at the various joints.

Size

The Vizsla is a medium-sized, robust, but lightly built hunting dog. A large rangy appearance detracts from the aristocratic bearing that has long been associated with the breed. Certainly, too small a male may lack bone and substance, and too large a female may have too much. The desirable size has always differed with the breeder, governed only by the

disqualifying heights in the Standard. Overall appearance, balance, gait, and, above all, purpose and attitude must be given more emphasis as long as the dog is within the required limits.

Temperament

Not many Breed Standards describe a dog as "demonstratively affectionate" as does the Vizsla Standard. Any shyness or nervousness in the breed should be penalized, as should aggressiveness. The Vizsla is always willing to please, but training and corrections must be done gently, as a strong reprimand will make a Vizsla unsure of himself. He will accept discipline in an intelligent manner if it is not meted out with a heavy hand. He will be an eager, happy worker in the field or in the home, and always sensitive to the environment around him.

Being afraid of thunder, as so many Vizslas seem to be, usually has no relation to gun-shyness, but relates more to the fear triggered by a sudden drop in barometric pressure. On occasion even the steadiest working field dog will show nervousness in a thunder storm and need comforting.

CANADIAN KENNEL CLUB VIZSLA (SMOOTH) STANDARD

Origin of Breed

The Vizsla is of Hungarian origin, where various records indicate its history as going back many centuries. It was the companion hunting dog of the early warlords and landed aristocracy who used it for general purpose hunting. It was known in Hungary as the "Yellow" pointer. In North America it is used primarily as an upland bird dog, where its excellent scenting and retrieving characteristics have been widely acclaimed. It is a strong swimmer and also retrieves well in water.

General Appearance

The Vizsla is a short-haired, medium sized sporting dog. It conveys the impression of an alert, muscular, well-balanced animal with a distinctive and aristocratic appearance.

Temperament

The Vizsla is intelligent, calm, obedient, and easy to train. It is a sensitive dog which becomes attached to its owner and develops a strong but not overly aggressive protective instinct. In the field, the Vizsla is an eager, happy hunter which is at home on land and in the water.

Size

The standard size, measured at the withers, for the Vizsla is 58.42cm for males, and 55.88cm for females. A dog of good bone and substance in this size range shall weigh from 22.68 to 29.48 kg. A bitch weighs about 4.53 kg less. The length to height ratio should be about 1:1.

Coat and Color

The hair of the Vizsla should be short and dense and should lie close to the skin. Each hair should be thick and elastic and the coat should have a glossy sheen.

The correct color is a golden-rust, sometimes described as the golden color of the crust bread. In some strains slightly lighter or darker shades may predominate. A white mark on the chest under 5.08cm (2 in.) diameter is permissible but not desirable.

Head

a) Skull. Should convey an impression of being lean and muscular, with a median line down the forehead. The top line of the skull should be straight. The skull tends to be comparatively narrow in relation to its length, with that of the male being slightly wider. The occiput is slightly visible. The stop should be slight and sloping rather than abrupt.

b) Muzzle. The muzzle should be approximately the same length as the skull. It should be narrow, end squarely, and have clean straight lines.

c) Mouth. The jaws should be strong and well developed teeth meeting in a scissors or even bite. The lips should be smooth and well developed and cover the teeth tightly. The lips extend in a level line ¾ of the length of the muzzle.

d) Eyes. They should be almond shaped, bright and intelligent in appearance. The color is in harmony with or darker than the color of the coat; they should be moderately deep set. The eyelids close neatly and cleanly with no overlap. The nictitating membrane should not be overly exposed.

e) Ears. The ears should be thin, silky and moderately tapered with rounded ends. They should just meet under the jaw, or reach to the corner of the mouth, but should not extend as far as the canine teeth. They should be set about 1.27cm below the level of the skull and hang close to the cheek.

Neck

The neck should be of medium length in proportion to the body. It must be well muscled, with a definite arch at the nape and widened to blend smoothly into the forequarters. The skin of the neck should be smooth and tight.

Forequarters

a) Shoulders. The shoulder blade should be of medium length and must be held tightly in place. The angle formed by the shoulder blade and the humerus should be approximately 90°. The musclulature should be firm, smooth and clearly defined.

b) Upper arm (humerus). The bone structure should be heavy, smooth and well covered by strong firm muscles. The skin should be firm, pliable and smooth. The upper arm should be equal in length to the shoulder blade.

c) Lower arm. Strong, big bones with good muscles. The legs should be straight whether viewed from the front or side. The angle at the elbow joint should be approximately 135°.

d) Pasterns. The angle that the pastern makes with the lower leg should be nearly straight (175°-180°).

e) Paws. The paws should be cat-like with tightly closed toes and big rough pads. The feet should be webbed. The nails should be short, firm and well curved, and their color should be similar to that of the eyes, nose and coat. Dew claws should be removed.

Body

a) Topline. The topline should be broad and smooth and is slightly arched over the loin and croup to the base of the tail. There is a slight depression at the junction of the withers and the back.

b) Chest. The chest should be deep reaching down to the elbows and moderately broad. A cross section of the chest is oval with well-sprung ribs, narrowing between the elbows to permit free and easy leg movement. Width of the chest between the forelegs is at least 15.24cm for a male and 12.70cm for a bitch.

c) Loin. It should be broad, strong and well muscled.

d) Croup. It should be heavily muscled and smoothly rounded to the base of the tail.

e) Abdomen. The abdomen should be trim and neat with moderate "tuck up."

Hindquarters

a) Hipbone (pelvis). This is the framework which forms the basic support for the hind legs. These pelvic bones should be wide and strong. The musculature attaching these bones should be very well developed and gives strength to the hindquarters.

b) Upper thigh. This bone should be heavy, straight, round and smooth. Muscle attachments should be very powerful, broad and evenly distributed. The angle at the hip joint should be 90°.

c) Lower thigh. Should be well muscled. These bones should be longer than the femur. The angle at the stifle joint should be 110°-120°.

d) Hocks. The angle at the hock joint should be from 125°-130°.

e) Paws. Same as the front.

Tail

The tail set is lower than on the other continental pointing breeds. In motion it is carried outstretched, at or above the horizontal level. A portion is docked, approximately ⅓ so that the tip of the shortened tail is level with the juncture of the upper and lower thigh. It should be thicker at the base than at the tip.

Gait

Viewed from the front, the dog's legs should appear to swing forward in a free and easy manner, with no tendency for the feet to cross over or swing wide. Viewed from the rear the gait should be true tracking. The topline is level when the dog is in motion, while the head is carried high and the tails "flags" constantly at the proper level.

Faults

a) Very nervous dogs should be heavily penalized.
b) Very dark or very light color coat.
c) Hare feet.
d) Light yellow, green, blue or pop eyes.
e) Throatiness.
f) Dogs 4.53kg over or under the standard weight.
g) Dew claws not removed.
h) Roached, hollow, or camel backs.
i) Too steep a croup.
j) Undershot or overshot bites.

Disqualifications

a) A dog 5.08cm or more over or under the standard height.
b) White markings over 5.08cm on the chest or white markings anywhere else other than the chest.

The Vizsla conveys the impression of a well-balanced animal with a distinctive and aristocratic appearance. Shown here is Ch. Loughran-Field Sundance Boelte, owned by David Pomfret.

3

Selecting a Vizsla Puppy

MOST dog behavior specialists agree that the forty-ninth day of a puppy's life is the optimum time to go to his new home. However, several states in the U.S. have now passed laws prohibiting the sale of puppies under the age of eight weeks. Even if this is not a law in your state, do not accept a puppy under the recommended forty-ninth day. If a puppy is removed from his littermates and dam at too early an age, he will relate poorly to other dogs as an adult, and become overdependent on his human owners. A puppy needs the interaction with littermates, and the corrections his mother gives in the first seven or eight weeks of his life in order to establish behavior patterns for life.

The young puppy that you select is going to be a member of your family for the next fourteen or fifteen years. Choosing him should be an enjoyable experience, and a reliable and dependable breeder will gladly help you with your decision.

WHERE TO FIND YOUR VIZSLA PUPPY

A good puppy that is a pleasure to live with is the result of much planning by the owner of the bitch. Thought, and care of both the mother and her puppies,

39

Select your new puppy from a clean, healthy, well-cared for litter.

should be evident whether you are picking your Vizsla for field training, show or obedience competition, or a pet. The puppy you choose must be healthy, happy, exuberant, friendly, and raised in a clean environment. It is virtually impossible to have confidence in a breeder whose young puppies are too dirty and smelly to hug.

Finding a Vizsla breeder may require a little research. If there is a local all-breed club, it should be able to tell you whether it has any Vizsla owners as members. Attend dog shows, field trials, and training classes in your area. Vizsla breeders and exhibitors have a good communications network and hear of litters or planned breedings in other parts of the country.

The best references will be from the VCOA membership list. Writing or calling its secretary will give you a choice of breeders in your area. None of these referrals are recommendations; they are merely contacts. It will be up to you to locate the right puppy for your needs.

Do not hesitate to order a puppy unseen from another part of the country if the breeder has a good reputation. Breeders depend on their

Your new puppy should be friendly and out-going and show no signs of shyness or fear.

Look for a puppy with clear, bright eyes showing he is healthy and worm-free.

Look for intelligence, natural curiosity, and a happy attitude in selecting your new puppy.

reputations, not only for producing excellent dogs, but for fairness and honesty in all dealings, and any failure is very quickly known in "dog circles."

In your search for your new puppy, you will find that, through the years, established breeders have developed certain characteristics in their dogs for easy recognition of particular lines. These include a darker or lighter coat, a dark or light eye, a certain-shaped head and muzzle, top line or tail-set. All of these Vizslas fit the interpretation of the Standard, however you may find one "type" more acceptable than another. Learn to read and understand a pedigree. "Champion lines" do not necessarily mean that your new puppy will have a champion sire or dam. Look for some consistency in the pedigree which shows desirable line breeding.

If you are visiting breeders, you should be able to see the dam and get an idea of how her puppies will look at maturity. No honest breeder can guarantee that an 8-week-old puppy is going to be a top-winning field or show dog, only that the potential is there based on the breeding behind him.

MALE OR FEMALE?

The choice of sex is usually a decision based on your future plans for a puppy, but it will also involve personal preference. The male is usually larger than the female and if size is a consideration this may influence your decision. Both sexes are happy, healthy, friendly, outgoing, and intelligent. Both are "demonstratively affectionate" but the young male demands and requires more attention. Males are sweet, soft, dogs and need more reassurance than females. If he stubs his toe he is a bigger baby about it and needs to be comforted.

Both are mischievous diggers. They are lovable, exuberant, but tractable dogs that take training easily, and both are sensitive when corrected as they have a strong desire to please.

If a bitch's twice–yearly seasons are likely to bother you and there are no plans for breeding, she can be spayed by 8 months of age. Male or female — both will make wonderful companions and friends.

PICKING A FIELD PUPPY

The Vizsla is born with a natural instinct to stalk and point everything from a lizard to a grasshopper. The majority can easily be trained to be excellent companion gundogs but if you want one to eventually go into field trial competition, selecting just the right puppy is going to be more demanding than finding the best available show or obedience puppy.

Aim for litters from sires or dams that work as field dogs, or at least come from hunting and field stock. It would be nice if, because a puppy's sire and dam were field trial champions, each puppy in a litter would be automatically good at trialing. Unfortunately, that is not always the case. Do remember, when you are considering a puppy, to look for a breeder who has raised his litter with an eye toward developing naturally, from an early age, their curiosity and sense of adventure.

Try to attend field trials and watch dogs in competition to get a clear view of what you are after. Do not hesitate to ask owners about the trial records of their dogs. Most breeders are striving to breed Vizslas of true trial caliber with Dual title potential. You should be looking for a puppy from parents that have not only proven their working ability under actual field conditions, but who also meet the Vizsla standard. The qualities to look for in both the parents and offspring are: physical soundness, intelligence, correct size and conformation, a stable temperament, and a tremendous desire to hunt.

When looking at a litter there are many ways to test puppies for intelligence and alertness. One way is to take a tennis ball, roll it past all the puppies, and see which one is the most interested in the movement. Then separate the puppies that indicate a quick mind and, one at a time, roll the ball past each one. (Puppies that function well with littermates are sometimes insecure when by themselves.) Lastly, fasten a bird wing to the end of a pole, wave it back and forth in front of each puppy, and look for the puppy that shows aggressive interest and desire. When you are down to final selections, have a friend drop a book or clap

When selecting a puppy for field training look for one which displays natural curiosity and a tendency to "flash point" a bird wing.

his hands to see which puppy has natural curiosity about the source of the sound.

Unethical breeders have been known to breed their Vizslas with Pointers to give them a far-ranging dog in the field. Avoid a litter with questionable large amounts of white (a disqualification in the show ring) and aim for the qualities of the Dual Vizsla. The recently organized Magyar Vizsla Club was formed to promote the purebred Vizsla and educate the new buyer. Remember that the Vizsla has always been bred to be a close working field dog.

PICKING A SHOW PUPPY

There are numerous breeders across the country whose Vizslas have made outstanding achievements in the show ring. These breeders have established a reputation for breeding very closely to the Vizsla Standard to meet the demands of judges in the show ring. That is not to say that these dogs are incapable of winning at field trials — they are, as is evidenced by the long list of Dual Champions, NAVHDA, and hunting titles — but if you have established that you are interested in show ring competition, a breeder will help you pick your new Vizsla puppy with that future in mind.

A 7– to 8–week old puppy will go through a lot of physical changes as he grows, but if he closely resembles one of the parents you will be able to make an educated guess as to his appearance at maturity. You will want to choose a puppy with a nice blunt, or square muzzle, not snipey. The muzzle should have moderate flews, without being excessive. The eyes should be an amber color or darker, never yellow. The teeth must come together in a correct "scissors bite." (An incorrect bite in puppy teeth seldom corrects itself in the adult mouth.) The neck must be smooth and clean with no throatiness or loose folds of skin under the throat. The front legs must be straight, with strong pasterns. The feet should be rounded and tight, with the toes close together. At this age the feet may point out a little, but as the puppy grows and his chest spreads, his front legs will straighten.

Look for a nice length of neck, even in a

Right: There are different head types, all within the standard. A narrow, snipey look is the least attractive. Look for a nicely rounded head with a deep muzzle.

Below, left: Selecting a show puppy at eight weeks of age with the hopes of winning the coveted Best in show is every exhibitor's dream.

Below, right: At eight weeks of age, this puppy shows the excellent reach of correct movement.

7–week—old puppy, and the length of back in balance with the neck. A long-backed dog will have a longer reach and stride than one with a short back. The rib cage should be nicely oval. Too round a rib cage interferes with front movement and will cause a dog to move "out at the elbows" or "toe in."

A balanced puppy is characterized not only by the proportion of head size, neck, chest depth, and the ratio of body to legs, but also by the angulation of the fore and the hindquarters. "Angulation" refers to the bend in the

thigh bone meets the lower thigh. Do not expect to be able to recognize correct angulation and movement in a puppy. Many experienced breeders are unable to do it. They do, however, have an eye for a good puppy that just seems to put it all together.

The back should be strong and level with a slight rise in the croup before it slopes down into a tail set a little lower than most sporting breeds. The correct tail length should measure even with the knee joint. The hocks should be strong and turn neither in nor out at this point.

Selecting a show potential puppy that will fulfill all the expectations of his new owner should start with a litter from Champion parents. This puppy is Cariad's Surfstone Szuka.

joints and their influence on mechanical function and efficiency. The Vizsla should have moderate angulation which strongly influences the length of stride and freedom of motion. In picking a puppy, not only for show potential, but for work in the field, consideration must be given to how well he will be able to perform at maturity. If he has correct angulation as a puppy, he will have it as an adult. Angulation does not change with growth.

In an ideal front, the upper arm should slope down and back at approximately the same degree of angulation — preferably around 105°. The same should apply to the rear where the

They will strengthen considerably with correct exercise.

There should be no evidence of temperament problems in a puppy. If you have been able to see the parents you can judge for yourself from their behavior how their puppies will develop. If the dam, in particular, is a happy, outgoing, friendly dog, there is a good chance her puppies will be too. She is the parent that has the greatest environmental influence on the puppies. A puppy should not be timid about greeting strangers. On the other hand, he should not be stubborn and headstrong by refusing to be held and examined.

Do not turn down your choice of a puppy

because of a *small* amount of white on either his chest or feet. Although most breeders do not care for white to appear in their litters, allowance is made for a small showing in the Standard. The record–winning show dog in the U.S. had a small diamond on his chest which appeared in future generations of winners.

If you do not have the time or interest to pursue any "career choices" for a Vizsla puppy, inform the breeder that your puppy will not go that route, and will also not be used for breeding. Most breeders like their first-choice

his vaccinations, will be housebroken, and partially trained. The hard part will have been done for you and you will be getting a wonderful pet.

You may even find a breeder who has a spayed champion not needed in his breeding program. The Vizsla is a wonderfully adaptable breed and such a dog would love to get the attention of a one-to-one relationship instead of getting lost in the shuffle of a busy breeder or kennel. This older dog can easily fit into a home with children who lavish attention on

Decision time, with the selection finally narrowed down to two choices.

puppies to go to exhibitors and breeders, if possible, in order to maintain their reputation for producing top quality dogs. However a puppy bought just as a pet has had the same thoughtful care which went into each puppy in that litter.

Many breeders keep the pick of their litters for themselves to evaluate for future use. However, a choice show potential at 8 weeks can have a misplaced tooth at 16 weeks. A choice field potential puppy can suddenly turn gun–shy. Do not hesitate to ask the breeder if he has an older puppy available for a pet that has not lived up to his expectations. Usually this older puppy will have had the best of care, all

A puppy exploring on his own.

At 7 months of age, Szuka is already showing the style and class that will make her the top winning Vizsla bitch.

Ch. Cariad's Surfstone Szuka, three years later, has shown all the promise that her pedigree indicated.
Owner: Paul Gornoski
Handler: Bill Pace

him, or lead a quiet life with an older retired person whose old dog has died and who does not want an active young puppy.

If you prefer, and can find, an older Vizsla puppy already trained and ready to start a show or field career, you are in luck. But be prepared to pay a higher price, as this puppy is probably already showing the potential for greatness. You may also be asked to sign a contract with the breeder agreeing to continue the training and showing.

PAPERWORK

When you buy your puppy you are entitled to receive from his breeder an individual form to register him with the AKC. If the breeder has not received these forms back after registering the litter, he is required to give you information identifying your puppy in the meantime. This should include the name of the sire and dam, their registration numbers and the date of your puppy's birth.

When you do receive the registration form for your puppy, fill in the information carefully. On the front side put a choice of names.

On the back side fill in Section B, sign the form, and mail it, with a check, to the AKC. It will be returned to you with the puppy now transferred to your ownership. Place this registration in a safe place. You *must* send in the blue slip *within twelve months of the date it was issued* by the AKC. After that time your dog will not be eligible for registration.

Most breeders will also include in their packets for the new owners, a four– or five–generation pedigree, the Vizsla Standard, a history of the breed, feeding instructions, and vaccination and worming records.

Ask the breeder what kind of guarantee he gives concerning the new puppy's health. A reputable breeder will stand behind a guarantee to take the puppy back if he does not work out in his new home, or eventually shows a fault such as size, bad bite, hip dysplasia, or any other fault which would eliminate him from showing or breeding. They will either offer a refund or replacement puppy. Ask for a written contract spelling out such guarantees.

It will be up to you to take your new puppy to your veterinarian to be checked over within a few days of purchase. Take along the shot and worming record and follow your veterinarians recommendation for a schedule of care.

INSTRUCTIONS: PLEASE TYPE — OR USE **PEN. NO PENCIL.** Erasures or Corrections may cause return of application for an explanation.

SEC. A. TO BE COMPLETED IN FULL AND SIGNED BY OWNER OF LITTER (AND CO-OWNERS, IF ANY)

Check one and only one box

1 ☐ I (we) still own this dog, and I (we) apply for a LIMITED REGISTRATION–OFFSPRING WILL NOT BE ELIGIBLE FOR REGISTRATION and to have ownership recorded in my (our) name(s).

2 ☐ I (we) still own this dog, and I (we) apply for full registration and to have ownership recorded in my (our) name(s).

3 ☐ I (we) certify that this dog was transferred DIRECTLY TO THE FOLLOWING PERSON(S) ON

MUST be filled in by owner(s) of Litter

PRINT NAME(S) OF PERSON(S) TO WHOM DOG WAS DIRECTLY TRANSFERRED _____ mo. ___ day ___ year ___

ADDRESS _____

I CERTIFY, BY MY SIGNATURE, THAT I AM IN GOOD STANDING WITH THE AMERICAN KENNEL CLUB.

Signature _____ Signature _____

OWNER OF LITTER AT BIRTH   CO-OWNER (IF ANY) OF LITTER AT BIRTH

SEC. B. TO BE COMPLETED and SIGNED BY THE PERSON(S) NAMED IN SEC. A ABOVE, PROVIDED the person(s) owns the dog at the time this application is submitted to the A.K.C. If the person(s) named in SEC. A has transferred the dog to some other person(s), obtain a Supplemental Transfer Statement form from the A.K.C. Instructions for its completion and use are on the form.

I apply to The American Kennel Club to have Registration Certificate for this dog issued in my(our) name(s), and certify that I/we acquired it on the date set forth above DIRECTLY from the person(s) who Signed Sec. A above, and that I/we still own this dog. I agree to abide by American Kennel Club rules and regulations.

New Owner's Signature _____ New Co-Owner's Signature _____

New owner must complete this Section (PRINT)

Name _____
Address _____
City _____ State _____ Zip _____

Complete only if co-owner is named in Section A (PRINT)

Name _____
Address _____
City _____ State _____ Zip _____

Fees must accompany application. See top left corner of the reverse side for the required fees. Make checks payable to the American Kennel Club — DO NOT SEND CASH. Application becomes the property of the American Kennel Club when submitted.

You should receive a blue litter registration slip with your puppy. Fill it in with your name and address, sign, and return to the AKC with the correct fee. In 4 to 6 weeks you will receive the dog's individual registration certificate with the registered name that you selected printed on it.

Three-month-old Kamet Keri grew up to become CHAMPION Kamet Keri. Owner, Kay Thrasher.

4

Your Vizsla's First Year: Care and Development

THE first year in your Vizsla's life is an exciting period of development; a time of physical and mental change as he leaves his littermates and dam and bonds with his new family. How he is cared for in the first few months will establish the behavior pattern for later in his life.

HOMECOMING

Bringing a new puppy into your home is a wonderful time for everyone but it can be a frightening experience for the puppy. Try to bring him into a quiet house without a lot of friends and family crowding him. New smells, voices, and surroundings are going to confuse him. Let him explore each room on his own and make the first approach to all the "strangers."

Try not to alarm the puppy with a lot of new commands all at once. Cuddle and hug him and save the strong corrections for a later time. However, if he jumps on furniture which you have no intention of allowing him on, remove him gently and distract him with a toy.

Having decided on a call name for your puppy, start using it immediately and often. Do not use a name that will rhyme with, or sound like, an obedience command you intend to use later. Puppies respond more quickly to two-syllable names, especially when used in a happy tone of voice. Use your puppy's name when giving praise, calling him to eat, or encouraging him to come to you.

FEEDING PROGRAM

From now on the person who is feeding and caring for the puppy will, in effect, take the place of his mother. A bond is being established that will have a permanent influence on him. At no other period in his life will your puppy have the ability to achieve as strong a bond or rapport with humans as he will at this age.

If you have brought your puppy home at 7 or 8 weeks of age he will be staying on a schedule of four meals a day for at least the next two weeks. Try not to make any changes in his schedule until he has become comfortable in his new surroundings.

Your puppy should be on a good dry kibble meal, specially made for puppies, with a high protein content for good bone and tissue growth. This dry meal will be the basis of his feeding for the rest of his life, even when you later switch to an adult product. Use the same product, if possible, that the breeder has been feeding. Any sudden changes in diet can cause diarrhea.

Soak the kibble in a small amount of warm water to soften it a little, and add a small amount of boiled hamburger or canned dog meat. Once a day give him a pet vitamin tablet, or add the ground vitamin to his food. Good occasional additives can be cooked egg, cottage cheese, juice from vegetables, oils from canned tuna or sardines, but table scraps should be discouraged to prevent a fussy eater.

When you are unable to be home to feed the puppy his midday meal, you should make arrangements for someone else to come in and

Waiting until her puppy has tired from playing gives Christina a better chance of cuddling her.

take care of it. By the time your Vizsla is 10 weeks old, the night meal can be dropped and he will stay on three meals a day until he is 4 months old, with the amounts being increased as he grows.

Too much activity around your puppy at mealtime may distract him from eating, and in that case try feeding him in a quieter area or even in his crate. He may miss the competition of littermates eating from a shared pan. For that reason it could take him a few days to get accustomed to eating alone. It may even be that his food is a little cooler or warmer than that which he was in the habit of eating. Anything can put off a fussy eater but as soon as he settles into his new routine he will gain back any weight lost during this period.

If your puppy is too fat (being fat is not an indication of good health) decrease the amounts being fed. Too much weight on young bones and cartilage can cause problems later.

If, for convenience sake, you have to change your puppy's kibble make a choice of which commercial food you prefer and stay with it.

Table 4-1
First Year Feeding Chart

Age	Type of Food	Frequency
7 - 10 weeks	dry puppy formula kibble with additives	4 times a day
10 weeks to 4 months	dry puppy formula kibble with additives	3 times a day
4 - 6 months	dry puppy formula kibble with additives	2 or 3 times depending on condition
6 months - 1 year	dry puppy formula kibble	2 meals daily
1 year and over	maintenance or high protein kibble depending on work and energy needs	1 or 2 meals daily

Your puppy will be confused if you keep changing diets every week. If he looks good and eats well, do not make any major changes. A Vizsla thrives on consistency even though serving him the same food day in and day out may become boring to you.

Your Vizsla will get his adult teeth from 4 to 6 months of age and may go through a period of not eating. If so, keep him on three meals rather than cutting him down to two. Do not try to entice him with table scraps or special cooking as it will be easy to turn him into a fussy eater. Continue to add cottage cheese, vegetable and meat broths, and cooked egg to his dry meal and meat diet.

Because your puppy's rapid growth rate starts to slow down during the latter part of his first year, use proportions to keep him in good weight, but not overweight. The growing puppy needs amounts sufficient in quantity and quality to maintain him in good physical condition. Use common sense to adjust the amount of food given according to his growth spurts, activities, and weather. Any dog will eat less in hot, uncomfortable weather.

Make sure he is on a high–quality, nutritionally balanced, dry meal made especially for growing puppies, one which includes a higher protein and vitamin content. It is usually safer, with regards to avoiding bloat or gas, not to use a self-feeder. Instead, moisten the dry meal with a canned meat or add some cooked liver or hamburger and water before serving to

Just like a small child, a puppy needs frequent naps.

eliminate the high consumption of water after eating dry food. Keep fresh water available separately.

The use of vitamins and calcium supplements should not be necessary if your Vizsla is already eating a meal with sufficient amounts added, as most of them are. Such supplements can sometimes be toxic if given in too high a dose. If you are concerned about your puppy's coat being dull, or dry itching coat, or if he has suddenly developed a yen for grass, you may want to consult your veterinarian about improving or correcting your dog's diet.

The dog being trained or running in the field should never be fed before any type of exercise.

He should be left to rest after he has finished working and should not be fed until his entire system has had a chance to slow down. If he is only fed once a day, his one meal has to be of sufficient quality and quantity to maintain him in good condition and supply the extra energy needed. Because of all the energy he is using up, the working field dog's diet should be of utmost concern.

It is important to your Vizsla's regimen that a schedule is adhered to whenever possible. Not only will it keep his bowel movements regular but it will relieve any stress on his part.

Small children and puppies must have constant supervision.

CHILDREN AND PUPPIES

If there are small children in the home, explain to them that a puppy is not a new toy but a living creature that must be handled gently and correctly at all times. This puppy will grow up to be their friend and protector, but in the meantime he and the children of the house need to get to know each other.

Have the children sit on the floor when they want to hold the puppy. Young children make strange noises and movements which will alarm the puppy if he came from a breeder without children. Instruct children to be quiet and calm to help him adjust to the many new experiences. They should let the puppy come to them instead of them chasing after him. Remember that puppies' teeth are like sharp needles that can unknowingly cut into a child's thin skin. Supervise constantly.

Instruct everyone that the correct way to pick up a puppy is by firmly supporting both his front and his rear. The sensitive jaw of a young puppy can be severely injured by a fall. For the same reason do not ever leave him sitting alone in a chair.

Just like a small child, a young Vizsla needs frequent naps. Explain this to your children and make sure they understand that the puppy can not be handled constantly. A Vizsla takes on the personality of his family and environment. If there is noise and a great deal of activity around him, his rest periods will be short-

ened and he may become stressed, tense, anxious, nervous and overactive. This leads to frequent complaints that the Vizsla is a "hyper" breed. It may simply be that his owner has a "hyper" household.

A parent should never stand by and allow a child to hurt or tease a puppy in any way. As the puppy has to learn control in all things, so does a child. Teasing a young puppy will teach him defensive biting and aggressiveness. A puppy should learn that human hands and actions are associated with pleasure and comfort rather than pain. A child who slaps or hits at him is going to make him hand-shy and nervous. From that point he may become excessively submissive or overly defensive and turn into a "fear biter."

A child should be made to understand that the puppy's crate or bed belongs only to the puppy. It is his place to run to when he wants to escape the noise and confusion around him. Children should also be instructed to leave a puppy alone while he is eating. A puppy has a short attention span and can easily get distracted from finishing his food.

Do not allow a small child to give the puppy an unsafe toy, an old shoe, or even a cookie. Your puppy is closer to the level of a youngster, and hand-feeding will encourage him to grab food from the child.

Your Vizsla will be a close companion to your child for many years to come.

A Vizsla is very like a child in many ways but you are not going to be able to ask him to mind. You will have to tell him, and in no uncertain voice either. You have to be the boss, the pack leader, a disciplinary figure. Both children and puppies are in a constant state of learning, the difference being that children grow up trying to reinforce and establish their position in society, while the puppy grows up to accept his part in it.

There are many aspects of caring for your Vizsla which should be left to adults, but there are some which can be shared with children who are at least 3 years of age or older. A young puppy just leashbroken will follow after a child sooner than he will an adult, and is still small enough to be controlled. A young child can take a share in the grooming, if only running a brush down the puppy's back. Letting a child share the responsibility of a simple job, such as keeping the water bowl filled, will make the child aware of the dog's need for attention and love. On shopping days he can help select dog food in the grocery store, and put it away when you get home. A new toy selected by your child with special thoughts for his pet will give him a learning experience on safe toys. Having your child accompany you on trips to the veterinarian's office will teach him about the puppy's need for health and good care.

Adolescence can be a trying and emotional time for a child. Unable to relate to adult, the adolescent often turns to his dog as confidant and friend. Always tuned to the emotional state of his owner, a Vizsla easily fills the need for understanding in a young teenager.

It is going to be hard bringing a young puppy into a home with children and then putting all kinds of restrictions on both of them. If you have small children, it will mean constant supervision of both, and a lot of patience. Vizslas adore children and naturally gravitate to them. As they both grow, the bond they form will be a joy to remember.

OLDER PETS AND PUPPIES

A resident older dog should never have to feel threatened by a new puppy if you are considerate and do not ignore the elder. For some older dogs life takes on a new excitement with a companion to keep them company, but it may take some time.

A young puppy can be rough and annoying to an older dog that has had your individual attention for a long time, and until the new addition has been accepted supervision may be necessary. After the initial trial period is over, you may find that the older dog takes the place of the puppy's mother, disciplining him if he gets too rough. The young puppy learns by imitation, and a "Come" obeyed by the older dog teaches the youngster basic commands. A puppy being taught to walk on a leash will readily follow along with the older dog.

You will have to make sure that a puppy learns to respect your older dog's food dish in particular. Feeding the new puppy in his crate will eliminate the need for your older dog to protect his food. Crating a new puppy will also give you the time to give individual attention to the older dog, thus avoiding a jealousy problem. Although the new puppy is going to need a lot of your time, it is never fair to push the older dog into the background and forget that he has been your wonderful companion for many years.

An older pet will enjoy the company of a puppy if the puppy is not rough and annoying.

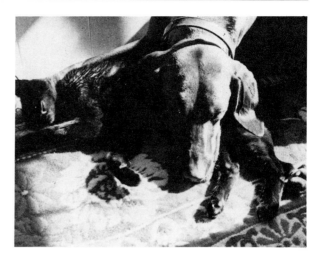

This Vizsla's companion is a Burmese cat.

A cat is a territorial creature and may object strongly to another animal brought into the home, especially a busy puppy that refuses to leave him alone. A puppy will gravitate to your cat, not only out of curiosity, but because he can not believe that another animal would not want to play with him. Luckily, a cat can easily get out of reach of a puppy by jumping up on top of a cabinet or refrigerator, but you will have to supervise and correct your new puppy for a long time.

Some cats and dogs adjust quite well and can even learn to play and romp together, but care must always be taken that a cat does not get cornered and threatened to the point of using his nails for protection. An eye injury can become serious and possibly blind a dog.

SAFE TOYS

From the time a Vizsla puppy is 5 weeks old he will enjoy carrying small toys around in his mouth. He is a natural retriever and if he can not find anything to bring to you, he will take your wrist in his mouth to show affection. Giving a young puppy soft, washable, stuffed ani-

mals to carry will encourage the desired soft mouth, but if he starts destructive chewing of them, he must be corrected.

The need for toys to be available at all times is particularly important. A young puppy has a short attention span and needs things to do to keep him out of mischief. Playing with toys will keep his interest and help prevent boredom.

Select toys carefully for safety to make sure they cannot be torn into small parts which your puppy may swallow. Rawhide chews are often recommended but pieces chewed off can expand and swell in a puppy's stomach, causing intestinal blockage. Large rawhide chews may last longer and be practically indestructible. Be sure to buy American—made products as many of the imported ones have been treated with chemicals.

A tennis ball is safer than a rubber ball with a bell inside and will provide self-exercise for a young puppy. Rubber squeaky toys should never be bought for a Vizsla as they will quickly be destroyed and eaten, showing up in the stool as bright-colored pieces of vinyl.

Nylon products are a better choice for a chew toy or bone. They come in various shapes and sizes and are a very safe toy, made of indestructible nylon. There is also a variety of them that are made of a softer nylon and these seem to be accepted faster than the harder nylon products. They will give hours of entertainment and help puppies through their teething stages. If your puppy does not show enough interest try boiling them in chicken or beef bouillon to add flavor.

A fairly large marrowbone from the meat market is always enjoyable for a Vizsla. Boil it to remove the marrow and it will stay clean but retain the flavor and odor.

Toys designed for tug-of-war games should be discouraged as they could cause a misalignment of the teeth, or encourage aggressive behavior unless your puppy is taught to relinquish on command. Do not give your puppy an old shoe or sock to play with and then punish him when he chews new ones; he can not be expected to understand the difference. A Vizsla puppy will proudly carry a stick or stone in his mouth, but if he stops to chew, take them away and give him a safe toy instead.

A puppy gets bored with the same old toy, just as a young child does. You will be surprised at how happy your young Vizsla will be when he receives a new toy.

SLEEPING ARRANGEMENTS

For the first few nights, bedtime will be a time during which you will have to harden

A puppy has a short attention span and needs safe toys to keep him out of mischief.

Place your puppy in a crate near your bed at night so he will not be lonesome.

your heart against your puppy's loneliness, and resist the urge to bring him into your own bed to keep him from crying. He has had a lot of excitement and experienced sudden changes and he should be tired, so hopefully if you ignore his cries, he will soon fall asleep.

Putting your Vizsla puppy in a crate which is placed alongside your bed should go a long way toward comforting him and may smooth the adjustment. Remember that Vizslas do not like to be alone, so if you do not use a crate give your puppy some other form of bed near you, with a clean, folded blanket and a toy for comfort.

Take your puppy out to eliminate for the last time just before you are ready to go to bed yourself. If he does wake up during the night and is only whimpering a little, reassure him quietly that you are nearby. As soon as he realizes he is not alone he will probably drift back to sleep. But if he starts to sound desperate, no amount of hushing is going to work. You are going to have to take him out to eliminate before either of you can sleep.

If you are not a "morning person" your life is in for a big change. Do not expect your young Vizsla to sleep late into the mornings. When he wakes he will be ready to start his day — and yours.

By the time your Vizsla puppy is past 5 months of age, has been completely housebro-

A Vizsla needs exercise to get rid of excess energy.

ken, has had some basic training and is communicating well with you, he will also be wanting to spend a good deal of his time with you. This is usually the time when he will graduate to sleeping on your bed at night. Most Vizslas do. It is not spoiling your dog to allow it; it is part of the bonding process. If you are away from home for a good part of the day, this is a time for contact and attention with your dog. You will be sharing your "den" with him. Do not play or wrestle with him on the bed, though. He must understand that the bed is for sleeping or quiet communication. Letting your Vizsla sleep on your bed provides extended but undemanding contact between you and him and builds trust and confidence.

IMMUNIZATIONS AND HEALTH

Your puppy's breeder will probably have included with the feeding and care instructions, the health certificate from the veterinarian certifying the types of vaccines given and the dates when the next series will be due. It is important that your puppy gets the complete series of vaccines needed to ensure his protection against disease.

The immunity he received from his dam at birth will have been diminishing and the vaccines that he is injected with will stimulate his immune system to produce his own antibodies. Consult with your veterinarian on which type he favors, what is included in the series, and the dates due.

Infectious diseases can be contracted by your Vizsla in various ways, depending on the disease. For most of them, prevention is the only option, and that is why it is important to avoid any delay in getting your dog completely immunized. He will need the appropriate shots throughout his puppyhood and then annually for life.

Regularly take a sample of your dog's stool to your veterinarian to test for the presence of worms. Microscopic examination is needed for

Table 4-2
Suggested Immunization Schedule

Age	Interval	Type of Vaccine
6 to 6 1/2 weeks	first shots	Distemper Measles vaccine (effective regardless of maternal antibodies present in puppy's system). Killed Parvovirus vaccine (given separately or in combination).
10 to 12 weeks	4 weeks	DA2PL+CPV+CV (Distemper, Hepatitis (Adenovirus Type II), Parainfluenza, Leptospirosis, Canine Parvovirus, Corona Virus (These are given in various combinations or all in one. Follow recommendation of your veterinarian.) Bordatella. Lyme disease when available in your state.
14 to 16 weeks	4 weeks	Booster shot of all above DA2PL+CPV+CV, bordatella, lyme disease. First Rabies Shot.
1 year	8 months	Booster all vaccines.
Annually as adult	1 year	Booster Distemper, Hepatitis, Lepto, Parainfluenza, Parvo and Corona Virus, Bordatella vaccines.
1 year	1 to 3 years	Rabies booster (Varies according to state and local laws. Vaccine is good for 3 years after initial booster at I year).

positive identification of most intestinal parasites. It is necessary to your Vizsla's health that both an immunization and a worming schedule be adhered to strictly.

Table 4-3
Suggested De-Worming Schedule

8 weeks	Check fecal and worm for round or hookworm if present
16 weeks	Re-worm for above and check fecal to make sure it is clear
16-20 weeks	Blood test for heartworm if recommended. Start on heartworm preventative
Every 6 months	Recheck fecal and treat if necessary
Any time	Check fecal if puppy or dog has persistent diarrhea, vomiting, pot belly and poor condition, or if roundworms or tapeworm segments are visible.

GROWTH AND DEVELOPMENT

The 8– to 16–week old Vizsla develops both mentally and physically at a faster rate than at any other time in his life. By 4 months of age, your puppy will be about sixteen inches at the shoulder. The growth rate then slows considerably over the next few months and by six months a male will be about twenty inches tall. A Vizsla usually does not reach his adult height until around one year of age.

Your puppy will gain at least 1½ pounds a week. His body and head will lengthen, and by the time he is 12 weeks of age you should have some idea of his body proportions at maturity.

The thirteenth, or floating, rib that was in evidence until the twelfth week, rounds out as your puppy's rib cage spreads. The ribs should be covered with enough fat under the skin so that they barely show. The ribs will continue to spread with the chest, reaching almost to the elbows, although body development will not be complete until he is well past 2 years of age.

The shape and length of the rib cage is important in a sporting dog as it affects the heart and lung capacity, which determines the endurance of a dog in the field. A chest that reaches down to the elbows is essential to provide space for the expanding heart and lungs. Even with the adequate depth of chest, a nar-

just a few weeks after hitting this fast growth spurt he will even out nicely as if it never happened.

At 8 weeks of age a male puppy should have both of his testicles down into the scrotum. Sometimes one of them will "float" up and down but when the dog is relaxed you should be able to feel both of them. The testicles should feel rather firm and be of almost similar size and shape. By 12 weeks both of them

The fastest growth rate will be in the first six months of your puppy's life. This is Mariah at five months of age.

Your puppy may hit a period of development when his rear is higher than his front, but toplines rapidly level out.

row-fronted dog would lack the necessary width. However, the rib cage must expand without becoming barrel-chested, which would restrict correct movement.

Your puppy's legs will seem to grow faster than any other part of him and he may go through several gawky stages during his first year. Some puppies stay perfectly balanced, however, and never reach those stages. Those are the ones that probably turn into top—winning dogs in the show ring.

The majority of puppies will go through a period, around 7 or 8 months of age, when the rear is higher than the front. Amazingly, in

should have descended into place. If one of them is completely retained in the abdomen, the dog is described as being monorchid, or unilateral cryptorchid. If both testicles are retained this is called bilateral cryptorchidism. Either condition will eventually require surgery to remove the possibility of problems with the retained testicle. Since a male only needs one testicle to sire a litter, a neutering is usually recommended to avoid the continuance of what could be a genetic problem. The presence of both testicles in the scrotum is necessary for competition in the breed ring at an AKC show.

At ten weeks of age, this cute male's ears look too long, but his head will eventually catch up to them and he will balance out.

Balanced angulation of front and rear is evident in this four-month-old puppy.

Your Vizsla puppy may show a darker line of color in his coat, mainly going down his back, which is an indication of the shade his hair will be at maturity. There should be lighter shades of color on the sides of his neck and shoulders which form an area called the saddle. He will retain these lighter areas throughout his life.

Eyes should darken by 10 weeks of age although in some breeder's lines a Vizsla may have a lighter eye color until he has finished cutting his teeth after 16 weeks. The eye color should blend with the coat color. Yellow eyes are faulty and undesirable.

Teeth

By 12 weeks of age the sharp needle-like points of your puppy's deciduous teeth will be worn down and they will not be as painful if you inadvertently connect with them. Remember to refrain from encouraging him to play tug-of-war games that may change the normal position of the teeth as his jaw grows.

By 16 weeks your Vizsla will start losing some of those baby teeth and replacing them with the permanent set. The first ones lost will be the incisors which are the six top and bottom teeth between the large corner canines. Next to go are the large canines. One of the baby canines may be retained as the new one grows in alongside of it. Since the canines have longer roots that are slower to be absorbed, try giving your puppy marrowbones or rawhide chews to loosen these teeth before consulting the veterinarian about pulling them. However, if the baby teeth do not loosen, causing the adult canine teeth to come in at an angle, they will have to be extracted surgically. The premolars and molars come in last. The total adult set numbers forty-two teeth, with twenty on the top and twenty-two on the bottom. It is rare for a Vizsla to have any teeth missing unless as the result of an injury.

Your puppy's gums and mouth may be tender for several weeks while he is cutting teeth and he may refrain from eating all his meals.

Since the last molar will not come in until he is almost 6 months old, he may experience some weight loss. Be patient. Keep him on a good high–protein puppy meal, and he will gain back any loss as soon as his teeth are no longer a problem.

Gait

Vizsla puppies are great exponents of the bouncing gallop, never walking into a room,

dent. He should be light-footed and graceful, and a joy to watch.

Even at this early age, a Vizsla puppy should pick up his feet purposefully and cleanly, never shuffling them. Faulty front quarters with over–angulated shoulders show up in a puppy moving forward from his elbows instead of swinging out from his lower shoulder blades. A pup with this problem will appear to have his back half moving faster than the front to keep from stepping on his front feet.

At the other extreme, a "mincer" will take

At a fast walk, a puppy uses only part of his potential front and rear extension.

As he increases speed, his legs move farther forward, developing a longer reach and extension.

but bouncing into it. In fact, this movement continues well into their adulthood as their actions show the exuberant happiness so characteristic of the breed. A developing 5–month–old will not yet have reached the clumsy stage and that is a good time to look at movement and gait.

Basic mechanics of movement can be observed in the walking puppy, as his legs travel slowly with action staggered on all four of them. At a walk he needs and only uses part of his potential front and rear extension and reach, but as he begins to put on speed his legs will begin to move farther forward, momentum will increase, and with his longer steps, an easygoing trotting stride will become evi-

short stilted steps. Such a dog usually lacks the front angulation. He will move out from the shoulders with flashy, fast steps, appearing to cover a lot of ground, but having to work harder at it.

Stand directly in front of your puppy and watch him coming to you in a straight line. As he increases speed to a trot, his legs should tend to converge under the midpoint of his body. This convergence, if seen by pawprints, would be evidenced by a single line, referred to as single tracking, which is the correct action for a sporting dog. Correct movement on a puppy will not change as he grows; unless influenced by lack of exercise and muscle tone.

Figure 4-1
Convergence of Feet When Single Tracking

Pawprints of opposing diagonals at a trot illustrate how the feet converge to touch a center line.

GROOMING

A young puppy's coat requires minimal attention, but he should be groomed or brushed weekly. The prime function of this attention is to train the active puppy to accept and submit to necessary restraints while he is still mentally flexible and can be easily managed. Vizslas love the attention of brushing but still they must be taught to stay still for it. Getting your Vizsla into the habit of being placed on a grooming table, or any other raised surface,

while still a young puppy will prevent backaches for you, his groomer. Besides the weekly coat brushing, his nails will need trimming, his teeth must be checked for any accumulation of tartar, and his ears will require special attention to prevent wax or yeast build-up.

Several times a week, place him up on your grooming table. Do not let any part of his grooming become a punishment; but use this time to enforce some basic obedience commands such as sit or stay. He should never be left unsupervised while on a table.

Right: Basic grooming equipment includes a fine-toothed flea comb, rubber curry brush, lava stone, rubber grooming glove, and scissors.

Below: Teaching a puppy to accept grooming on a table will also aid in other training, such as stacking and baiting, as demonstrated here.

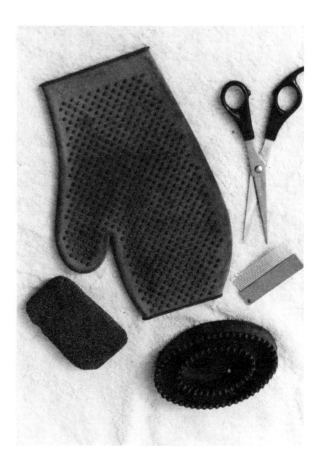

Above: Ch. Cariad's Classic Mariah, a Champion at eight months of age.
Sire: Ch. Cariad's Masterpiece
Dam: Ch. Cariad's Pride N Joy
Owner: Marcia Folley

Left: This eight-week-old puppy selected by Marcia Folley grew up to become Ch. Cariad's Classic Mariah.

Kamet Cheyenne Rebel at 4 months of age.
Sire: FCH & AFCH Randy Duke
Dam: Ch. Kamet Keri
Owner: Kay Thrasher

Kamet Cheyenne Rebel at eleven months of age. A Vizsla will usually reach his full height by a year but will not be fully developed until two years of age.

With a dog that stays as close to your side as a Vizsla it will be easy to notice if your dog is a little down. Maybe all he will need is a little attention to make it right, or he may not be feeling well due to an upset stomach or diarrhea. Stay tuned to your Vizsla's emotional state as well as his physical. It can be an indication of something serious.

Coat Care

Accustom your Vizsla puppy to grooming by running a rubber curry brush over him weekly. This will also give you the chance to check his skin for any dandruff, burrs, injuries, or allergy and mange problems. Running your hand over the coat against the hair, or using a small flea comb, will disclose any external parasite problem.

A good digestive system and intestines free of parasites are the first requisite for healthy hair since any clogging of the system with poisons from those sources will inevitably work to the detriment of your Vizsla's coat. Your Vizsla should always have a shiny, clean coat, nourished from inside.

Depending on the season, your Vizsla will shed his puppy coat around the end of his first year when reaching puberty or, in the case of a bitch, her first season. The new coat usually comes in darker and will be his true color. A rubber brush will be the easiest way to get the short, stiff, dead hairs out of his coat and hasten new growth.

In cold winter climates the Vizsla will grow a thicker undercoat, especially on the neck and shoulders, that will need special attention in the spring. A dry coat from a heated house can benefit from wheatgerm capsules or peanut oil added daily to the diet.

The Vizsla Standard allows for whisker trimming, and if you decide that you would like your dog's face clean, it will be easier to start trimming the whiskers while he is still a puppy to get him used to having them snipped. A Vizsla has such a pretty face and the whiskers do not really enhance it. It is still debatable whether the whiskers actually serve a functional purpose.

Bathing

Vizslas love water, whether they are swimming or playing in it, and they enjoy baths or showers as soon as they become accustomed to them. Start while your dog is young — in fact most puppies need a bath more than adults do since they tend to roll on the ground playing.

Bathe your Vizsla whenever you think he needs it. You are the one holding and hugging him and if you think he needs a bath once a week, then do it. However, do remember that too many baths will rob his coat of natural oils, so unless he is really dirty or smelly, it might not be as necessary as you think.

Use a shampoo specially formulated for either your puppy or your adult, whether it is a flea shampoo or merely a cleansing shampoo. Rinse well and dry him, remembering the inside of his ears. Do not leave him in an air-conditioned room or in a draft while he is still damp.

Nail Care

Nail cutting is the one aspect of grooming with which most dog owners have difficulties. Nails will have to be clipped regularly for the rest of your Vizsla's life so the earlier you get him to accept it, the easier the job will be.

The quillotine type of nail cutter is the best tool to start out cutting a puppy's nails, but as the care of the nails gets easier for both you and him, an electric nail grinder tool is faster. The Vizsla should have well–arched toes, close together, and nails kept short will keep both the feet and the pastern area strong. A weekly trimming will be enough to keep the nails from touching the floor.

Make sure that your Vizsla has had plenty of exercise, as the best time to get him to settle down to having nails trimmed is when he is tired. Sometimes it is possible to do the job on a younger dog while he sleeps in your lap.

The secret of successful nail trimming is knowing how far to go without cutting into the quick, causing bleeding. The quick is the

Ch. Kamet Keri, shown as a puppy at the beginning of the chapter.
Sire: DCH & AFC Rippi of Webster Woodlands
Dam: Ch. Debreceny Dijana
Owner: Kay Thrasher

Proving that a Vizsla can get along with other pets, this one has a raccoon as a companion.

Your bed is going to be the natural place for a young Vizsla to take a nap.

Nail grooming equipment can be either nail clippers or an electric nail sander.

line running through the center of the nail, and you can see it easily if you hold the foot up in a good light.

If you are worried about cutting into the quick, cut off only a small amount of the nail at a time. If you accidentally cut the nail too short and the quick bleeds, do not panic. It will bleed quite a bit but press a cold wet cloth tightly against the end of the nail until the blood clots, or apply some styptic in the form of powdered ammonium alum. After cutting the nail, follow up by smoothing the edges with a grooved nail file if necessary.

If your young dog protests too much about having his nails cut, do one foot at a time, brushing his coat for a few minutes in between. Progress like this until all toes are tackled. Doing rear feet first may give you a head start. Do not tolerate any protests. Long nails are easily snagged on crates, fences, or brush and can be severely painful when torn.

Your dog is like a young child and he will learn to accept nail trimming if you keep at it. If you find, for any reason, that you are not able to keep him groomed, make regular visits to a groomer.

Figure 4-2
Trimming Nails

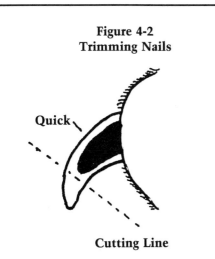

Cutting Line

The quick is the line running through the center of the nail. It will bleed profusely if cut into.

Five-month-old "Star", owned by Brent Aronson, takes a minute to rest while looking for birds.

5

Your Vizsla's First Year: Behavior and Training

THE average Vizsla puppy displays friendliness and gaiety with an overwhelming demonstration of affection both to his owners and strangers, especially in a home environment where he is always secure and comfortable. No matter what the future plans for your puppy include, you should deliberately widen his exposure, from puppyhood on, to include strange places, sounds, situations and people.

SOCIALIZATION

Trips to your veterinarian should be counteracted by joyful excursions elsewhere so that your puppy does not associate auto rides with unpleasant experiences. Vizslas thrive on trips to shopping centers or parks. People are always curious about the breed, gravitating to the aristocratic style and attractive color. Owners should always welcome these encounters with strangers and allow their dog to greet them. Ask a stranger to pet your puppy by scratching him under the chin or behind the ears. This will teach him to lift his head for attention. Patting a puppy on the top of his head will give him the idea to approach strangers with his head down.

At the same time that you are getting your puppy used to the big wide world, try to expose him to other breeds and encourage short play sessions with friendly dogs that will accept a puppy. Your young Vizsla will gain confidence in himself when he finds that nothing he is exposed to poses a threat. A puppy will learn through his imitation of another dog. If your Vizsla is being brought up with an older shy, retiring dog, chances are that he will also behave in this manner. The older dog that gives a happy enthusiastic welcome to everyone will be your greatest asset in teaching a young puppy. Confidence will make him a better all-round companion no matter what is asked of him.

EXERCISE

Vizslas are adaptable; many live in high-rise apartments, getting their daily exercise from riding up and down in an elevator and a walk around the block. But even in most situations of this kind, the owner usually finds some way to take his Vizsla to the park or a field on a weekend to really let him exercise.

Exercise is important to both the mental and the physical well-being of your Vizsla. Quite often a young dog will get sudden bursts of energy and go wildly tearing through the house, around the dining room table and up and down on the sofa. He even may, quite without warning, start racing around and round the yard until he gets it out of his system. Whether this is just boredom or a sudden need for more exercise is uncertain, but for any dog to develop properly, he must have a chance to "blow off steam." He might not necessarily be unhappy in a limited space, as long as he is with loved ones, but rarely is a Vizsla well muscled or a good mover under those conditions.

Ch. Piper's Moonstruck Moppet, UD, was trained and shown by her young owner Christy Coffee, in both obedience and junior showmanship. *Photo by Jill Landers.*

Muscle development is a continuous process beginning the moment the puppy is born and progressing throughout his life. Getting your Vizsla outside regularly for walks, play, and jogging sessions is essential, but consider some form of indoor exercise too. You will have to be careful that he does not slip or fall on a smooth floor so select an activity which he can handle safely.

A young puppy can be taught to fetch or retrieve at the same time he is being exercised. Simply rolling the ball down a hallway and sending him to retrieve it will last until he gets bored or tired. This is also a good activity for a small yard, or can be enlarged upon to include a long–distance chase in a field or park when he can be trusted off the leash. Another canine playmate to romp with will give him

Exercise is important to the well-being of your Vizsla.

Muscle development will be a continuous process.

added incentive. The Vizsla with a big yard or field to roam in will quite often be found sitting on the doorstep wanting someone to keep him company and this may also be an incentive for his owner to play with him.

The young dog being trained for field work will always be getting exercise but he should never be encouraged to go off and hunt on his own or he may develop the habit of working for himself and not for his owner. The dog whose hind-quarters need an extra bit of tightening may benefit from trotting up and down a hill, a beach, or uneven ground. Romping or swimming in a lake or pool will also tighten these muscles. It is the consistent push that develops the power in legs, lungs, and back, so essential to a sporting dog.

The importance of powerful musculature on a show dog is often overlooked. The Vizsla, like most sporting breeds, should be shown in working condition. Many dogs that look like first place winners when standing still, drop right out of contention as soon as they are moved across the ring. Unfortunately, many Vizslas are unsound in movement due to undevelopment of muscles because of sedentary lives. Vizslas do need exercise to present a

healthy appearance and relieve their boredom. Short, regular bouts of activity are more beneficial than long but infrequent ones.

EARLY TRAINING

The sooner your puppy is taught to behave and "mind his manners", the easier he will be to live with and the fewer bad habits he will develop. There is no one way to train a dog, nor is there any set age at which formal training should begin, but after a few days of letting your new puppy "settle in" he should be secure enough in his new surroundings to be ready for early basic training.

Vizsla puppies grow so fast that they cover, in one year, what most children cover in eight to ten years. During your puppy's first year you should outline, in your own mind, a few basic plans for habit patterns you may wish to set up and then adhere closely to a training program.

Whether the plans include field training, the show ring, or a companion that you can live with, the close contact during this early period will do much to give your Vizsla courage, confidence, and a knowledge that he could not gain if he were to stay in a kennel environment. It is essential that good rapport with people and especially you, the owner, is established during this time, as his emotional development is linked with his physical and mental growth. Your Vizsla puppy will form a strong bond with you in this first year that will last for life.

Since the Vizsla puppy is so cute and smart, it is easy for the new owner to tend to allow him to do anything he wants to when he is small, and then have to correct problems when he is older. To take the extra work out of training, teach your dog good habits while he is young.

A dog is actually capable of learning anytime after the age of 3 weeks, at which point it is the simple imprinting of the human presence on him. At 12 weeks, with a series of vaccinations behind him, he can be started in a puppy kindergarten class, and at 6 months, formal obedience lessons can be undertaken. In the meantime his learning process starts the day he comes home with you, and continues throughout his life.

Crate Training

The dog cage, or crate, is a sanctuary for your Vizsla. From the day you bring him into your home, give him a place he knows is his. It is important for his peace of mind and well-being and can make the difference in adjusting well to his new home and environment, or not. The crate should never be used as a form of punishment but should be viewed by your young Vizsla as a place where he can escape to, in order to rest or nap in peace away from family activities. Most Vizslas love a crate and adapt easily to its use. It should not take more than a few days before your puppy is going into his on his own.

A wire crate is best as it will give your dog adequate ventilation and visibility. He can watch the family activities around him but feel protected from them. There are many good

Place your puppy's crate where he can watch the family activities but still nap undisturbed. A crate is the only guarantee that he will not get into mischief when left alone.

crates on the market which fold up and can be carried like suitcases and easily moved from room to room. You will find a crate indispensable not only in your own home, but when visiting friends and relatives. Confining an active puppy in someone else's home ensures an invitation and a welcome, especially as it will keep him from soiling the floors and carpets at will.

Make sure that your attitude toward using a crate is a positive one. Remember that you are doing your puppy a real favor, as his crate training will reduce his fear, insecurity, and stress.

As he gets older, you will find your Vizsla going into his crate by himself if the door is left open. He has recognized it as being his and readily welcomes his time spent there in peace. You will be using a crate for most of your Vizsla's life for one reason or another. Getting both yourself and your puppy used to his crate now will be a benefit for life.

Get a large enough size to be comfortable for your dog as an adult — approximately 24 x 36 inches. Place the crate in a corner of the family room or kitchen during the day. Keep a washable blanket, never newspapers, on the floor of the crate along with several safe toys. Make sure the crate is not in a draft from air conditioning or heat ducts.

Wait until your puppy is tired, ready for a nap, and has been fed and taken out to eliminate before attempting to crate him. If he cries, do not let him out. Because he is already tired, he will soon settle down for a nap. If you put your puppy in his crate at the same time each day he will quickly adjust to a schedule of rest. It will make your life easier if he is not constantly underfoot when you are attending to household chores.

If you are away from the house for short periods of time, confining the puppy to his crate means that you will not have to worry about what kind of mischief he is getting into while he is alone. Not only will you not have chewed furniture, or a mess on the floor, but you will also have a happier relationship with your puppy if he is not a problem.

Use the crate as a housebreaking tool as a dog will generally not mess in his sleeping area. He should not be confined for any more than three hours at a time during the day, and he should be taken out to eliminate immediately upon release. Since he will not be able to soil at will, he will learn control of his bowels that much sooner, and associate his toilet duties with being outside.

Housebreaking

The hardest problem confronting the new puppy owner is housebreaking. When you bring your young Vizsla home, he will probably be in the habit of eliminating on newspapers, both in the whelping box and on the floor. But if weather permits, there is no reason to delay outdoor training.

When he opens his eyes in the morning, immediately scoop him up in your arms and run, do not walk, to the nearest exit. Go out with him and give plenty of praise as he does his business. Feed him breakfast and repeat the same procedure. Take him to the same spot each time and he will associate the odor with the deed.

When inside, confine your puppy to an area with washable floors. Watch him for signs and if he suddenly stops playing and looks for a place to squat, pick him up and run outside with him. Each time he wakes from a nap, after each of his meals, take him outside. Take him out before bedtime and stay with him until you are sure he has had a bowel movement. He should be able to get through the

---

Table 5-1
Suggested Housebreaking Schedule

Time	Activity
6:00 a.m.	Walk puppy. Return to crate. Place water in crate or pen for day.
7:00 a.m.	Feed Puppy.
7:15 a.m.	Walk puppy and have brief play time. Return to crate or pen.
10:00 a.m.	Walk puppy and spend time with him afterward.
12:00 noon	Feed second meal. Walk 15 min. later Give pup a play time, then return to confined area.
3:00	Exercise and potty the puppy. Return to confined area.
5:00	Feed third meal.
5:15	Walk pup. Bring pup into house with you.
7:00	Walk pup, followed by brief play time.
9:00	Feed fourth meal.
9:15	Walk pup. Remove water from crate. Put puppy in crate near your bed for the night.

night. Expect to go out with an 8– to 10–week–old puppy a minimum of ten times per day.

As he gets older your puppy will have better control over his functions and you will be bragging that you have him "housebroken," but actually it is you that has been trained to get him outside in time. Despite all your despair that he is not learning, one day around 14 weeks of age, something clicks in his brain and suddenly he has learned that it all belongs outside.

Never punish your puppy for an accidental puddle in the house by rubbing his nose in it. A Vizsla is smart and sensitive enough to know just from the tone of your voice that he has "goofed." Clean the puddle up with vinegar and water solution to kill the odor and do not make it a traumatic experience for either of you. Accidents will occasionally happen and while he is learning he needs your encouragement and help.

Unless there is someone home most of the time with your young puppy, the training will be a long and frustrating job. It is unfair to expect him to go more than a couple of hours without making a puddle. In fact, if he is not confined to a crate, it will seem as if he is making small puddles every few minutes.

If you have to leave him, make sure you have taken him outside to eliminate first, and take him out again as soon as you return. While you are away, if he is not in a crate, confine him in a room with newspapers covering part of the floor. Do not punish him for anything he did while he was alone, especially since it was your fault for not being there to take him out when he needed it. Remember to praise him when he eliminates outside where he should.

Leash Training

By the age of 10 weeks, your Vizsla puppy should be introduced to both a collar and leash. Start with a regular collar that buckles on and is made of soft material. Do not use a slip collar, or choke chain, on a puppy this young as you can cause damage to the soft cartilage

in the throat if you do a lot of pulling with the leash.

Leave the collar on your puppy for several hours at a time even though he will stop whatever he is doing to scratch persistently at it. Make sure the collar fits correctly and will not allow the puppy to get his chin under it, and never leave it on when he is unsupervised.

When he has become sufficiently accustomed to the collar to ignore it, attach a lighweight leash and let him run and play, dragging the leash behind him. Soon he will get used to the weight of the leash attached to him and it will be time to get him accustomed to the leash restraints. The timid owner who encounters frantic resistance to this early training is usually conned into stopping it, with the misconception that it will be easier to handle when the puppy gets older. But your puppy will only grow larger, stronger, and more determined, and protest again, so it is always better to start this early.

Most Vizsla puppies adapt to the leash without protest, but the first few times he will probably want to go the other way when you try to entice him to follow you. Do it his way to start, and let him lead the way.

Do not try to control him the first few times on a leash. You have to build his confidence before you can get him to walk quietly by your side. If he still balks drop the leash on the ground, walk a distance away from him, squat down to his level, and call in a coaxing voice. Since he will hate being left alone, he should come flying to you. Praise and reward him with a hug or a dog treat.

Another basic method is to train the puppy to come to you as the first step. When the puppy, finding himself on a restraint, lies down with resolute immobility, walk in front of him, stoop down a few inches from his face, and call his name accentuating the call with positive jerks on the leash. He will come, or be dragged, those few inches to you and you should reward him with lavish praise and hugs. Repeat the performance, always using an encouraging voice and short positive jerks. Move slightly back from your puppy each time, forcing him to advance. When he unhesitatingly runs to you at the sound of his name and

A young puppy being leash broken will follow after a child faster than he will an adult.

This young Vizsla is leash trained and under control at fourteen weeks of age.

"Come," it is time to begin to encourage him to walk quietly at your side.

When he has accepted walking on the leash, insist that he not wander in every direction on his own. Keep the leash shortened so that he stays on your left side, and coax and praise continuously with slight tugs on the leash. Make everything fun for him and you will soon have a puppy trotting along proudly at your side, unafraid, with tail wagging and head held high.

Discourage your puppy from sniffing at the ground — a great natural temptation. Set a brisk pace and do not allow him to stray towards nearby bushes or ground scents. Animation and silliness, such as his taking the leash in his mouth to carry, are welcome at this age.

The more severe corrections can come when he is older.

Teaching your puppy to eliminate while he is on leash is vitally important. If you do not have a fenced yard which enables him to do his job on his own, you will have to start leash training early. The leash and collar may distract him from his toilet at first so keep repeating in a calm voice to "Hurry up." As soon as he is finished, give a lot of praise. He will soon associate the words with his toilet acts.

Leash training and housebreaking should be done within the confines of your yard if possible until your Vizsla has had the time to build up his immunity to diseases with his full series of vaccines.

Coming when Called

Before your new Vizsla can come, he must learn his name. Every time you look at, play with, or feed him, say his name. Let him get used to the sound of your voice and only use a happy tone, never an angry one.

Sit on the floor while he plays and call him to you. As soon as he comes to you, reward him with a piece of cheese or a dog biscuit, and lots of praise. Repeat several times, calling his name and "Come" everytime he wanders off, rewarding him each time he comes back.

Keep your voice light and happy and avoid adopting a menacing position. If your puppy does not pay attention to you the first few times, squeeze a rubber squeaky toy, jingle some keys, make clicking noises with your fingers or mouth, or rattle a box of biscuits to get his attention. When he comes back to you, give him lots of praise. Never call your Vizsla to you to scold or punish. Every call to you should be a pleasant experience.

As your puppy gets accustomed to his new surroundings, he will show more independence, especially if he is enjoying himself outside, and you are calling him to leave his exploring and come into the house. If he turns a deaf ear to your pleas, the time has arrived for the come on leash command to be taught.

Attach a long, light lead to your Vizsla's collar and let him wander in whichever direction he chooses. Call his name and "Come" as you immediately give a slight tug on the leash and reel him in to you. Praise him as he comes.

It does not matter at this point whether he sits or jumps up on you. The important thing is that he responds to the call. Let him wander off on his own again without saying anything to him for several minutes. When he forgets that you are on the other end of the lead and focuses his attention elsewhere, call his name and "Come" again. Immediately, give the leash another short jerk to get his attention and as soon as he looks at you, praise him in an excited voice, and reel him in.

Spend only a few minutes each day with this exercise. Do not use it constantly while the puppy is on the leash. Give him time to explore and then, when he is not expecting it, give the command. Once you are getting reliable instant responses try it without any jerking of the lead, and finally completely off lead.

If your puppy fails to respond when you remove the leash, go back to working on the lead and stress the fact that he *must* come when called. Make it more fun by running backwards as he is coming after you. Praise, praise, when he reaches you.

Staying Alone

In every puppy's life there will be times when he will be left in an empty house, alone. So, you need to help him accept and adjust to the fact that someone will not constantly be by his side.

Begin by setting up his crate, or bed, in a permanent place and leave him there while you go about your chores in other parts of the house or apartment. If you are sure he does not have to eliminate, do not let him out if he cries. Stay in another room, out of sight, but where he is still aware that you are nearby.

Your puppy will soon learn that your activities do not constantly involve him. As he adjusts to not always having you at his beck and call, he will be able to adjust to being left alone without stress.

It is cruel to expect an 8–week–old puppy to stay in his crate more than three hours at a time. If that does not fit in with your schedule, make sure that you arrange for someone else to come in and care for him in between. It will lessen his time alone, give him his meals and exercise on time and relieve his tension so that he will be able to nap quietly. As he adjusts to confinement the time periods that he spends alone can be gradually lengthened.

Do not make a big deal out of the process of leaving home. Give your puppy plenty of time to exercise and play, place him in his crate or room with plenty of safe toys for company, and leave a radio, turned on to a talk show, within hearing range. Leave the house quietly without any fuss. When you return home, do it in the same quiet manner. Take him outside immediately to eliminate. After that, spend time playing with him and be lavish with your praise and affection. Show him that you will always come back for him and there is nothing to worry about. Communicating to your puppy that you will be coming and going fairly constantly will help him learn to stay alone without anxiety.

BEHAVIOR PROBLEMS

A Vizsla never needs a heavy hand for any type of correction. All he needs is the sound of displeasure in your voice and firm gentleness in the corrections or training. Vizslas are highly intelligent animals and training your puppy correctly will give him confidence in himself. The Vizsla's lovely temperament is probably the characteristic that sets him apart from other breeds. How you handle and develop your dog's personality from the start will mean all the difference in this wonderful dog. You can not put him aside and ignore the affection and attention he will want to give.

Jumping on People

The Vizsla is a happy, outgoing, and sociable breed and if your puppy is being raised with love and affection, he will probably expect the same from everyone. However, if you allow him to jump up on you to lavish all that attention, he will also do it to visitors. Short of discouraging non-doggy friends from visiting, you will have to train your puppy not to jump up on people. And even if your friends like dogs and do not mind being greeted, muddy feet on clean clothes are not regarded with any degree of leniency.

One of the ways to prevent your Vizsla from jumping up to greet you, is to get down to his level immediately as he tries to reach your face. He will be enthusiastic about getting all the kisses and hugs he has been waiting for.

The alternative is to teach him not to jump up at all. As he starts to jump up, immediately

A puppy can jump on a young child, knocking him down. This three-month-old Vizsla is being restrained with a leash.

press the palm of your hand against his nose and say "No" or "Off." Then turn your back on him and walk away. He will soon learn that jumping up and pawing is no way of greeting you and that you are displeased with him. If pushing his nose down with your hand does not work, grasp both of his front paws firmly and thrust him downward. As a last resort, time a jab to his chest with a raised knee as he jumps up. But gently, please. Do not discourage the affection.

You must be consistent with the training. Do not expect him to understand that he is welcome to jump on you if you are in old clothes but not when you are in good ones.

Climbing on Furniture

Maybe other breeds are content to lie on the floor, but a Vizsla seems to enjoy higher elevation. Although a sporting breed, the Vizsla is a very socially oriented dog who loves to be on your lap as you read or watch television.

Giving your Vizsla his own chair is the easiest way to handle his sleeping on the furniture.

Give your puppy a blanket on the floor near your chair if you do not want him on your lap.

Of course the easiest way to handle this desire to be on furniture is to allow it, or allow it on one particular chair. It is very simple to throw a cover on a chair to protect it, and teach your puppy that it is the only furniture on which he is permitted. If you are never going to allow him on furniture, do not allow it as a puppy and then try to change the rules later in his life.

If you do not want your Vizsla in your lap every time you sit down, give him an alternative that will still enable him to be close to you. Place a thick folded blanket or a dog bed on the floor near your chair and be consistent with your commands. Do not allow him up with you. Do not reason to yourself "just this once won't hurt," as you will only confuse him.

Whether it is his crate or a blanket on the floor, get your Vizsla used to the command of "Go to bed" in the place he truly knows is his. Catch him before he wants his nap on the sofa or chair, give him a hug and a kiss, and a toy, and place him where he should be sleeping. A crate is the only guarantee, however, that he will never be on the furniture when you leave him on his own.

Destructive Chewing

A Vizsla is born with the retriever instinct and, because of that, is very mouth-oriented and loves to be constantly carrying something. That sometimes graduates rapidly to chewing on sticks, stones, toys, and even chair legs. If you wait for your Vizsla to outgrow this "phase" you will have to replace shoes and furniture long before he decides to move on to another phase. Instead of trying to teach him *not* to chew, teach him what is permissable and safe to chew.

Keep a good variety of soft, stuffed animals, rawhide chews, both nylon bones and hard marrowbones for him to carry and chew. Give a sharp "No" if he starts to chew on anything that is not allowed. Puppies and adults have both been known to swallow items, including nails, bolts, needles, and tinfoil, all of which can cause intestinal problems.

Teach children to put away books, toys, shoes, and belongings and not give your Vizsla the opportunity to get into trouble. Do not give your young dog an old sock or shoe to play with and then scold him for damaging a

A rawhide chew toy may possibly keep a young Vizsla from chewing on the chair leg.

A bored Vizsla puppy will soon resort to digging for amusement.

good one. He can not be expected to know the difference and the inconsistency of corrections will confuse him. You can not change an in-bred tendency, so channel it in the right direction with corrections and praise.

Biting and Nipping

A Vizsla puppy will chew on everything his mouth comes in contact with and that will include your fingers and toes. He has to be immediately corrected when this happens. Puppy's milk teeth are sharp little needles, and your first impulse, when he nibbles at you, may be to swat his face. However, slapping will result in a hand-shy dog that will back away every time you reach for him, so avoid this instant response. Instead, use a stern voice command of "No" and grab him by the scruff of the neck and give him a couple of good shakes. If he tries to turn and bite at your hand while you are shaking him, be even firmer in the correction.

While most of your Vizsla's training is done in a quiet, gentle manner, this is a time for sterner measures. He must learn that chewing or nibbling on someone is not permitted. If allowed to continue, he will always be testing you by using his teeth as a protest tool when he does not want to obey. Stopping such practices at an early age will ensure an adult dog that does not have a biting problem.

Digging Holes

Vizslas love to dig, and freshly planted flower beds or gardens seem to hold a special attraction. If your puppy would confine the digging to an area without any grass or flowers, the damage might not be of any consequence, but once started he will be having too much fun to quit.

Digging can become exceedingly persistent in a young Vizsla that is left alone in the yard without toys or another dog to play with. If the digging habit is allowed to continue, it is difficult to break. Scolding does not seem to work. Apart from filling the holes with large rocks to discourage the digging, the only alternative seems to be constant supervision, and plenty of exercise.

Vizslas enjoy the companionship of other dogs and do not like being alone.

6

The Young Adult Vizsla

Every Vizsla owner thinks that his dog is unique in his intelligence but when owners get together and compare notes, they find that each Vizsla is intelligent, friendly, sociable, happy, and interesting. There is never a dull moment with a Vizsla in the home and watching him develop from puppyhood to adulthood will be satisfying and amusing. A Vizsla never loses his sense of humor and will find ways to entertain himself and his family well into old age.

GROWTH AND DEVELOPMENT

By 14 months of age both the male and the female will have gained their full heights, but they will continue to mature as their rib cages spread and their chests widen and drop.

A male should look like a male. He should not look small and feminine. He should have an attractive head, heavier than the female's, good bone and strength without any coarseness, and an ideal height of 24½ inches. A female should be smaller, finer boned, with a soft, feminine head, but she should still show strength of body. The ideal height is about 22 inches as a smaller bitch may lack substance.

Both the young adult male and female have well-developed chest and rib cage.

Although both are clean and elegant, the size and substance differ in the adult male and female.

Cariad's Classic Mariah shows the lovely head and expression of a feminine bitch. Posing with Brooke Folley.

The Boelte's young male, Skylar, poses among his Christmas toys. The Vizsla's wonderful personality makes him fun to live with.

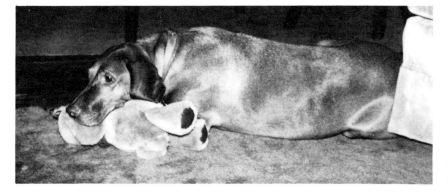

A young adult Vizsla enjoys a soft stuffed animal to carry around.

As a full-grown adult, the weight of a bitch will usually average around forty-eight pounds, and that of a dog, around sixty pounds. Enough weight should be maintained to keep the ribs from showing, but a Vizsla should never be allowed to get fat or soft.

Your young male will start lifting his leg to urinate by the time he has reached 1 year of age. This is when his hormones start working and he reaches the age of "puberty". He will start marking his territory, covering areas where other dogs have been.

Most males have a moderate amount of discharge from their prepuce. If you are concerned about the appearance of this discharge, or even the color of the discharge, or excessive licking and cleaning activity, it may be a sign of infection and you should consult your veterinarian about the problem. As your male Vizsla gets older he should have an annual physical examination of his organs since treatable disorders of the prepuce, testicles, and prostate glands will be common.

The female will usually have her first season, or "heat", between the ages of 10 and 15 months, but it is not that uncommon for the first heat to be delayed past that, even to almost 2 years. After the first season, most bitches will come back into season every six to seven months.

The first signs of your bitch coming into season will be the swelling of the vulva. It may actually stay slightly enlarged for a few weeks before the bloody discharge starts. She may keep herself clean so that you miss the first few days, but when she starts to bleed in earnest and drips on the carpeting, keep her confined to her crate while indoors, or in pants with a protective pad.

The consistency, color, and odor of her discharge will change around her tenth day in season and will attract males. It is very important that she is not allowed outdoors without supervision at any time during her season as a determined male can climb a fence to get to her. If you live in the city or in a residential area, take her outside on a leash to eliminate and bring her back in immediately. She can make up for the exercise she is missing after her season is over.

Putting protective pants on a bitch in season will prevent blood spots on carpets.

Your female's complete cycle will last twenty–one days, although she will not be ovulating, or releasing eggs for fertilization, during the entire period. Rather than risking an unwanted pregnancy from a roaming male, it is the owner's responsibility to keep a female in season confined.

Quite often, after a young bitch has finished with her first season, her vulva will remain swollen for several weeks and her breasts will be enlarged and hard with blue discoloration around them. This could develop into a "false pregnancy" where she may eventually show signs of lactation, build a nest, and adopt articles and toys as surrogate puppies. If left untreated, the symptoms will slowly disappear by themselves, but if you are concerned about them and her personality changes, ask your veterinarian if hormone treatment is warranted.

A male Vizsla will reach full growth and development between two and two and one-half years of age. Shown here is Ch. Taunee's Loki Santana at that age.

In her first show at six months of age, this puppy shows confidence and poise resulting from early training.

Ch. Cariad's Czigany Malie finishing her championship title at nine months of age.
Sire: Ch. Dorratz Diamond Jim
Dam: Ch. Cariad's Pride N Joy
Owner: Stacey Thomson

The only reason not to have a bitch spayed (removal of the ovaries and uterus) is if you have made plans to show or, eventually, to breed her. If that is not the case then it is wise to have her spayed before she has her first season. It is certainly not true that a bitch should be bred at least once in order to fulfill her mat-ernal instincts and prevent frustration, or even to have a long, healthy life. She can enjoy good health and happiness if never bred. The younger you have a bitch spayed, the more likely you are to prevent any chance of unwanted pregnancies, infection, false pregnancy behavior, or the development of breast cancer. A spayed bitch will never attract unwanted males and can not be bred by them. She will not accumulate fat or be sluggish and lazy any more by being spayed than if she had not been. These conditions arise from a decrease in exercise.

Neutering (having a male's testicles removed) may make him less inclined to mark his territory, especially indoors, and may make him less interested in picking a fight with another male. It should discourage him from roaming and looking for a bitch in season. It will prevent infection or cancer as he grows older, and may eliminate sexually linked behavior problems, such as the obnoxious habit of riding a person's leg.

TEMPERAMENT AND BEHAVIOR

As your Vizsla grows into his young adulthood all his energies and intelligence need to be channeled into correct behavior patterns in order for you to keep control over a dog that is a wonderful con artist. No matter how good-natured your Vizsla is, you should remember that behavior never stays the same. Your dog is constantly learning and developing. Interactions with people will have a strong effect on any expression of affection. Vizslas love to show affection and usually respond to everyone they meet. Because of their happy, exuberant, loving nature they are easy to love and spoil; and because of that you may lose the essential control.

Somewhere around the age of 14 months a male Vizsla will start testing that control. His hormones will have been working from the age of 11 months and his "testing" of wills can be compared to that of a teenager who is starting to question authority.

From your sweet, sensitive, soft male there can sometimes emerge a stubborn and resistant streak. He may refuse to get out of your favorite chair, and even talk back when asked to obey. If he senses that you are uneasy and uptight about his behavior, he might become even more tense when you try to exercise control over him. You have to be a figure of authority to your Vizsla at every point in his life. He has to learn that even with all the hugs and kisses, you are still the boss.

If you have already done basic obedience training, a continued plan of advanced work has beneficial effects at this age. Obedience provides a subtle and enjoyable way to enforce your authority without any threatening position. Training is also a good way to dissipate a lot of his surplus energy and give him an outlet for his exuberance. A contented and relaxed dog is less likely to chew, bark, or misbehave, and a confident dog learns to accept control from any family member once an effective pattern of behavior has been established.

Female Vizslas do not seem to go through any stubborn stages. They usually accept any corrections as a matter of course and then in a quiet, subtle way jump up in your favorite chair as soon as your back is turned.

Both dogs and bitches will be protective guardians, even though they are not aggressive in any way. The protective instinct develops strongly in their second year as they learn to discriminate. Used for many years to guard the famous St. Stephen's crown in their native Hungary, Vizslas are not usually thought of as guard dogs in the U.S., but the underlying characteristic will become evident if it is ever needed. Certainly, Vizslas do not perform as well as most guard breeds because of their low aggression ranking, but they do give a good alarm and warning when a doorbell is sounded, or when an owner is being threatened.

FEEDING PROGRAM

To the confirmed show ring exhibitor and the field trial follower, the condition of a Vizsla may mean two separate things. To the show person, for a dog to be in condition signifies that state of his appearance which enhances him to the judge's eye and enables him to go into the show ring and win. A show Vizsla must be adequately fed to maintain a shiny coat, clear eyes, and a happy, healthy attitude. He must be in good working condition, although not as lean as the field Vizsla.

To the field enthusiast, his Vizsla must be lean, muscular, and definitely not carry any extra weight that may keep him from performing in the field for long hours. However, a Vizsla running in the field should not look gaunt, with bones sticking up. Since a field dog will utilize more of his food than a dog that stays quiet most of the day and only gets exercise

is a safe rule to judge more on the basis of his looks and actions in attempting to determine how much food he should have, than to try to specify the amount.

Growing puppies need a high–protein food since they are almost constantly active and burn up more energy. If your young adult is still using up every bit of food he takes in, you may want to keep him on a puppy meal containing a higher percentage of protein than most adult meals. Some of these foods contain

The Vizsla working in the field should be lean and muscular in order to keep him performing for long hours.

Stay with a good quality dog kibble and meat, adding vegetables occasionally.

on a weekend, he must be on a high–protein diet. It should be able to maintain the excitable and active hunting dog in all kinds of weather with adequate energy and weight.

Both appearances desired are only the superficial ones which do not really show the well dog. This is where the proper feeding comes in that will equip your Vizsla to live a happy and healthy life. A dog correctly conditioned from the inside out will hold that condition against greater odds than the one whose outer appearance may be camouflage.

Food provides growth and energy, but the exact quantity your Vizsla may require for his maintenance, growth, and work will depend on his own individual rate of metabolism. It

as high as a thirty-one percent protein. However, only you will be able to "eyeball" your own dog and make the decision.

Whichever food you do decide to feed for correct maintenance, stay with it. Do not keep skipping from one brand to another because a friend tells you that their dog likes it. You will only get a fussy eater from all the changes.

Every breed has fussy eaters, and Vizslas are no exception. Apart from cooking special meals for him constantly to try to peak his interest in eating, force-feeding may be the only alternative if you have to get some weight on a dog.

Mix the regular amount of meal and meat with a little bit of warm water. Add a full tablespoon of peanut butter and a tablespoon of honey and mix well. Holding your dog's mouth open with one hand, take small balls of the mixed food and place it well to the back of his mouth with the other hand. Hold his mouth closed gently, allowing him to chew and swallow, but not spit it out. Feed him two meals a day, increasing the amounts as needed for a faster weight gain.

For any dog, you can occasionally add vegetables and juice, cooked egg, cottage cheese, fish, meat gravies and broth, or soups to the meal for variety without getting a fussy eater. Most dogs love broccoli, asparagus, carrots, green beans, and even melons and apples. Any of these are better for your Vizsla than cookie and cake snacks. The important thing to remember in feeding him is routine. It may get boring for you, but Vizslas thrive on consistency.

Strenuous exercise should not be permitted for an hour before or after eating a meal to ensure good digestion. Any evidence of diarrhea or vomiting is cause to withhold a meal until the problem is resolved.

COPROPHAGY AND PICA

The most unpleasant of all phases of raising a dog is when he takes to eating stool. This practice, referred to as coprophagy, is still an unsolved mystery in dog behavior. There is simply no clear explanation as to why some dogs do it.

At one time it was thought to be a problem affecting mostly bitches once they had a litter to keep clean. Others now believe the dog is cleaning up after himself rather than be punished as he was when a puppy if he made a mess on the floor. Still others claim it is a sign of boredom, nutritional deficiencies, or the use of preservatives in dogs' food. It is argued that preservatives give the food an appealing odor that survives the digestive process, but using meat tenderizers, garlic powder, or monosodium glutamate, all of which would give the stool a bad odor, does little to discourage a dog with this habit.

Unfortunately, the habit can not be ignored if you are to enjoy your Vizsla to the fullest. If you are unable to correct the problem with a change of diet or the adding of enzymes, the only way to control it is with complete sanitation practices. Set up an establihsed eating and exercising schedule for your dog, and remove all feces immediately.

Pica is the craving of unnatural food by your dog, such as ashes, dirt, or grass. Some dogs love eating grass. Whether they do this because they need extra fiber in their diets, or because they have an upset stomach and are using the grass as an emetic to make themselves vomit, it can be as much of a habit sometimes as coprophagy. If the grass has not been chemically treated, there is usually not a problem if your Vizsla "grazes." A change in diet may be warranted, and a stool sample should be checked for parasites.

TRAVEL

Most Vizslas love riding in a car, which makes traveling with them a pleasant experience. A young dog should be started out on quiet, short rides which can be gradually lengthened. If you have tackled the problem of a carsick dog during puppyhood, he will be over it by the time he is old enough for longer trips to dog shows and field trials.

Carsickness is a by-product of fear and nervous reactions. The usual remedy for a dog that vomits on rides is to leave him at home but this is precisely the wrong approach. Carsickness can be cured if you take the time to acclimatize your Vizsla to riding. Take him for short rides to visit other doggy friends to help him understand that there will be fun waiting for him at the end of the trip. Instead of walking him to the park or fields for his exercise, drive him there so that he learns to associate the car with good things.

You can make sure your dog has not eaten for several hours before riding, but even that will not prevent carsickness.

The moment you notice he is going to get sick in the car, pull over to the side of the road

Most Vizslas want someone to keep them company outside and will sit on the doorstep instead of exercising themselves.

and take him out on leash to relax. Avoid the "roller coaster" roads and sharp turns. You should soon have a puppy anxiously waiting to go with you on every trip.

No matter how long or short the trip, your dog should be crated. If a crate has been part of your puppy behavior modification program, he will already know the crate to be his sanctuary, and taking it along will make him feel safe and secure even in a strange place. If your puppy continues to get carsick, try turning his crate so that he is facing towards the front of the car instead of sideways or backward. This may help.

Traveling in a crate while in a car or van, or even a motor home, means your dog will stay still. He will not jump from seat to seat, wrestle with children, take up more than his share of room, or knock your elbow while you are driving. He will not get thrown through the

windshield in case of a sudden stop, and he will not escape out of the car door when you stop for gas.

Having a crate in a motel room means that your Vizsla will have his own place to nap while you are out sight-seeing or dining and the maid will not open the door and let him out. The motels which allow dogs will welcome you as a responsible guest. Hopefully, you will have taught him not to bark while crated. Make sure to take along his favorite toys to keep him company in his crate, and a rawhide or chew toy to keep him busy.

If you are unable to place a set-up crate inside your car to hold your dog, there are steel dividers which can fit between the front and back to confine him to an area and prevent him from jumping into the front seat with the driver. There are also dog seat belt harnesses, available in pet supply stores, which will hold your dog in place and prevent him from jumping around inside the car.

Get in the habit of putting a collar on your Vizsla every time he gets into the car, even if you are only going around the block. His collar

Traveling with your Vizsla can be made safe and enjoyable with him secure in a crate.

should be of flat nylon or leather material with a brass identification plate displaying your name, address, and telephone number. One form of permanent identification that you may consider for your Vizsla is having a number tattooed on his inner thigh. There are several "lost dog" registries which use different forms of tattoo identification. Check with your local kennel club or your own veterinarian for more information. Tattooing is painless and only takes a few minutes with no anesthesia needed. But even if your dog has the tattooed identification, his collar should always hold information which can be used immediately.

When traveling by car with your Vizsla, keep his leash handy for emergency stops. Keep it fastened to his crate and you will not have to waste time looking through all your luggage for it. In fact, it is a good idea to take two leashes to be on the safe side. Never allow your dog out of the car in a strange place without a leash on him. He may panic and bolt. No matter how much you think he will obey, keep a leash on him.

Most rest stops on interstate highways have an area where you can exercise your dog. Be a responsible dog owner and keep a roll of paper towels, or plastic bags, and a pooper scooper

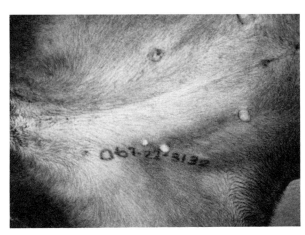

Tattooing is the best way for a permanent identification on your Vizsla, but the number must be registered with a lost-dog registry.

These Vizslas have leather collars with proper identification tags and are ready to travel.

handy for cleanup after your dog. Do not allow your dog to sniff at other dog's feces.

Before traveling, make sure your Vizsla's immunizations are current as the risk of exposure to a virus or disease is higher in rest stops and other public areas. Get boosters as needed, especially for Parvovirus and Coronavirus, at least two weeks before your trip.

Take enough food and water for the entire trip so you will not have to make any dietary changes. If you will be gone for an extended time, fill a large jug with water before you leave home and add to it each day of the trip so that the new water is diluted with the old, or purchase bottled water. Try to keep as close to your dog's feeding schedule as possible in order to avoid digestive upsets.

Pack a separate bag with medications and health supplies for your Vizsla. The most important thing will be an anti-diarrhea drug. (Whether in pill or liquid form, be ready to give your dog a dose at the first sign of trouble.) Include in his bag a thermometer, ear and eye ointments, antihistamines, foot powder, hydrogen perioxide, shampoo, iodine, an antibiotic and any medication your dog may be on, including his heartworm preventative. Include a bottle of *Pepto-Bismol®* to soothe an upset stomach or nausea. You will also need to pack a good flea and tick spray for him.

Daily exercise will be a necessity if you want to travel with a happy dog. Exercise helps avoid constipation, stress, and boredom. It will be good for bored children too. With supervision, children can take their Vizsla on walks in campgrounds, rest stops, and parks. A dog is a wonderful introduction and your children and dog can meet new friends that way. Your dog will be willing to nap in his crate if he has frequent walks.

While traveling during the day in hot weather you may find yourself restricted to the use of fast-food drive throughs since you will be unable to leave your Vizsla in the car. But, if you are lucky, you might be able to park under a shade tree, and with your dog securely in his crate, leave all the windows on your car open. Of course, this is only to be recommended if you are going to be in a position to keep the car within sight.

Table 6-1
Checklist for Traveling

- Crate
- Water from home
- Food and bowl
- Toys
- Collar with I.D. tag
- Leash
- Medications
- Health certificate if required or record of immunizations
- Dog's bedding

Remember that the temperature inside a closed car in hot weather builds up at a frightening speed and a dog can die within minutes from the effect of heatstroke. Heatstroke can cause a dog's temperature to reach as high as 106°F. Breathing becomes rapid, mucous membranes turn bright red, and there are severe muscle spasms. The dog steadily weakens, coma sets in, and death follows rapidly. It is a critical situation and you should never take the chance of it happening.

Planes

Plane travel with your pet is easy, fast, and can present less stress most of the time than the long trip by auto. Instead of a wire crate, you will be required to use a molded plastic shipping crate specially designed for safety in air travel. Borrow one from a friend or buy it from a pet supply store so that you can get your dog used to it for several days before the trip. Most airlines also sell them. The correct size for an adult Vizsla is the #400. Place your dog's blanket in the bottom of the crate, along with a toy, and put proper identification on the top of the crate along with your flight number and destination. Using red paint or tape, put arrows on the crate indicating the crate's correct position, or use the words "This end up."

Educate yourself on the easiest way to fly with your Vizsla by asking other dog owners. Find out which airlines take the best care with the animals. When making plane reservations for yourself, specify that you will also be bringing a large dog as "excess baggage." There will be a charge each way, and the number of live animals per flight is limited in most cases.

If you are traveling during hot weather, choose a flight that will leave and arrive in the coolest parts of the day. A non-stop direct flight is always best whenever you are traveling with a dog.

Try to carry as much of your dog's own food as possible and hope that the local stores at your destination will carry his brand. Include his medications, health records, and rabies certificate. Do not feed him for several hours before the flight, and make sure he has had plenty of exercise and water.

Plan on getting to the airport a minimum of one hour before the flight time. You will need that much time to get your dog checked in and a porter to take your crate and dog to the loading area. Put your Vizsla in his crate yourself, and give an extra check to be sure the crate is securely fastened together and the grill door in place.

Tranquilizers are not recommended or needed and sometimes have an adverse effect on your dog.

Before boarding the plane, if you haven't seen your dog loaded, tell the gate steward that you are traveling with a dog, and to please check if he is aboard. Make sure you get positive confirmation that your dog has been loaded. If you are not on a direct flight, you will have to go through the same problem of confirmation each time you change planes.

If you are traveling out of the country, you will have to check the regulations and restrictions on bringing your dog with you. Several countries, including Hawaii, enforce lengthy quarantine.

By using sensible precautions, air travel with your Vizsla is safe and you will be able to enjoy the fun and competition of distant dog shows and field trials, or just relaxing vacations without having to leave your companion at home or in a boarding kennel.

Dogs being shipped by plane without the owner will be required to travel as air freight. The freight office will usually need the dog two hours before the flight time. Make your reservations early with non-stop flights, if available. Weekday travel is advisable as many freight offices have limited hours and may be closed on weekends. Dogs traveling as freight are limited by weather temperatures and are usually restricted in extreme hot and cold.

Travel with your Vizsla does not have to be limited to auto or plane trips. Your Vizsla can accompany you on hiking trails and camping and back–packing trips. You will have to inquire at each national park you may want to use to find out if they will allow a dog to accompany you, as the rules are not the same in every area. It is important to keep your dog on leash at all times and clean up any feces he may leave on a hiking trail or at a campsite.

There will, of course, be times when it is better for your dog to remain at home. He should not travel if he is old, feeble, or recovering from any debilitating illness or surgery. It is also advisable to leave a pregnant bitch at home.

Your Vizsla will have to share in every family activity.

Shown working toward his OTCH title, triple champion Cariad's Kutya Kai Costa made history for the breed when he became the first dog of any breed to win a title in obedience, conformation, and field.

7

The Vizsla in Obedience

OF the many "career choices" for your Vizsla, none is more readily available to the average owner than obedience. Even before you consider a field or show career for your dog, some basic obedience training will be helpful. Obedience training is the best way to get your Vizsla's attention and love. It will make him easier to live with and it will be an enjoyable hobby for you. It can be enjoyed merely for the purpose of developing a more mannerly pet, or for performing in obedience trials at different levels of competition.

Vizslas love obedience work. They are extremely intelligent, fast, graceful, willing performers that love to please. Very sensitive, they do not do well under a heavy hand. Do not use any harsh, extreme corrections; the tone of your voice is enough. Lay a good foundation with the basics and let the fun start in advanced work with jumping and retrieving exercises.

Your Vizsla will always attract attention because of his beauty and enjoyment while working. If you have overtrained or overcorrected to the point that you have a dog working with his tail between his legs and obviously not happy, you would be doing the breed a disservice to show him at an obedience trial where he would not make a respectable impression on exhibitors or spectators.

There are lots of obedience books on the market, lots of theories, and lots of methods. You should decide whether a companion dog that you can train to

Ch. Cariad's Classic Mariah, studying the AKC obedience regulations.

be a pleasure to have around is your main interest, or whether you are also interested in competing for obedience degrees. You can teach obedience at home with the help of one of the books, but if competition is your aim locate a good local training class.

Pre-novice, novice, intermediate, and advanced training classes are held in almost every community. They are sponsored by all-breed kennel clubs, humane societies, and training clubs specializing in obedience. Sometimes individual persons, experienced in training, hold private classes. Whatever you choose, let your young Vizsla mature physically and mentally before beginning formal obedience lessons. The majority of classes do not accept puppies until they are 5 or 6 months of age for that reason.

If you have any doubts at all regarding the qualifications of the people who are teaching obedience in an area convenient to you, start with the basics at home. When your Vizsla is a little older and you have gained experience through teaching the exercises yourself, then you can try the classes without so many reservations. You will now know enough to say "No" to anyone who you feel is approaching your Vizsla in an attempt to cow him with a heavy hand.

TRAINING TIPS FOR TEACHING AT HOME

If you are training your dog by yourself, select a training area that will allow you and your dog to work without distractions, whether it is your yard, a park, or an empty field. At this point you need his undivided attention.

Pick a cool quiet time of day to work. Make the sessions pleasurable for both of you. Keep the training sessions short, especially at first. Start with fifteen–minute sessions, work up to twenty, and finally thirty. If you are keeping it fun, a 5– or 6–month–old puppy should be able to listen and learn for that short time.

Do not attempt to teach more than one new exercise a day. Keep the commands short, but importantly, make them the same each time you give them. Practice each old exercise for several minutes before attempting a new one.

Do not feed your Vizsla for at least two hours before training and make sure he has been exercised sufficiently. Use praise, not food, as a reward. Praise should be given in warm, friendly tones. In this way, he learns to associate words with action and then praise.

EQUIPMENT

You will need only two pieces of training equipment to start with: a six-foot leash and a training collar. Green or black cotton webbed leashes are made for obedience training. They are easy on your hands and strong. A training collar is called a choke and is a necessity for making corrections. A medium–weight nylon or chain should be used and the correct size is important. Place a tape measure around your dog's neck and up over the occiput, pulling it snug. Add three inches to that measurement

Obedience leash, chain choke collar, and leather collar. Basic needs for obedience training are few.

The correct length of the choke chain should have no more than three extra inches.

To make up the collar, lift one ring above the other and drop a loop of the chain down through the bottom ring.

The collar is put on over the dog's head so that it pulls in an upward direction. The lead gets fastened to the upper ring. There should be no more than three inches between the tightened collar and the ring for the leash.

and you will have the correct size for your Vizsla. It is advisable to use a nylon choke collar for a very young dog when starting, as the sound of a chain on his neck may make him uneasy. A chain may also pull the little hairs in his coat.

To make up the collar, simply hold one of the rings in each hand. Lifing one hand above the other, drop a loop of the collar slowly down through the ring held in the lower hand until the two rings meet. Put the collar over the dog's head so that it pulls in an upward direction. Then fasten the lead to the ring which passes over the dog's neck. Never allow your dog to wear this type of collar when he is not being trained. It can catch onto things and slowly strangle him.

BASIC LESSONS

The first basic rule to understand is that you are not asking your Vizsla to follow a command; you are telling him. Be firm. If you pay attention to what you are doing, praising and rewarding the exact behavior you want, your dog will learn easily, happily, and correctly after just a few times.

Sit

Your puppy can learn to sit soon after he has learned how to walk on a leash. With him on your left side, gather the leash in your right hand so that there is only a slight slack in it as it goes to your dog's collar. Leave your left hand hanging empty at your side. At the same time you are telling him to sit, pull up gently on the leash with your right hand and gently push his hindquarters down to the ground with your left hand. Every time he sits, be quick to praise him.

It does not matter how he sits. Training for straight sits is only important for obedience trials and that type of formal education can come later. All you want right now is a dog that is friendly and reliable. He will soon sit

Teach your Vizsla to sit by pulling up on the leash with your right hand at the same time that you are pushing down on his rear with your left hand. Penlee's Harann Best Bet Yet, owned by Betty Anderson

as soon as he sees your left hand move towards his rear, and as soon as he has associated the word with the action, use it frequently around the house.

Heel

This exercise is quite often ignored by pet owners since the only time their Vizsla might have to walk on leash is on a trip to the veterinarian's. But the heel is one of the basics of dog obedience, and it is necessary to make your dog a true companion. Your Vizsla must learn to stay near you when walking, no matter how interested he is in other things.

Do not make sudden jerks and pulls with the leash. Just hold it tightly enough that your

Left: Heeling is the basics of dog obedience. Your Vizsla should learn to walk close by your left side with his shoulder in line with your left leg. Ch. Victor's Star Attraction, SH, CD, owned by Judy Richie. *Top, right:* If your dog is lagging, encourage him to keep up with you by patting your leg and praising him. *Bottom, right:* Come to a halt slowly and, giving the command to "Sit," pull up on the leash with your right hand and touch his rear with your left.

dog is comfortable when he is near your left leg, but very uncomfortably tight if he tries to move from that position. Keep the leash in your right hand, leaving your left hand free to give him a pat every so often.

Once he has learned to stay close by you while on leash, loosen the leash a little and encourage him with a pat on your leg, repeating "Good boy" and "Heel" in a pleasant voice. Patience and praise are the key. Correct him by urging and coaxing, instead of a lot of pulling on the leash.

When your Vizsla starts walking easily beside you, begin making turns and changing directions. It will make it more interesting to your dog and keep his attention on you. Practice doing circles to the left and right. Use trees and garbage cans as an obstacle course. Repeat "Heel" often.

Once you have him heeling nicely by your left side, start using the sit command every time you halt. Keep your eye on your dog at all times and as you are coming to a stop be ready with your left hand to touch his rear end.

To put your dog into a stand, walk him into a standing position, being careful not to pull up on the leash.

Hold the leash in your left hand and swing your right hand across to a halt in front of your dog's nose, giving the command of "Stay."

Turn and face your dog, still telling him to "Stay."

Go to the end of your leash with your dog on a stand-stay. This teaches him control from a distance.

Do not say anything to your dog unless he moves, then be quick with both the hand and voice command to "Stay."

When he sits readily as you halt, you will know that he has learned the exercise and the command.

Continue to vary your speed of heeling and sitting so that your Vizsla has to pay attention. Go from a fast pace to a slow one, constantly talking to him with praise.

Heeling will probably take longer than any other exercise you teach him. Combining it with the sit he has learned will give you a well–behaved dog that will automatically sit when you come to a stop. Patience and repetition, plus a relaxed attitude, will make for pleasant sessions, and a happy dog.

Stand

The basic stand will take longer compared to the short time taken for the sit. It is a required exercise in obedience competition, and a necessity in the breed ring where a dog has to be able to stand, sometimes for extended periods. Even if you do not plan on either of these competitions, your Vizsla should learn to stand quietly for an examination by your veterinarian.

It is easier to teach it from a standing position rather than getting him back up on his feet once he has sat down. Remember not to pull up on the leash or try to control him. Simply stop walking and do not encourage the sit. Instead, try scratching his back while giving the command "Stand." If he starts to sit, scratch him on the rump and in his anxiety for the scratching to continue, he will rise into contact with your hand.

Keep repeating the stand command quietly, along with praise. The stand exercise will extend into a stand-stay since he will learn he is supposed to stand until he is told to do anything else. The more praise you give him, the quicker he will learn, as a Vizsla loves to be able to please his owner and receive praise.

The hand signal for stay is done by holding the leash loosely in the left hand, swinging your right hand across your body and bringing your right palm to a sudden halt just in front of your dog's nose. As you swing your hand out, and at the same moment that you bring your palm into position, give the command "Stay!"

Now calmly start backing away from your dog to the end of the leash. Do not say anything to him unless he starts to move. Then quickly step forward, and bring your hand across in front of his nose again, repeating "Stay" in a sterner voice.

Sit–Stay

Surprisingly, it is usually easier to teach your dog to sit and stay after you have introduced the notion of being told to stay while standing. Since he has learned the command he can readily adapt it to his sit.

As in the stand, hold the leash in your left hand and leave him after giving him the command to stay, only this time leave him in a sitting position. Move away from him, quietly repeating the command "Stay." Do not praise him at this point as a Vizsla instantly responds to praise with a bounce and a wagging tail, and you do not want any movement from him.

If he does not remain in place, go back and repeat the procedure. Lead him to the spot where you want him to sit and leave him again. As he gets more dependable and is able to stay in place for several seconds, use a longer lead so that you are able to go farther from him. Go to the end of your lead and stand facing him, but do not say anything to him if he is still.

When you return to him give a lot of praise in an excited voice so that he knows he has really pleased you. Practice the sit and stay exercise in the house to keep reminding him that he must stay wherever he is told to. As you go from room to room put him into a sit–stay where he can see you, and gradually increase it to include out–of–sight sits. Remember always to give a lot of praise when returning to him.

Down-Stay

Since any dog will feel vulnerable in a down position, you may get strong resistance to this

To teach the sit-stay, place your dog in a sit by your left side.

Giving the command to "Stay," turn and face him.

Giving another voice and hand command to stay, slowly back up to the end of your leash.

Stand quietly at the end of your leash and do not talk to your dog unless he moves.

After your dog is reliable on a sit-stay off leash, practice it in the house with you being out of sight.

Above, left: Your dog may panic if you use too much force for the "down." Do it calmly and gently as you quietly keep giving the command.

Right, top: Kneel by your dog and, reaching over his body, grasp him by each foreleg.

Below, left: Lean some of your body weight on his shoulders as you pull forward on his legs until his chest is on the ground.

Below, right: With training, your dog will drop to the ground on command.

command until he understands that he is not being threatened in any way.

Place your Vizsla in a sit by your side and, kneeling down next to him, slide your left arm over his shoulders and grasp his foreleg. With your right hand, grasp his right foreleg just below the elbow. Now lean some of your body weight on his shoulders as you pull forward on his legs, giving the "Down" command.

Since his body is in a straight line with the pressure centered on his breastbone, your Vizsla may find this an uncomfortable position and turn over on his side. Let him lie any way he might want to. At this point the only important thing is that he has learned the exercise.

Some dogs will resist for several times before learning a reliable down. However, you should find that once your dog learns the command, it is just a matter of practice. You may have to persist by pulling his forelegs out in front of him and pushing him down from a sitting position for several days until he will go down simply by you pointing to the floor and giving the command.

As in the sit and the stand-stay, practice leaving him with a strong "Stay" and walk a distance from him before turning to face him. When he has become reliable, do the exercise in different rooms in your house by disappearing from his sight.

AFTER BASICS

If you are interested in obedience competition, you will need to go to training classes and learn how to teach your Vizsla to "finish" or go to heel position from a "recall," and all the finer points of body language and handling. There, you will get the necessary off-leash work and your dog will be exposed to distractions similar to those faced at a trial.

If you plan to continue with the fun and challenge of obedience competition, you will need a copy of the current Obedience Regulations, published by the American Kennel Club, 51 Madison Ave., New York, N.Y. 10010. These will contain the complete regulations

Teaching your Vizsla to retrieve over a low jump will eliminate the boredom of basic beginning obedience.

for performance and judging, explain how titles are won, and disqualifying conditions.

OBEDIENCE TRIALS

A licensed trial is an event where dogs perform exercises according to the rules established by the AKC. The dogs are judged on their performances of each exercise. In order to receive a qualifying score a dog must earn a minimum of 170 points out of a possible perfect score of 200 at each trial. The 170 points must be made by earning more than half of the points allotted for each exercise. For a dog to earn an obedience title he must get a qualifying score in three trials, under three different judges.

Obedience trials may be held separately or in conjunction with either all breed or specialty (single breed) dog shows. Practice events, called matches, provide opportunities to prepare for "the real thing." Your local kennel club or training class can help you learn about dates, locations, and entry procedures.

The Classes

There are three levels of competition at obedience trials. The first level, Novice, consists of basic heeling both on and off leash, sit, stand, down and recall. Qualifying in three trials will give your dog a Companion Dog (CD) title.

The second level, Open, takes the basics farther with all off-lead work, and adds jumping and retrieving on command. If your dog has three qualifying scores he will earn a Companion Dog Excellent (CDX) title.

The third level of competition is Utility. It includes a scent discrimination test, directed jumping and retrieving exercises, silent hand

Winning High in Trial and High Combined score at the VCOA National Specialty in 1988, is Ch./OTCH Autumn Gold Jaz of Witts End.

Ch. Sandyacre Poquito Chili Bean, UD, SH, winning High combined in trial at the Rio Salado Vizsla Club's specialty. Owner, Maria Fajardo-Zucconi.

signals, and a group examination. Three qualifying scores by your Vizsla will earn him a Utility Dog (UD) title.

TRACKING TESTS

Tracking tests provide yet another way to enjoy the excellent scenting ability of your Vizsla. Training him to track will be fun, interesting, and educational as he first learns to follow your scent and then that of a stranger, retrieving an article dropped at the end of the trail. You will learn how the weather conditions and wind currents can affect your dog's scenting ability in the field and how his keen sense of smell could be used to help save a life.

Tracking can be started with your Vizsla at any stage unlike the other obedience degrees that must be earned in order of complexity.

The initial tracking training can be done at home if you have a field or yard of proper size (the track must be 440 to 500 yards long and the dog is trained on a harness which is attached to a leash between thirty and forty feet in length). There are excellent books available which teach tracking at home, but if possible, try to locate other trainers in the area. The enjoyment and companionship of other dog owners, regardless of breed, will make for a wonderful new experience for both you and your Vizsla.

OBEDIENCE TRIAL CHAMPIONSHIPS (OTCH)

In July 1977, the AKC established rules for a new title for Obedience competitors. Points

High in Trial winner Ch/OTCH Autumn Gold Jaz of Witts End at VCOA National in 1986.

Ch. Coffee's Tijuana Moonshine UDT was trained to all her obedience titles by her young owner Christy Coffee.

Ch. Lyon's Brewster of Harann, CDX, owned by Joy Lyons.

Ch. Penlee's Cutter, UD, in Open obedience. Owned by Joy Lyons.

Ch. Piper's Moonstruck Moppet, UD; Ch. Piper's Kid Coffee, UD, VC; and Ch. Piper's Tijuana Red, UD. A trio of titled Vizslas owned by Karen Coffee.

can now be awarded to a dog that has already earned his Utility title and whose owner wishes him to continue in Obedience trials, in a competitive spirit; for a higher title.

The requirement for an Obedience Trial Champion title is earning 100 points — not an easy task, as a dog has to earn those points by placing first or second in Open B or Utility class competition. Points are determined by the total number of dogs competing in the class.

The dog competes in the regular Open and Utility class against dogs at different levels of training — those still working for their CDX or UD and those others also competing for points on their obedience trial championship. It takes an owner with a lot of dedication to the sport of obedience, and a happy, intelligent, and wonderful working Vizsla to earn an OTC.

At this writing, only five Vizslas have completed requirements for an Obedience Championship:

Triple Champion Cariad's Kutya Kai Costa, owned by Robert and Marianne Costa (1980)

OTC. Gold In Hills Janos, owned by Blaine and Melissa McGaughey (1981)

OTC. Barben's New Year Baby, owned by Curt Morsell (1983)

OTC. Bouman's Lady Circle, owned by Mark and Janice Bouman (1986)

Ch. and OTC. Autumn Gold Jaz Of Witts End, owned by DeLoise Witt (1987)

Ch. Taunee's Loki Santana, CD, a top-producing sire of fifty-two champions, was selectively bred to only sixteen bitches.

8

The Vizsla in the Show Ring

As you marvel over the beauty and smooth movement of your young Vizsla, the lure of the show ring may become more and more appealing. Forget the fact that you have never even gone to a dog show before. You have seen the "big one" at the Garden on television and know that your Vizsla is just as pretty. The Vizsla is exhuberant, vivacious and fun to show.

EARLY TRAINING

If you plan to show your dog, it is very important that you start conditioning and training your puppy just as soon as he has settled in and adjusted to his new home. After he has had a chance to get used to the feel of his collar, and the pull of the leash, gradually begin training with a "show lead." You can choose from several types of show leads, from a thin chain with a lightweight lead attached, to a one–piece thin leather lead. Whichever you prefer, it should be used for show training and the show ring only. Do not use this kind of lead for any obedience work.

The lead goes on around your Vizsla's neck, snugly up behind his ears and is kept in that position so that it does not slide down his neck. If you are using a thin choke chain, it goes on so that it tightens and releases across the back of his neck the same way an obedience training chain works. Remember to keep all training for the show ring light and happy. Once you have taken the enthusiasm out of a young Vizsla nothing on earth can put it back.

The lead will be held in your left hand only, with the end gathered inside your hand. The correct place for your puppy to move will be in line with your left leg and out from your body about one foot. Do not let him get in the habit of moving too close and crowding you.

The Vizsla moves beautifully with a far-reaching gait. Try to get in the habit of moving out with longer strides yourself, and you will see your dog reaching out with his movement also. Practice at a walk until you have coordinated your movement. Your lead should be an extension of your arm, and your dog thus becomes an extension of yourself.

Practice making "figure eights" as your puppy has to learn inside as well as outside turns. When both you and your puppy have learned control, increase your pace gradually to a smooth, slow run. Do not use mincing steps. Once you have mastered the movement and lead work with your puppy, the next step is to have control of him while standing still.

Left: Lightweight leads are used for the conformation ring. If a thin choke chain is used, it goes on the same as the obedience collar but is kept high on the neck, just behind the ears. A thin lead is then attached. *Top:* Training for the show ring starts at a young age. This three-month-old puppy is already stacking beautifully.

Bottom: Teach your dog to stop and stand in a correct position, with his feet pointing straight ahead.

The Vizsla should have a far-reaching, light-footed movement whether he is in the show ring or in the field.

Early training will teach control no matter what your future plans are for a young dog.

When you come to the spot where you want your puppy to stop and stand, give the command to stand as you tighten up slightly on the lead. Simultaneously, extend your right hand in front of his face. If he attempts to sit every time you stop, slip your left toe under his belly and lift up gently; he must learn not to sit while he is wearing a show lead.

When he seems to have mastered stopping and standing, stand in front of him and face him. Keep your body straight and do not lean over him. Do not worry at this point if he is not setting his body up correctly as you are only teaching him control. As you proceed to improve with movement and control, gradually loosen the lead so that your puppy moves out freely. Make sure he is staying correctly on your left side and does not run unexpectedly in front of you, tripping you.

Get your Vizsla used to having his teeth examined while he is still young because a judge will examine the mouth in the ring to make sure your dog has the correct scissors bite called for in the Vizsla Standard. Handle his mouth gently if he is still in his teething period as it may be sensitive. The correct way to show the judge your dog's bite is to place your right hand under the jaw and your left hand over the bridge of your dog's nose. With the left index finger, lift up the upper lip. Do not let the mouth sag open; the teeth must be shown in the correct bite position.

If you will be showing a male, he must also become accustomed to having his testicles examined. Touch them lightly each time you groom or train him. A judge always checks a male to ascertain whether both testicles are down into the scrotum.

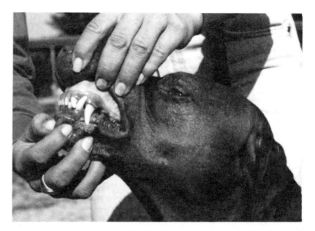

The correct way to show the bite to the judge. The mouth is closed and the teeth together in a proper bite position.

Ch. Rotkopf Tia d Russet Leather
Sire: Miklos Heliker
Dam: Ch. Rotkopf's Regina of Sageacre
Owner: Bev Wanjon

When setting up correctly, the front legs will be the same distance apart on the ground as they are coming out of the shoulder.

With your right hand holding the muzzle, lift the left leg at the elbow and place it in position.

Holding the muzzle in the left hand, use your right hand to set the right front leg in position.

As you continue to train your Vizsla puppy for the show ring, a practical investment will be an inexpensive closet door mirror. Before working on "stacking" your dog, place the mirror against a wall so you can watch while you work. Stacking, or setting up your dog, simply means putting him into as natural and favorable a stance as is possible, for the judge to view and go over him.

Start with your Vizsla's front. His forelegs should be exactly the same distance apart on the ground as they are coming out of his body. Holding his muzzle with your right hand to keep his head facing straight ahead, reach over his back with the left hand and, grasping the left leg at the elbow, lift it and position the leg with the foot pointing straight ahead. Change hands and do the same thing with the right leg. If done correctly, both front feet will be under their respective shoulders, with the toes pointed straight to the front. Do not try to change the position of the feet by handling

them. Always move them by lifting at the elbow.

Now set the rear. Taking the muzzle in your right hand to keep the head straight, run your left hand down your dog's back so he can feel you going to his rear. Your dog's rear legs should always appear perpendicular from the hock joints to the ground, and turn neither in nor out at the hocks. The rear feet should be the same distance apart as the hip bones.

Keeping an eye on the mirror, reach over your Vizsla's back and firmly taking hold of his leg at the top of the hock joint, move the leg to where you want it. Then do the same with the other rear leg, still keeping your right hand on the muzzle. Remember always to set up the legs on the judge's side first.

Do not let your dog lean on you. After you have stacked him, either kneel beside him or stand away from his body, with your right hand under his muzzle and your left hand holding the tail out. Your puppy is not going to hold

Ch. Cariad's Szultan Barat
Sire: Ch. Taunee's Loki Santana, CD
Dam: Ch. Cariad's Gypsy Sprite
Owner: Robert Branden

Stacking the Rear

Holding the head facing straight ahead, run the left hand over the rear in preparation for placing the left rear leg.

Still holding the head straight, lift the rear left leg at the hock to place it in the correct position.

The rear can be set up by reaching over the dog's back, or from underneath.

Set the right rear leg last. The rear feet should be the same distance apart as the hip bones.

Correct presentation of your Vizsla. The head and body are straight, and the tail is held out gently.

that stack for any more than a few seconds at a time, but do not get impatient with him. The more you practice, the more understanding he will have of what you are trying to make him do.

Before you consider entering an AKC point show with your young dog, get some ring experience by going to match shows. These are practice shows for both you and your puppy, using many of the licensed show procedures. They will give both of you exposure to slippery floors, congestion, noise, crowds, and strange under the regulations of the AKC. If you are planning to show your dog, write to the AKC for a current copy of *Rules Applying to Registrations and Dog Shows*. While you are still training your young Vizsla and waiting for him to mature, take the time to attend a licensed dog show and watch the judging procedures. Nothing else will give you quite the understanding of how the classes are judged and the points awarded. It may be confusing the first few times, but usually most exhibitors will be happy to explain to a newcomer.

Match shows are fun to practice with puppies. Bob Branden's four-month-old Poppy wins the sporting group.

dogs, and they cost a lot less to enter than a point show. You may find notices of local match shows in the newspaper or store windows, or you can call your local kennel club.

AKC CONFORMATION SHOWS

Any purebred dog eligible for registration with the AKC may compete at licensed dog shows provided that he can not be disqualified

While at the show, locate the show superintendent's area and ask to be put on his mailing list for dog show premium lists for your area. Unlike a fun match where you enter on the day of the show, AKC licensed show entries must be sent in advance.

You can also find out about upcoming shows from your local kennel club, training class, or by checking the national dog magazines. The American Kennel Club publishes a list of licensed shows in its official magazine, *Purebred Dogs, The AKC Gazette*. You will find show dates and addresses for superintendents listed in *Dog World*, available on the newstand. The *AKC Gazette* lists all pertinent information necessary for entering any show and includes a wealth of interesting and educational information as well.

The premium list contains the name of the club holding the show, the date and location, map and directions, motels in the area, hours of the show, cost of an entry, the closing date, and the address of the show superintendent. It also includes each judge's breakdown of breed assignments.

In order to enter an AKC licensed show you must fill out an official entry form. *Copies are not acceptable unless they also have the rules copied on the back of the form.* It is acceptable to scratch out the name and date of the show printed on the form and substitute the name and date of another show if you cannot obtain the correct form. Blank forms may be used for any show, and can be obtained from any superintendent or by writing AKC.

Entries close two to three weeks in advance of the show. This date is printed on the front of the premium list, and entries, correctly filled out and including the fee, must be in the hands of the superintendent by this date. No exceptions will be made.

Entry forms need to be filled out completely or they will be rejected. The information you need to complete your entry can be found on your Vizsla's AKC registration certificate.

The Classes

The regular classes offered at an AKC show are Puppy, Novice, Bred By Exhibitor, American Bred, and Open. All of these classes are divided by sex.

The Puppy class is for dogs that are 6 months of age and under 1 year. Your puppy is eligible for entering on the day he becomes 6 months old and can show in this class until the day before his first birthday.

The Novice class restricts you from entering if your dog has already won championship points, or if he has placed first three times in

---

Table 8-1
Checklist of Supplies To Take To A Show

Essential Items

For Me

Judging Schedule
Jacket with pocket, and comfortable shoes
Clothes brush and grooming smock or apron
Wet-wipes or washrag and paper towels
Trash bags
Pooper scooper
Rain gear

For My Vizsla

Drinking water and bowl
2 Show leads and collars (one to wear & spare)
Grooming tools
Crate with pad or rug in it
Several terrycloth towels
Liver or other bait
Rawhide chews and favorite toys
First Aid kit includingdiarrhea medication

Optional Items

Folding chair
Cooler with lunch or drinks
Dolly with wheels to roll crate & supplies
Change of clothes and/or shoes
Overnight bag including any needed medications

Grooming table
Shade cloth
Exercise pen
Obedience equipment (if also competing there)
Dog food (if overnight trip)

Ch. Russet Leather Proud Warrior, owned by Mark and Bonnie Goodwein, was Best of Breed at the VCOA National Specialty in 1989 and has one Best in Show win. Handled by Cindy Lane.

Novice, or once in any Bred By Exhibitor, American Bred, or Open class.

The Bred By Exhibitor class entry has to be owned or co-owned by its breeder, or by the spouse of the breeder, and must be handled in the class by one of the breeders or by a member of their immediate family.

The American Bred class is restricted to a dog born in the United States from a breeding that took place in the U.S.

The Open class is for any dog 6 months of age or older.

At some shows "non-regular" classes will be offered for veterans (over 10 years old), stud dogs, brood bitches, 12-to-18-month puppies, or other categories.

Championship Points

To gain a Championship title on your Vizsla you must accrue a total of 15 points in competition at any licensed AKC shows. In those 15 points there must be two wins that are major points, won under two different judges (a major being 3, 4, or 5 points). Points are determined by a scale for your area and how many you win depends on how many Vizslas you defeat that day. The highest number of points you can win at a single show is 5.

THE SHOW RING

The judging program for each show you enter usually arrives in the mail about a week before the show date. It includes the time each breed is judged and the judges do adhere fairly close to that schedule. They will not wait for anyone so always make plans to be at the showground at least an hour before you are due to be judged. That will give you time to find your ring, get your dog settled down and accustomed to the noise and other breeds, and to watch the pattern of judging which your judge is following.

Best in Show winner Ch. Lyon's Brewster of Harann, CD.
Sire: BIS Ch. Penlee's Cutter UD
Dam: BIS Ch. Harann's
    Tulipann
Owners: Joy and William Lyons

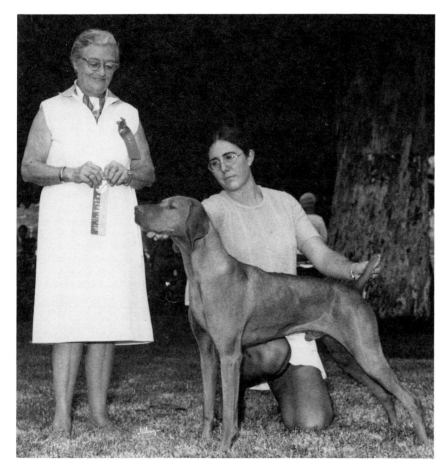

Ch. Totton's Jo-B Russet Leather, top winning Vizsla in 1972.
Sire: Ch. Napkelte Vadasz Dalos
Dam: Burnt Gold Becket of
    Randan
Owner: Bev Wanjon

Get your armband from the ring steward and put in on your upper left arm so that the number can easily be seen by the judge. Stay at the ring side to be ready when your number or class is called.

Order of Judging

All male classes are judged first, one class at a time, starting with puppy class (if there are entries). There are four awards in each class.

After all the male classes are judged the first place winner in each class comes back into the ring to be judged again. From this group the judge awards one dog the title of Winners Dog, and it is to this dog that the points are awarded.

The Winners Dog leaves the ring and the second place dog from the same class from which the winner was selected comes in to compete with the remaining first-place winners for the title of Reserve Winners Dog. No points are awarded for this win except if for some disqualifying reason the Winners Dog is found to be ineligible for his win, he loses it and the Reserve Winners Dog gets the points.

When all the male classes have been judged the bitches are judged in the same manner, with one of them being awarded Winners Bitch and the bitch points.

The last class to be judged is the Best of Breed competition. This class consists of all the entered Champions, and the Winners Dog and the Winners Bitch. If there are veterans'

Figure 8-1
Classes at an AKC Show

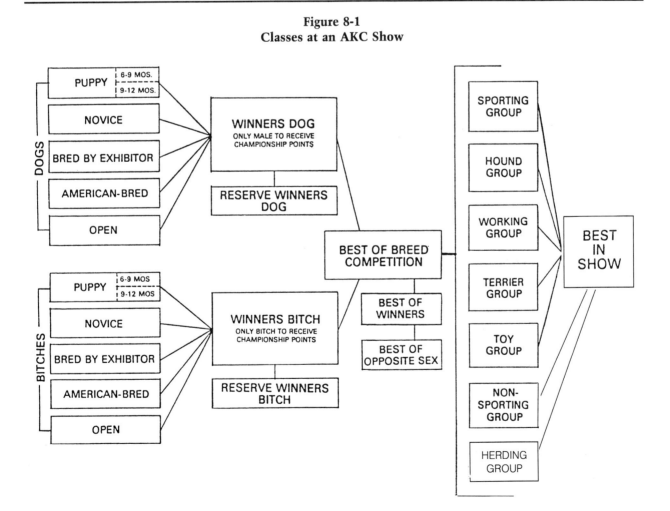

Best in Show winner Ch. Lyon's Skipjack of Harann
Sire: BIS Ch. Penlee's Cutter, UD
Dam: BIS Ch. Harann's Tulipann
Owners: Joy and William Lyons

Ch. Piroska's Tick Tock of Renbrok
Sire: Ch. Great Guns Riding High
Dam: Renie's Amber Gypsy
Owner: Marilyn Fowler

Ch. Camarily Rambling Rose,
CD, Winners Bitch at the 1979
VCOA National Specialty.
Sire: Ch. Rich's Pirosch Aranya
Dam: Ch. Sloane's Palinka
Owner: Robert Sloane

classes, these winners also participate. From this class the judge will pick his Best of Breed, Best of Winners, and Best of Opposite Sex.

The Best of Winners is chosen from the Winners Dog and Winners Bitch. The winner may be able to gain additional points if the other sex had more entries and higher points. For example, if 4 points were awarded the Winners Bitch and only 2 points were earned by the Winners Dog, but the male was chosen as the Best of Winners, he would gain the highest number of points available that day, which were 4. The bitch would still retain her own points however.

The judge will also pick his Best of Breed winner and his Best of Opposite Sex. The Best of Breed winner will go on to compete in the Sporting Group with other sporting breed winners. The winner of the Sporting Group then competes with the winners from other groups for the coveted Best in show award.

Gaiting and Ring Patterns

There are several patterns of movement which a judge could request but only three of those are commonly used. They are the circle, triangle, and the straight line, or "down and back" as it is called.

When you first enter the ring, whether it is alone or with others, the first movement is usually a command to "Take them around." Always circle to your left, or counterclockwise, with your Vizsla on your left. Start off easily and flow into a smooth faster movement.

Only you are going to know which is a comfortable speed for both you and your dog. If you have practiced well you will be able to feel when the "timing" is right. The judge does not want to see how fast your dog can move, but rather if he can move correctly.

After the initial go-around your judge will examine each of the dogs individually. Keep your dog correctly stacked and do not fuss with him as the judge starts to check the head, eyes, bite, shoulders, testicles and hocks. The best way to call attention to a fault is to fuss with

it. Readjusting a slightly turned toe while the judge is going over your dog is the first thing he will notice.

As the judge examines your Vizsla, get your hands out of the way. Steady your dog, but do not hamper the judge. As he moves to the rear of your dog, hold your dog's head firmly and adjust any front leg or foot which may be out of line if you can do it without disturbing the rear.

Do not let your dog take command in the ring. One of the tricks he may try is holding a foot in the air and refusing to put it down. Do not let him get away with it. Gently push him in the rib section to force his line of balance over to the side being help up. This will necessitate his replacing the foot or falling flat

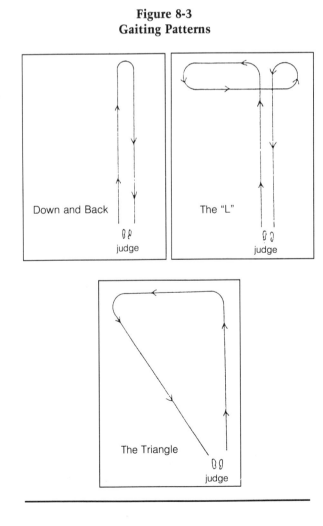

Figure 8-3
Gaiting Patterns

on his face. Do this any time your Vizsla's weight is not on a foot.

If your Vizsla protests about being stacked and tries to shy away by creating a bend with his body, immediately with a finger, poke him in the ribs on the side being bowed, forcing him to readjust to the proper position.

The cowering dog is another problem. If your dog is tired, scared, or physically down on his pasterns, you need to distract him away from cowering by baiting with food or a small toy and also asking in a low voice, "Where's the bird?"

If you find your Vizsla leaning back, a hand just below an elbow can prod him back into an "up on the toes" look, or place a very sharp fingernail just below his last rib and push forward. Keep corrections subtle and practice them in training class before you try them in the ring.

After the judge has examined the dogs individually he will have them move, one at a

Left: Ch. Kamet Rocket
Sire: FCh/AFC Randy Duke
Dam: Ch. Debreceny Dijana
Owner: Kay Thrasher.

Below, left: Ch. Brance N Carob's Solo's Son
Sire: Ch. Chestry and Carob's Solo Sun
Dam: Ch. Brance N Carob's Shenandoah
Owner: Marion Coffman.

Below, right: Ch. Rotkopf's Super Charger, CD, JH, Best in Specialty winner, VCOA National Specialty winner, 1981. Owned by Michele Coburn.

time. The simplest pattern you may be asked to do will be the straight "down and back." Move your dog straight away from the judge to the farthest point you can go in the ring, turn your dog around the outside of your body, and return in a line to the judge, stopping just a few feet in front of him. Your dog should be in a position directly in front of the judge while you stand off to the side. Make sure your dog stops with his feet and body pointing straight ahead.

The triangle pattern is also popular with judges as they can see the dog moving away, from the side, and the front. It is an easy pattern to do with no changing of hands. Just picture a triangle in your mind. Keeping your dog on your left side at all times, leave the judge in a straight line and move to the end of the ring. Turn left, and move across the ring as far as you can. Turn at a slight angle and return in a straight line to the judge.

Right: Best in Show winner Ch. Penlee's Cutter, UD
Sire: Ch. Dirigo Gambler's Marker
Dam: Ch. Firebrand's Constant Comment
Owners: Joy and William Lyons

Below, left: Ch. Csopi V Hunt, CD, top winning Vizsla in 1967.
Sire: Ch. Csisckas of Goncoltanya
Dam: Gellert Csintalan
Owner: Bertha Butler
Photo courtesy of J. Hunt

Below, right: Ch. Jin Ja Richards, winner of sixty Best of Breeds and four Group placings, was on the top-ten list for 1973-1976. Owned by Richard Zappacosta and Rosanne DeVergiles.

If you are showing indoors with rubber mats on the floor, make sure that your Vizsla moves on the mats to give him good footing.

One pattern that is not often called for, but should be learned, is the "L." Again, just picture "L" in your mind as you move. Leave the judge in a straight line and move to the end of the ring. Turn left and go to the next end. Change hands as you turn around and return to the judge over the same path you used moving out, this time with your dog on your right in order not to put your body between your dog and the judge.

No matter how many handling classes you attend, there is nothing like the experience of actually being in the ring. You will soon learn to watch the judge and your dog, and to make sure you do not fall over the ring barriers.

Insufficient training or improper and faulty handling can result in a lower placing than your Vizsla deserves and could conceivably ruin an otherwise promising show career. In a wider sense and of even more importance to the breed as a whole is the impression your dog would project to the spectators. The Vizsla is a classy, showy breed that loves attention. School yourself to be at ease in the ring with your dog. If you are tense and nervous it will communicate to your dog and he will display the same emotional stress.

Remember, if you do not win one day there is always another show and another judge with another opinion. You will see bad dogs and bad judges, and it may be hard to keep up confidence in yourself and your dog. Handling well means that you must have a positive attitude in spite of all the disappointments.

Your Responsibility as an Exhibitor

It is estimated that between twenty-five and thirty dogs can be judged in an hour and each judge has his schedule set for the day. It is the sole responsibility of each exhibitor to be at the ringside and ready when his breed is called, and not delay the judging in any way. It is also the exhibitor's responsibility to be sure that

Table 8-2
Courtesy in the Show Ring

Do not crowd the dog in front of you.

Don't block the judge's view of another dog.

Be polite to the judge and other exhibitors.

Do not make excuses to the judge about your dog or yourself. He must judge your dog as he appears

Keep bait and toys from distracting other entries.

Avoid making loud noises to attract your dog's attention.

If another handler blocks your dog from the judge's view, be courteous but firm in requesting him to move.

If another exhibitor deliberately interfers, you may ask the steward to move you, or you may file a complaint with her.

If you do not understand the judge, you may ask him to clarify. Paying careful attention to the dog ahead should avoid this problem.

Always take time to congratulate the winners.

his Vizsla has been properly exercised and has eliminated before ring time. Not only is it an embarrassment to you if your dog fouls the ring, but it will irritate your judge if he is delayed while the floor is being cleaned.

There is nothing so exasperating for a judge as an exhibitor who is not paying attention. Watch the handler or class ahead of you so that you are prepared for the pattern of movement your judge will want you to do. Have your Vizsla under control in the ring and set him up smoothly and quickly. The judge will not have the time nor is it expected of him to stand by and wait while you try to set up an inexperienced dog.

It is your responsibility to present a clean Vizsla to the judge. Not only a clean, shiny coat, but clean teeth, mouth and ears. If you have a bitch in season, it is suggested that you quietly mention that fact to the judge as he

Ch. Cariad's Surfstone Szuka places Best of Opposite Sex at the VCOA National Specialty in 1987. Owned by Paul Gornoski; handled by Bill Pace.

starts to examine her, so that he will not get any discharge or odor on his hands.

PROFESSIONAL HANDLERS

In show after show you will be competing with professional handlers. These are people who have spent years in the show ring, probably starting as junior handlers or breeders handling their own dogs. As they became more proficient at it, they progressed to handling for other people and being paid for it. They have to be good at it. Many of them make their livings traveling and showing dogs throughout the country.

An amateur may not always be free to travel to shows — he may have restricting job or family commitments — or he may not be interested in learning to handle his own dog, and in these cases a professional handler is the only answer. Some clients carry their own dogs to shows and deliver them to the handlers at the ringside. In this way they are able to watch their dogs in competition and share in the enjoyment and satisfaction of a win, without the anxiety and nervousness of having to do the handling themselves.

Once you have decided that a professional handler is the best route for you to take, take your dog's personality into account. Most Vizslas can not take any rough handling or training.

ity of the handler is what is judged, not the merits of the dog being handled.

The purpose of Junior Handling is to teach good sportsmanship, poise, correct handling, grooming and care of dogs to the breeders, exhibitors, and handlers of the future.

The Classes

The regular Junior Showmanship classes are Novice and Open, with both usually divided by age groups.

Ch. Willow Runn's Bold Brigadier, with owner Heather Christie, winning the Junior Showmanship class at the Newtown Kennel Club show.

Ch. Cariad's Lieberstraum Barat, being shown in Junior Showmanship class by owner Anglele Wright.

Whether your choice is a man or a woman, make sure that the handler knows a heavy hand will intimidate a Vizsla.

JUNIOR SHOWMANSHIP

Junior Showmanship classes are offered to encourage youth to get involved in showing. In Junior Showmanship competition the abil-

The Novice class is for boys and girls at least 10 years of age and under 18 who have not won first in competition in that class more than three times. If the class is divided by age, a Junior must be at least 10 years of age, but under 14, and the Senior must be at least 14, but under 18 years of age.

The Open class is for boys and girls at least 10 years of age and under 18 who have won the Novice class three times in competition. If divided by age, the division is the same as for the Novice class.

Debbie Bush handles her Vizsla bitch, Kedves, to win Best Junior Handler at the VCOA National Specialty in 1979.

Each dog handled in Junior Showmanship must be owned by the Junior or by a member of his family, which includes parents, grandparents, sisters, brothers, aunts, uncles, and even several half relatives, and foster children.

By learning to be at ease in the Junior Showmanship ring, a young handler will carry the attributes of courtesy, poise, confidence, efficiency and experience over into all facets of his life. His entire future will benefit from the association.

If you are the parent of a Junior handler, try not to do anything in the way of criticism that will take away his confidence in his handling. Do not stand outside the ring and glare at him if he is making a mistake or does not place in the class. Support his interest in handling with simple, quiet suggestions. With a constant criticism he may get the idea that winning is more important than good sportsmanship.

Give your child a chance to develop friendships with other junior handlers and to have an open mind to learn from them. Remind him that his responsibility to his dog has to come first, and encourage a healthy, happy attitude toward competition, whether it is in losing or winning.

The winners of the classes compete for the Best Junior Handler at each show. Juniors who win eight or more Open classes in competition in a single year earn the right to compete at the Westminster Kennel club show every February where the Top Junior Handler of The Year is chosen.

Rules and Regulations

Each dog that is entered in Junior Showmanship has to be eligible to compete in the breed or obedience ring. Since it is the handler that is being judged and not the quality of the dog, a spayed bitch, monorchid or castrated male, or dog with any disqualifying faults under a breed standard that would eliminate it from the breed ring, but leave it eligible for obedience, can be shown in Junior Showmanship. However, bitches in season cannot be shown.

RECORDS IN THE SHOW RING

Top–winning Vizslas leave their impact on the breed and draw the breed to the attention of show fanciers. The first Vizsla in the U.S. to take a Best in Show was Ch. Napkelte Vadas Dalos. Bred by Phil Wright in Canada and owned by William and Elsie Totton in California, "Danny" had his first top win on 24 May 1970. That win was followed by two more later the same year. Danny also became the sire of eighteen champions.

Ch. Debreceny Dezso was the second Vizsla to gain a Best in Show. Bred and owned by the Carpenters in Carmel, California, Dezso gained his first top win on 25 July 1970, at Ventura, California. He was also the breed winner at two National Specialties. A lovely, dark

Ch. Taunee's Loki Santana, CD, made Vizsla history with his record of seven Best in Show wins and 120 group placements.
Sire: Ch. Glen Cottage Loki Barat, CDX
Dam: Ch. Cariad's Gaybine, CD
Owner: Marion Coffman

Ch. Cariad's Surfstone Szuka, record winning bitch with four Best in Shows and 124 Group placings. Owned by Paul Gornoski. *Photo by Kernan.*

Ch. Boelte's Brant of Penlee, winner of two Best in Shows.
Sire: Ch. Taunee's Loki Santana, CD
Dam: Ch. Firebrand's Constant Comment
Owner/Handler: Pat Boelte.
Photo by Ashbey

Ch. Firebrand's Constant Comment, the first Vizsla bitch to earn a Best in Show. Owned by Betty Anderson. *Photo by Gilbert.*

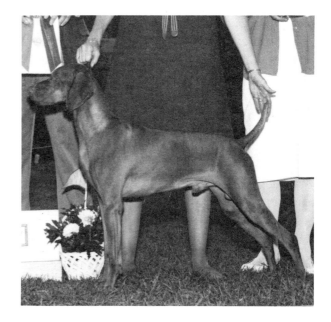

dog, he made a lasting tremendous contribution to the Vizsla breed as the sire of forty–nine champions.

Ch. Taunee's Loki Santana, CD made Vizsla history with his record of seven Best in Show wins and 120 group placements. He was fifth of all sporting dogs in 1974 and seventh in 1975. His record seven Best in Shows has stood for over seventeen years. A beautiful, elegant, stylish dog in the show ring, "Bear" also left a legacy as a top–producing sire with fifty-two champions. Owned by the author, "Bear" was handled by Bobby B. Barlow. "Bear's" sire was Ch. Glen Cottage Loki Barat, CDX, a member of the VCOA Hall of Fame and sire of thirty-one champions. "Bear's dam was Ch. Cariad's Gaybine, CD, the dam of sixteen champions.

Ch. Boelte's Brant of Penlee, owned and handled by Pat Boelte, Valhalla, N.Y., was the first Vizsla to be owner handled to two Best in Show wins. Brant's sire was Ch. Taunee's Loki Santana and his dam was the first Vizsla bitch to gain a Best in Show, Ch. Firebrand's Constant Comment. Proving that an outstanding, beautiful dog can get top wins without the use of a professional handler, Brant also won five Vizsla Specialties and had fifty-six group placings. He is the sire of twenty-eight champions to date, producing dogs with elegance, style, lovely heads, and temperament.

The first bitch to gain multiple top wins was Ch. Harann's Tulipann, bred and owned by Anne Denehy of Huntington Station, N.Y. "Tuli" had a record of four Best in Shows wins.

The record–winning Vizsla bitch to date is Ch. Cariad's Surfstone Szuka. She has had four Best in Show wins and 124 Group placings. Szuka is a double granddaughter of Ch. Taunee's Loki Santana and shows the excellent movement and style that his line continued to produce. She was bred by the author, owned by Paul Gornoski of Lakeland, Florida, and handled by Bill Pace.

Ch. Harann's Tulipann, winner of four Best in Shows.
Sire: Ch. Cariad's Trefas Szereto
Dam: Ch. Harann's Kristiana Penn V Duna, CD
Owner: Anne Denehy

Ch. Cariad's Classic Mariah
Sire: Ch. Cariad's Masterpiece
Dam: Ch. Cariad's Pride N Joy
Owners: Marcia and Milo Folley
Photo by Booth

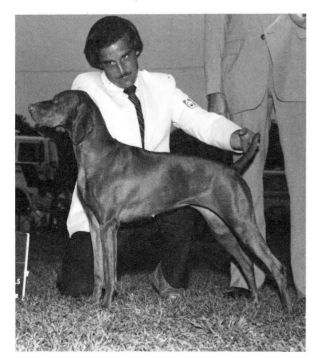

Triple Champion Cariad's Kutya Kai Costa retrieves a downed bird gently to his owner/handler Robert Costa.

9

The Vizsla in the Field

Vizslas are born with a natural instinct to stalk and point. Such desirable attributes as a good nose, style, and natural retrieving will be evident in a puppy from an early age and will make training him enjoyable and easy. It is obvious that the Vizsla needs to be taught by patient, kindly methods, regarding most of his early work as a happy game so that he will mature into a bold and happy worker. However, he should not be allowed to do everything he likes and then suddenly have to be corrected in an attempt to eradicate habits which had been encouraged at the start.

EARLY TRAINING

While your puppy is still young teach him to obey commands around the house, such as sit and come. You should have one major objective in mind — control. Control must be worked at gradually and steadily, so as not to take away your puppy's spirit and enthusiasm. Be consistent with each lesson and, at some point, your puppy will respond. Any response on his part to comply and perform correctly should be instantly rewarded with praise.

Voice tone is of major importance and you should give each command firmly and quietly. Make a conscious effort not to shout a command if your

Above, left: Living in the home and sleeping on the bed does not ruin the natural instincts of the Vizsla in the field.

Above, right: The same dog one hour later finds wild quail and stays on point.

Left: At fourteen weeks of age, this Vizsla puppy shows the natural tendencies to explore on her own.

puppy is not obeying. Encouragement and kindness are what is necessary in training a Vizsla at any stage.

Training to heel early is a must and should never be postponed as it is important to later off–leash control and acceptance of the check cord. As soon as you have started the basics of come and sit, attach a lead to his collar and teach the heel. He might not be too happy about it at first but shortly should be moving with head high and tail wagging.

Start taking your puppy out to strange areas where the grass is of different heights. Encourage him through various types of grass and cover. As soon as he is able to walk on the leash without pulling, you can begin to think about off–leash work with him. To start him off–leash, simply drop the leash and let him trail along as you walk. This is also a good time to incorporate the use of the whistle.

As you call his name and a "Come" use the whistle with the command. This will eventually be the signal while working in the field to call him to you from a distance. If he persists in not coming back to you, you will have to start using a longer lead, or check line, of about twenty feet in length. Letting him run loose, dragging the longer lead, give the command "Come" and either grab or step down on the cord, bringing him to a sudden halt.

When he has become reliable on a recall, either from a voice or whistle command, discontinue the use of the check cord until he starts working in the bird field.

Natural First Points

Every owner of a Vizsla wants to know if his puppy will point. Most puppies do, instinctively. One of the easiest methods to find out what your puppy will do is to use a quail wing attached to a fishing line and pole (without the fish hook, of course). What you are looking for is intense excitement and interest in movement.

Hold the fishing pole at an angle so that the wing is just touching the ground. With your puppy playing loose, jiggle the wing slightly until he sees the movement. He will stop, look at it, and then suddenly make a lunge to grab it. Flip the line and wing up before he grabs it.

Repeat the procedure several times, just moving the wing slightly to keep his attention. After several attempts to grab the wing, he will realize that if he stalks and points it, the wing will stay still. If he tries to pounce on it, flip it up fast. Stop before the puppy gets bored. At a young age he has a very short attention span. If it is overdone he might get discouraged if he is unable to get the wing. Also, since he is responding to movement and not smell, it will not hold his interest.

Introduction to Live Birds

Early successful training is dependent on the use of a lot of live birds. You want your Vizsla

---

Right: Your Vizsla should be encouraged in every way to show interest in a bird.

Below, left: Andre V Schloss Loosdorf (Joey) is shown in 1956 training photos done by V. Halmrast. Basics start with sight-pointing a bird wing attached to a pole and line. Owned by Joan Hunt.

Below, right: Joey is kept on a check cord to keep him from rushing in and grabbing the wing.

to retain his intensity so he must be able to find birds. Since game birds are expensive and, at times, difficult to obtain, it is acceptable to use live pigeons. Up till now your puppy has probably done nothing more than run around and play in the fields, sniffing and picking up strange objects, which is normal puppy behavior. He has not yet truly discovered how to use his nose. Finding birds will rapidly teach him to search for game using his scenting abilities.

and relocate it when it lands. Or he will come back to where he first found the bird and smell around the same area. He needs to learn to connect using his nose with locating something exciting — a bird.

Once the game is scented your puppy's instinct to point will be triggered and he should freeze in his tracks. The bird will also remain motionless to avoid being located. An uncertain nose and a wrong movement from your dog, because of a lack of the pointing instinct,

Joey has found his bird and shows an excellent style of pointing.

The handler encouraging Joey to "steady."

Place your live birds by first dizzying them and tucking the head under the wing to prevent them from flying off immediately. Place the bird in suitable grass cover, and bring your dog into the field on his long check cord. Come into the cover from a downwind direction to give him a chance to use his nose to locate the bird.

If he sees the bird and grass move, he will probably stop moving and stalk, or even flash point. Most puppies will flash, or sight, point and then rush in and try to catch the bird. Do not reprimand him too severely at this point. He will learn after several failed attempts when the bird takes wing, to follow its flight

will cause the bird to flush. However, both using his nose and the tendency to point are inherent in your dog, and correct training will bring about the proper balance.

The desire to "catch" is also inherent in a hunting dog once the bird moves, so you want the bird to stay still until flushed by you. Continued training with a check cord will bring about the control necessary to keep your dog from pouncing and grabbing the bird. For him to remain in a pointing position until the bird has been flushed, as the bird flies, and after the shot, is purely obedience to a learned command. The response to a "Whoa" must be constantly reinforced.

Joey has snapped to a point. The handler talks to the dog at all times, keeping him steady.

The handler is pushing Joey's hindquarters and the dog is resisting, resulting in a stauncher point.

Again, with Joey on point, the handler is giving a slight forward push on his back. Joey resists by pushing forward, getting a tighter point.

Joey retrieves the downed bird and delivers it to his handler's hand.

Release cages for whatever bird you are using can be purchased from most training equipment suppliers. The cage has a spring-loaded lid which flies open when a metal arm is depressed. It can also be released from a distance by using a length of cord attached to the release arm. When you use a cage with an unsteady dog on point, he can not dive in and catch the

The use of a release cage when planting a bird will give you a chance to train your dog to stay steady on point without the bird moving.

bird. By continued work with a check cord your dog is encouraged to hold his point until you release the bird.

Since a noisy approach by you may break your dog's concentration, the check cord and a calm "Whoa" will be a necessity. The angle of approaching him when he is on point is always an important consideration. Approaching him from the front or side to flush the bird instead of from his rear will keep him from interpreting your movements as a command to release his point no matter how quiet or noisy your approach may be. Always be careful never to walk between him and the bird if you can possibly help it, and never rush your approach. Excitement on your part is quickly transmitted to your dog, and this will lead to an unsteady point.

The moment your dog breaks his point, do not yell at him. Let the check cord out as he runs and then suddenly step on it, and dump him head over tail, bringing him to an abrupt halt. Bring him back to where he had been on point even though the bird is no longer there, and give a strong "Whoa" again. Keep him in that position for several seconds and after telling him the bird is "All gone" heel him off in another direction to hunt for another bird.

That will help to get his mind off the departed one.

Introduction to the Gun

Getting a Vizsla puppy accustomed to the sound of a gun is a most critical stage. Done incorrectly or even thoughtlessly by an impatient owner, it can result in problems which may be difficult or impossible to overcome. Introduced correctly, however, gunfire should cause no fear and will soon be regarded as a normal occurrence.

Sounds of gunfire should be introduced gradually while your dog's mind is occupied with something he enjoys — finding a bird. With the dog running freely ahead of you, shoot off a blank pistol. In the excitement of finding and chasing his first birds, a young dog will not have much reaction to the noise. He may stop momentarily and look at you, find nothing to concern him, and continue the chase. While he is still a distance from you and occupied with the chase, fire again. Provided he is still unconcerned, wait until he is closer to you before firing again.

How to carry the large pheasant instead of the smaller gamebird presents a different type of retrieving to this Vizsla.

When you are perfectly satisfied that your dog is not the least concerned about the sound of the blank pistol, you can change to a .410 shotgun. The introduction to the shotgun should always be done from a distance at first. If you detect a nervous reaction from your dog, you are pushing him too soon and should revert to the blank pistol for a time before reintroducing a shotgun. Patience will be extremely necessary.

Retrieving

Vizslas are natural retrievers and it would be unusual for a young dog not to have the tendency to chase a ball or stick when thrown. Retrieving is going to be required for a dog used in the field so it is well to start encouraging a young dog, especially when the desire exists.

So far your Vizsla has probably been retrieving as a fun game. Now you want him to do it for you, on command only, in order to ensure a steadiness to wing and shot.

The use of a canvas dummy in training will eliminate the necessity for strong corrections which can occur if you use a bird, even a dead one. Your young dog may find it hard to give up a bird.

Since the enforcement of a "Whoa" will be necessary, put your dog on his check cord and stand on the end of it. Give him the command to "Whoa" using a hand signal, and then toss the dummy. He may break when he sees the motion but will come to a sharp stop when he hits the end of the cord. Pull him back to you, and giving another command "Whoa", pick up the dummy yourself. He has to learn that he can retrieve it only when you allow him.

Repeat the process of throwing the dummy, while you continue to stand on the end of the cord. If he breaks again, correct him again in the same way, but if he obeys the whoa until you release him, give the command "Fetch" after taking your foot off of the check cord. If there is any hesitation in bringing the dummy back to you give a lot of voice encouragement. Praise him when he comes back to you with his retrieve.

Vizslas learn fast and willingly. As a natural retriever your dog will be in his true element. As soon as you are sure of your dog's steadiness in waiting for the command "Fetch", you can remove the check cord. Practice throwing the dummy in different directions, up close and far, and changing the length of time he has to stand and wait for the command. Never allow him to run in and retrieve as soon as the dummy hits the ground. He must wait for the command. It is not necessary that he sit when he brings the dummy back to you, but he should never be encouraged to drop it before you take it from him.

Add some fun to the exercise by tying bird wings around the dummy to keep his interest. He may become more possessive about it when it holds the bird smell, so be quick to enforce any command.

The "Whoa" is going to be the most important command your dog will learn. It will be necessary at every stage of his training and the dog that learns to obey it immediately is worth his weight in gold.

Much of the preliminary work of steadying the dog can be done in the home in spare time.

Steadiness to Shot

Steadiness to a thrown drummy is the first lesson in making a dog steady to wing. The next stage is teaching him to be steady to a gun being fired. Someone will be needed to help throw the dummy and fire the pistol for this exercise while your concern will be watching that your dog does not break.

As before, put your dog on his check cord, with your foot on the end of it in case he breaks in the excitement of a gunshot. Give him a sharp "Whoa" and signal your helper to throw the dummy and fire the pistol. Pause for a few seconds if your dog has stayed still, and then tell him to "Fetch."

Practice firing the pistol with your dog in a whoa, without throwing a dummy. After a pause, instead of sending your dog out, tell him "All gone" so he will not expect to retrieve every time a gun is fired.

Water Retrieves

Along with the early yard and field training, you must teach your young Vizsla to swim. Vizslas love to swim, especially if something is thrown into the water for them to retrieve.

When introducing your Vizsla to water for the first time, whether it is a lake or a swimming pool, walk out a short way into the water with him in your arms. When you are waist deep, lower him into the water letting him swim and follow you to the shore or steps. Never throw a young dog into the water. Most of the time the use of an older dog that is a willing swimmer will encourage a reluctant puppy to do likewise.

As soon as your dog is comfortable in the water, start throwing the canvas dummy, a tennis ball, or even a stick for him to retrieve. With a lot of praise and encouragement a water retrieve will be done with enthusiasm. Although not yet a requirement in Vizsla field trials the water retrieve is always useful and fun.

Right: The jump can be encouraged by sending the dog over narrow creeks which he will attempt to jump.

Below, left: Retrieving a bird that fell into the water during a day of fun in the field.

Below, right: These young puppies are taught water retrieves with a canvas dummy.

CONTINUED TRAINING

Careless introduction of the gun, plus the lack of insisting on a staunch point, will lead to numerous problems as you advance in training with your dog. In some cases it will mean going back to the very beginning, this time slowly and patiently.

Blinking

In the case of gun nervousness, the end result could be a young dog "blinking." Blinking is the tendency of a dog to ignore game while hunting even though he has already scented it and is aware of it. Since the dog associates the gunshot with flushing the bird, he reasons that if the bird is not flushed the gun will not go off. If he does find and point the bird, he may move away from it before his handler can come into position.

A dog that has been strongly handled in early training may also develop a tendency to blink. A threatening voice should never be used on a sensitive Vizsla and the "Whoa" command should always be given in a soothing, calm manner.

Hillary holds her point while the handler circles in front of her to flush a quail.

Quartering

The distance over which any individual dog will range while hunting can vary considerably, along with the owner's views on how far a Vizsla, supposedly a close-working dog, should range. A lot will depend on the type of ground cover and terrain where the individual is hunting.

Every dog should show enough independence to leave his handler and quarter ahead and to each side so as to cover ground thoroughly. He should leave the impression that in all the ground he has covered, he has not missed anything. A dog that runs only far and straight without quartering is quite useless. It is the handler who should maintain a straight course while his dog hunts and quarters the terrain.

A dog that consistently ranges too far can be controlled to a degree by experienced handling and the manner in which he is taught to quarter, or cover ground. Teach your dog to respond to whistle and arm signals if you find

that his working patterns are too far from you. If his range is too far to your right, give a couple of bleeps on your whistle to get his attention. When he stops to look at you, signal with your left arm as you start walking left. He should cross in front of you and start working his pattern on your left as you continue in a straight line again. With experience, any dog should make use of wind directions while hunting, and will quarter into the wind, developing a fairly even pattern of covering the field ahead and to the left and right of you.

If you have a young dog that is determined to hunt for himself and not obey directions, he will have to be put back on a long check cord until he learns instant response to verbal and whistle commands, along with arm signals.

Backing or Honoring

"Backing" means stopping during hunting and honoring the point of another dog. Ideally,

Advanced training for field trials will include teaching your dog to honor another dog on point.

on seeing another dog on point, your dog should stop immediately without command and honor the other dog by pointing also, whether or not he can actually smell or locate the bird. Many hunters will never need such a completely well-mannered dog unless they participate in field trials, but if you know someone with a good, well-trained dog he will be able to help you with training sessions if desired.

FIELD TRIALS

Field trials have been in existence for about the same length of time as dog shows, both having started only a few months apart in 1874. In that year the first field trial ever recorded was held in Memphis, Tennessee by the members of the Tennessee State Sportsmen's Association. That initial trial, with an entry of only eight dogs, became the beginning of a healthy outdoor sport that has gained the enthusiasm of people all over the country.

When the Tennessee Club faded out of existence after a few years, other clubs began to spring up around the nation. By 1907, scores of clubs were in operation and a total of 410 trials had been recorded. By the late 1940s, more than 20,000 dogs were being run in trials each year.

Field trials were given their initial big push by *The American Field*, the oldest sportsmen's magazine in America. In 1917 the Amateur Field Trial Club of America was organized and it devoted its attention to conducting amateur trials. This organization, along with the AKC, made a tremendous contribution to the development of pointing dogs by regulating and sanctioning field trials that comply with their rules and by recording wins and breeding records.

Since the first recorded field trial in 1874, the standards of performance for dogs have changed, particularly the element of range. At first, handlers were on foot as they directed their dogs around the course. Soon, however, wider–running dogs came into favor and handlers were permitted to complete the course on horseback. Although the Vizsla is a naturally close hunter, many handlers still make use of a horse in the backfield course in order to cover a larger area.

Field trials are one of the most exciting and highly competitive of all dog sports. A dog must live up to established criteria for performance while still competing against other entries.

The sport is costly and not easily accessible, and the birds need to be constantly replaced. The Field Trial Championship requires more work than many owners are willing to put into it. The distances you may have to travel to train or to reach the field trial grounds may be far and they may be in out–of–the–way places. While your Vizsla is in training, it must be constant, not just once in a while. He should be run on birds every single weekend, plus worked on the basics during the week. It is a time–consuming task.

However, from the first time you have seen your Vizsla in a rock-hard pointing position, so intense over the smell of a quail that he is actually drooling, you will probably become hooked on that way of life.

If you feel that you truly want to develop this natural ability of your Vizsla, but do not have the time or training to progress past the stage of a companion gun dog to a completely trained competitive field trial dog, professional dog trainers can do it for you. Choose one who is basically a Vizsla handler or who knows the breed well.

You will have to part with your dog for several months. The trainer will evaluate the dog's potential during the first few weeks and give you a report on progress. Inform him as to whether you want only a companion gundog or a finished dog ready for field trail competitions.

You will find that there is a constant influx of new Vizsla owners who are anxious to train and handle their own dog. Locate someone who owns a really good well-trained dog. Ask

Above: Ch. Melto-N-Futaki's Rapstone Red, SH, retrieving bird to Chauncey Smith. Owned by Lynn Worth.

Left: A downed bird must be retrieved willingly without any damage to it.

FCh. Futaki Lenke
Sire: Ch. Caesar
Dam: Futaki Lincsi
Owner: Chauncey Smith

FCh. Futaki Juliska
Sire: Ch. Hunor
Dam: Piri
Owner: Robert Perry
Handler: C. Smith

if you can work with him for a few seasons, especially to teach your dog backing. Make sure your dog is already under control or you may get turned down. Like all competitive sports, training a field dog has protocol, general practices, and fine points.

Go to field trials, as a spectator, to listen and watch. There are no set rules for training a field trial dog. There are as many different methods as there are trainers, but one method is sure to be the right one for you. You will find that handling at trials is both interesting and exciting. The essential thing is, of course, to have a really good dog and to be able to trust and handle him adeptly. Given this, there is no reason why anyone who trains his own Vizsla should not run him in trials and enjoy it.

Field Championship

A Vizsla will be recorded a Field Champion after having won 10 points in regular stakes in at least three licensed or member field trials, provided that 3 points have been in one 3–point or better Open All–Age, Open Gun Dog, Open Limited All–Age, or Open Limited Gun Dog Stake; that no more than 2 points each have

Dual Ch. Szekeres' Kis Szereto, the first bitch in the history of the breed to become a Dual in 1970. *Photo courtesy of Chauncey Smith.*

been won in Open Puppy and Open Derby Stakes, and that no more than 4 points have been won by placing first in Amateur Stakes. A Vizsla needs to win at least 4 points in Retrieving Stakes at a field trial held by a Specialty club, also.

Championship points are credited only to dogs placing first in regular stakes. The number of points is based on the actual number of eligible starters in each stake.

Amateur Field Championship

A Vizsla will be recorded an Amateur Field Champion after having won 10 points in regular Amateur Stakes in at least three licensed or member field trials, providing that he has been awarded two first placements in such Stakes, one of which must be a first placement in a 3–pointer or better Amateur All-Age, Amateur Gun Dog, Amateur Limited All–Age, or Amateur Limited Gun Dog Stake. He also needs to have won 4 points in Amateur Re-

trieving Stakes at a field trial held by a Specialty Club. A dog entered in amateur stakes can not be handled by a professional trainer in that stake.

Stakes

A Stake is a unit of competition at a field trial or a testing level at a hunting test. Each Stake has its own entry requirements, its own judge, and its own tests.

Puppy Stakes — The Puppy Stake is for dogs over 6 months of age and under 15 months of age on the first day of the trial. A puppy must show desire to hunt, boldness, and initiative in covering ground and in searching likely cover. He should indicate the presence of game if presented, show reasonable obedience to commands, but should not be given additional credit for pointing staunchly. He is judged on his performance as an indication of his future as a high–class Derby dog. If the premium list states that blanks are to be fired, a dog that makes game contact shall be fired over. At least fifteen minutes and not more than thirty minutes is allowed for the test.

Derby stakes — The Derby Stake is for dogs that are over 6 months of age and under 2 years of age on the first day of the trial. The Derby dog must show a keen desire to hunt, be bold and independent, have a fast, yet attractive style of running, and demonstrate intelligence in seeking objectives and the ability to find game. A Derby dog must establish point but no additional credit will be given for steadiness to wing and shot. He must show reasonable obedience to his handler's commands. If the handler is within gun range of a bird which has been flushed after a point, a shot must be fired. At least twenty minutes and not more than thirty minutes shall be allowed for each heat.

Gun Dog Stake (Open and/or Amateur — This Stake is for dogs 6 months or older on the first day of the trial. A gundog must give

Piri, dam of the first Dual Champion, Futaki Darocz.
Sire: Urfi of Goncoltanya
Dam: Dgin
Owner: Bela Hadik

DCh. Futaki Darocz, first Dual in the history of the breed.
Photo courtesy of C. Smith.

a finished performance and be under his handler's control at all times. He must handle kindly, with a minimum of noise and hacking. A gundog must show a keen desire to hunt, must have a bold and attractive style of running, and must demonstrate not only intelligence in quartering and in seeking objectives but also the ability to find game. The dog must hunt for his handler at all times at a range suitable for a handler on foot, and should show or check in front of his handler frequently. He must cover ground but never range out of sight for any length of time. He must locate game, point staunchly, and be steady to wing and shot. Intelligent use of the wind and terrain in locating game, accurate nose, and style and intensity of point are essential. At least thirty minutes shall be allowed for each heat.

All-Age Stake (Open and/or Amateur) — This Stake is for dogs 6 months or older on the first day of the trial. An All-Age dog must

Left: Ch. Bratt's FK Satin Valentine
Sire: DCh. and AFCh. Janos VW Come Lately
Dam: DCh. Szekeres Kis Szereto
Photo courtesy of C. Smith.

Below: FCh. Futaki Jocko
Sire: Haans V Selle
Dam: FCh. Futaki Juliska
Photo courtesy of C. Smith.

give a finished performance and must be under reasonable control of his handler. He must show a keen desire to hunt with a bold and attractive style of running, and must show independence in hunting. He must range well out in a forward pattern seeking the most promising objectives, so as to locate any game on the course. Excessive line casting and avoiding cover must be penalized. He must respond to handling but must demonstrate his independent judgement in hunting the course, and should not look to his handler for directions. He must find game, point staunchly, and be steady to wing and shot. Intelligent use of the wind and terrain in locating game, accurate nose, and style and intensity on point are essential. At least thirty minutes shall be allowed for each heat.

Limited Gun Dog Stake (Open and/or Amateur) — This Stake is for dogs 6 months of age or older on the first day of the trial which have won first place in Derby, or have any placings in any Gun Dog Stake. A dog in this stake that encounters a bracemate on point must honor. Failure to do so must be heavily penalized. The intentional avoidance by a dog or handler of a backing situation must also be heavily penalized. A dog that steals a point must be ordered up by the judges. The running time for the heat shall be no more than thirty minutes unless stated differently in the premium.

Limited All-Age Stake (Open and/or Amateur) — This Stake is for dogs 6 months of age or over on the first day of the trial which have won first place in an Open Derby Stake or placed in any All-Age Stake. A dog encountering his bracemate on point must honor. Failure to honor when he sees his bracemate on point must be heavily penalized, and the intentional avoidance by the dog or his handler of a backing situation must be heavily penalized.

DCh. and AFCh. Bratt's FK Gippen
Sire: SCh. and AFCh. Janos VW Come Lately
Dam: SCh. Szekeres Kis Szereto
Photo courtesy of C. Smith.

FCh. and AFCh. Melto's Caprice
Sire: SCh. and AFCh. Bo Sassy Delibab
Dam: Ch. Willie N Berry's Calidar, CD
Owner: Lynn Worth

A dog that steals his bracemate's point must be ordered up by the judges. The time of the heat shall not be more than thirty minutes unless the running time is stated differently in the premium. A dog that is on point, or obviously working on game when time is up, shall be allowed a reasonable amount of time to complete his work.

In 1978 The Vizsla Club of America approved the qualification requirements for a National and National Amateur Championship Stakes for Vizslas as follows:

National Championship Stake for Vizslas — Open to any Vizsla 6 months of age or over that has ever placed first, second, third, or fourth in an Open All-Age Stake, Amateur All-Age Stake, Open Limited All-Age Stake, or Amateur Limited Gun Dog Stake in which at least thirteen dogs started in an AKC licensed field trial.

National Amateur Championship Stake for Vizslas — Open to any Vizsla 6 months of age or over that has ever placed first, second, third, or fourth in an Amateur All-Age Stake, Amateur Limited All-Age Stake, Amateur Gun Dog Stake, or Amateur Limited Gun Dog Stake in an AKC licensed trial.

Procedures for Running National Championship Stake

A National Championship Stake has two series. The first of these is a single course without a bird field, and it lasts thirty minutes. Blank pistols are used. The second is a single course with a bird field. Twenty–two minutes are allowed for the back course, eight minutes for the bird field, and time is called when the dog is on point in the bird field. Horseback handling will be allowed in both series. The dog must be under reasonable control of his handler. He must respond to handling, and hunt for his handler at all times at a range suitable for the course and terrain, either from foot or horseback. He must demonstrate the ability to find game on the course, and he must

DCh., AFCh., and NAFCh.
    Fieldstone's Tip Top Timmy
Sire: DCh. Rebel Rouser Duke
Dam: DCh. and AFCh. Rothan's
    Rozsda Kisanya, CD
Owner-handled by Paul Rothan
to the National Amateur
Championship.

show championship class in running style, birdwork, and manners at all times.

If a champion is declared, the title of National Vizsla Field Champion is bestowed. If the judges do not feel that the dogs measured up to championship caliber, a champion is not declared.

Procedures for Running National Amateur Championship Stake

A National Amateur Championship Stake has a single course with a bird field. Twenty minutes are allowed for the back course, eight minutes for the bird field, and time is called when the dog is on point in the bird field. Blank pistols are used in the back course. Shoot-to-kill is permitted for official gunners in the bird field. Horseback handling will be permitted. Bitches in season are not allowed to compete in this Stake. The dog must be under reasona-

ble control of his handler and must respond to handling and hunt for his handler at all times at a range suitable for course and terrain, either from foot or horseback. He must demonstrate the ability to find game on this course and must show championship class in running style, birdwork, and manners at all times.

If a champion is declared the title of National Amateur Vizsla Field Champion is bestowed. If the judges do not feel that the dogs measured up to championship caliber, a champion is not declared.

Added rules include: no shooting over puppies; no shoot to kill in the Derby Stake; both Puppy and Derby Stakes are a single course without a bird field; trial dates are the fourth weekend in October (alternate — one week before or after).

In the 1982 VCOA National Amateur Championship, first-place winner was FCh. and AFCh. Kataki's Riki Knoh.

Sire: DCh. Rippi of Webster Woodlands
Dam: Ch. Bratt's FK Kataki
Owner: Eugene Remmer

Ch. Rotkopf's Super Charger, CD, JH, VC. Best of Breed in 1981 VCOA National Specialty and sire of fifty-five champions. He is equally at home in the field and in the show ring. Owned by Michele Coburn.

———10———

The Versatile Vizsla

ONE of the reasons that the Vizsla is so appealing to the one-dog family is the versatility of the breed. There are so many options with this truly wonderful dog that the word "versatile" can have a different meaning with each owner.

To the Vizsla owner with no other desire than a loving dog to live with, a "versatile" dog can mean fun and enjoyment, protection, and guardianship. To some owners a versatile dog is one that can compete in obedience and conformation, gaining titles in both areas. But to most Vizsla owners, who truly love and believe in the versatility of the breed, the term also includes the breed's natural ability and intelligence in the bird field.

With the advent of the Obedience Champion title, it is now possible to earn a title in all three areas of competition: field, show, and obedience. To date, at least one Vizsla has accomplished that, and it is hoped that more will follow.

NAVHDA

On the continent, and among a group of people in North America who founded the North American Versatile Hunting Dog Association (NAVHDA), in 1969, the term "versatile" is interpreted to mean a dog that can point game, retrieve from land and water, and track wounded game. NAVHDA is a non-profit organization whose purpose is to foster, improve, promote, and protect the versatile hunting dog breeds. It does this by sponsoring field tests that truly test their versatility by providing standards for testing and evaluating the dogs, with the ultimate objective being the conservation of game by encouraging hunters to have dogs well trained in work both before and after the shot.

There are two types of versatile tests: Natural Ability tests, and Utility Field tests. In the natural ability test the dog is judged only on his hereditary characteristics, and is only eligible for the test up to 16 months of age.

Natural Ability Test

The Natural Ability test covers seven different hereditary characteristics which should disclose the latent natural abilities that are required to develop a dog into a versatile hunter. Natural abilities manifest themselves at an early age and any hereditary flaws will show up in a young dog. It is the Natural Ability test that a breeder looks to in order to assess his present breeding program or plan a future one. No other test is so important for the breeder who is honestly interested in improving his breeding program.

At least three judges officiate; one of them must be a senior judge. Dogs are run individually for not less than twenty minutes on native or liberated game. Each dog is tested for the following: use of nose, search, love for water, pointing, tracking, desire to work, and cooperation.

A dog that finds game fast and repeatedly and can productively scent game under various conditions has a fine nose, while any dog that has to search for a long time in an area where game is abundant leaves little doubt that he only possesses a fair nose. The dog should show eagerness, industry, stamina, and independence while searching and not waste time on barren land. A truly versatile dog must possess a natural love of water and must enter the water without hesitation to retrieve a non-game object. An ability to point must be demonstrated, and his point must be intense, convincing, and productive, even though he may break and chase.

Tracking ability is an important aspect for the versatile hunting dog, and the dog is required to track a running bird. The length of the track is not as important as the eagerness and intensity displayed by the dog. The desire to work is the hallmark of a good hunting dog. This desire must be expressed in every phase of his work by him displaying an eager and industrious attitude while hunting. The dog should at all times demonstrate a willingness to handle and to hunt with the purpose of producing game for his handler.

As might be expected, the Natural Ability test assesses all the natural characteristics aimed at evaluating the 16-month-old or younger dog. The utility test measures not only the natural ability but responsiveness and obedience. In critiquing the dogs in terms of hunting instincts and trainability, the NAVHDA judges also evaluate each dog for basic conformation and temperament.

Utility Field Test

The Utility Field test is designed to test a hunting dog's usefulness for the on-foot hunter in all phases of hunting before and after the shot, in field and marsh, and on different species of game.

The individual tests are divided into two groups: field and water. Each of these is officiated by at least two judges. In the field tests each dog is tested on the following: search, pointing, steadiness to wing and shot, retrieve of a bird, retrieve of bird by drag. In the water tests each dog is tested for the following: searching, walking at heel, remaining by a blind, behavior by a blind, retrieve of a duck.

Searching is a test of the dog's use of his nose in tracking a duck on the land, into the water, and on the water. It is also a test of the dog's ability to persevere in difficult reed cover and in the water. In the field, searching by the utility field dog should indicate one purpose — the production of game for the gun. A dog should be penalized for missing game during the search. The ability to point distinguishes the versatile hunting dog from other breeds, and the instinct to point should be clearly present.

A Utility Field dog should display self-control in the presence of game and when the gun is fired. He should be steady without a command until ordered to retrieve. A good retriever does his job happily and eagerly. On command he should go to the bird, pick it up, and return to his handler.

The drag test is one of the most satisfying tests of the versatile dog's retrieving ability. The important element is that the dog use the scent of either a dead bird or a furred animal on the drag, and retrieve it.

In the utility water tests, heeling is a test of practical obedience, where the dog should be able to follow his handler at heel, on or off leash. A course is set up using wooden stakes which lead to a blind on a lake where the remainder of the water tests are conducted. At the blind, the dog is tested for gun shyness, obedience, and control when the handler leaves his dog alone. The handler out of sight fires two shots and a dog under complete control should remain quietly by the blind until his owner returns.

Another behavior test at the blind is reliability in the presence of game and gunfire. A gun is shot and a dead duck is thrown into the air. A dog should remain silent and not leave the spot until the handler sends him to retrieve. The dog should swim and pick up the duck without hesitation and return to his handler, holding the duck until the handler takes it.

Each dog is judged throughout the entire test for the use of his nose, desire to work, stamina, cooperation, and handling and obedience.

Another function of NAVHDA is to help owners of versatile hunting dogs enjoy their dogs through proper training. Many hunters have never had the opportunity to learn firsthand the various steps involved in training before NAVHDA.

HUNTING TESTS FOR POINTING BREEDS

In 1985 the American Kennel Club designed their new non-competitive hunting tests, after the basic tests which NAVHDA had promoted, intended to test a hunting dog's usefulness for the on-foot hunter in all phases of hunting, except for the water retrieves. There being

---

Figure 10-1

**OFFICIAL AKC SCORECARD
HUNTING TESTS FOR
POINTING BREEDS**

Indicate whether Junior, Senior or Master

DOG'S NAME_____

BRACE #_____

HANDLER _____

Score all categories of ability on the basis of 0-10.
Do not score Retrieving in Junior.

1. HUNTING	
2. BIRD FINDING ABILITY	
3. POINTING	
4. TRAINABILITY	
5. RETRIEVING NOT APPLICABLE IN JUNIOR	
TOTAL	
AVERAGE *	

* Divide total by 4 in Junior, and divide by 5 in Senior and Master for overall average.

In order to receive a Qualifying score a dog must acquire a minimum of not less than 5 on each of the categories of ability (4 categories in Junior, 5 categories in Senior and Master) with an overall average of not less than 7.

(c) The American Kennel Club 1986

S191-1(5-86)

many owners of pointing breeds that do not compete in licensed field trials but who still want a type of structured activity related to them, the AKC wrote regulations for the hunting tests to allow these owners to test their dogs against a practical hunting standard. These hunting tests immediately became very popular as Vizsla breeders, in particular, were anxious to have some way of measuring their dog's natural abilities and, by insuring the continuance of them in a breeding program, promote the Dual Vizsla.

ness, and independence. He must show trainability, obedience to commands, gun response, and point. Only blank pistols are fired in the Junior class.

There are eight categories in the Junior class. Six of them have a score judged from 0–10, with 5 points considered a pass. The "desire to hunt" and the "bird finding ability" are judged from 0–20, with 10 points considered a pass. In order to qualify, the dog must score a minimum of 70 points. Four qualifying scores are needed for the Junior Hunter title.

The Junior Hunter must show boldness and independence while hunting.

Ch. Boelte's Bronze Brea on a firm point working toward her Junior Hunter title.

Dogs entered in these hunting tests are judged in one of three levels: Junior, Senior, and Master, based on the ability of the dog. Participating in any of these levels offers the owner both the fun of training and seeing his dog work, as well as the pride of accomplishment in earning an AKC hunting title certificate.

Junior Hunter

The Junior Hunter is judged and scored on his bird finding ability, plus his desire, bold-

Desire, speed, independence, and useful pattern of running are the elements of the hunting category. A dog that is out for a run in the field and does not seem to be hunting, or a dog that does not leave his owner's side to explore the territory, or that wanders around slowly should be scored low in hunting ability, even though there is more leniency at the junior level.

A dog which does a good job of hunting should find birds. The number of birds a dog finds should not necessarily be considered as important as the quality of the finds. Finding more birds than another dog should not result in a higher score since the dogs are not judged against each other. Their abilities are evaluated against the standard. A Junior Hunter must find and point birds to receive a qualifying score.

The Junior Hunter is scored on the basis of the intensity of his point, as well as his ability to locate birds. A "flash" point (a point in which a dog stops, only momentarily before chasing the bird), can not be graded as pointing.

The Junior Hunter is also graded on the basis of his willingness to be handled, his reasonable obedience to commands, and his gun response. "Gun-shyness" can not be tolerated in the makeup of any dog that is being evaluated as a hunting companion.

Senior Hunter

Judging for the Senior Hunter is stricter. Birds must be shot and the dog must retrieve willingly while being judged on handling, obedience, and gun response. The Senior

Ch. Victor's Star Attraction, owned by Judy Richey, has earned his Junior Hunter title and is now working on his Senior Hunter title.

DCh. Futaki Darocz, the first Vizsla Dual Champion, finished in 1965.
Sire: Ch. Hunor
Dam: Piri
Owner: Bela Hadik

Hunter will receive a disqualifying score if he fails to honor a bracemate encountered on point.

There are seven categories in the Senior Hunter class. In the categories that have 10 for a perfect score, a score of 5 is considered a pass. When 20 points are needed for a perfect score 10 points are needed to qualify. Five qualifying scores are needed for a Senior Hunter title unless the dog has already earned his Junior title. In that case, only four qualifying scores are needed, each with a minimum of 70 points.

As with the Junior, a "flash point" can not qualify for a grade. Senior dogs must point and hold the point until the bird is flushed. A dog which breaks before the flush can not receive a qualifying score.

A Senior dog is expected to be under control. The scoring of obedience and willingness to handle should reflect the level of response by the dog. Gun response is also evaluated under trainability. Gun response for the senior is evaluated when the bird is shot, or when a blank is fired over the dog on the backcourse.

Honoring is an additional element included under trainability. If a dog is given an opportunity to honor and refuses, he can not receive a qualifying score. If he does not have an opportunity to honor, he should be called back at the conclusion of the test to demonstrate his willingness to honor. The handler may give his dog a verbal command to honor, but if a dog steals his bracemate's point he can not receive a qualifying score.

At the Senior level, the dog is not required to retrieve to hand, but any dog which renders a bird unfit for consumption can not receive a qualifying score.

Master Hunter

The Master Hunter category is graded very strictly, without any degree of tolerance or leniency. This dog must give a finished performance showing a keen desire to hunt with a bold manner of running, displaying not only intelligence in seeking the birds, but also a willingness to work with his handler and not

DCh. and AFCh. Golden Empire's Doctor T
Sire: Piroska's Golden Empire, CD
Dam: Voros Tars Lady of Agoura
Owner: Michele Coburn

DCh. Sage Richards locates a pheasant.
Sire: Ch. Bayzil Richards
Dam: Ch. Elsa Richards
Owner: Richard Zappacosta

Ch. Sandyacre Poquito Chili Bean, UD, SH.
An accomplished performer in the obedience and
agility ring, he is also a therapy dog and a Senior
Hunter. Owned by Maria Fujardo-Zucconi.

DCh. and AFCh. Bratt's FK Gippen
Sire: SCh. and AFCh. Janos VW Come Lately
Dam: DCh. Szekeres Kis Szereto
Owner: F. and K. Mileikis
Photo courtesy of C. Smith.

range out of sight. After finding game he must
be firm to point, and steady to wing and shot.
He must honor not only during his bracemate's
point but through the entire flush, shot and
retrieve or he will receive a disqualifying score.
He must not require any restraint, either physical or verbal when honoring. In the Master
class the dog must retrieve absolutely to hand
without any assist from his handler.

This level is the true test of a trained and
finished gundog. A dog needs six qualifying
scores for his title unless he has already earned
his Senior Hunter title. If that is the case he
will need only to qualify in five tests.

All three of the classes are done on foot with
only the judges and the judges' marshalls on
horseback. Running time for each brace in the
junior class is at least fifteen minutes, and in
the Senior and Master classes at least thirty
minutes.

The AKC awards the suffix of Junior Hunter
(JH), Senior Hunter (SH) and Master Hunter
(MH) to qualifying dogs in each class.

VCOA VERSATILITY TESTS

Versatility tests were designed by the VCOA
to help in the overall improvement of the breed
by promoting the Vizsla as a versatile, attractive, obedient hunting dog; and to encourage
breeders to breed for the all-around dog. All
licensed Vizsla clubs are eligible to hold versatility tests as long as the club follows the
guidelines set up by the VCOA. Since the program is a VCOA event, the results of each test
are sent to the versatility chairman appointed
by the VCOA. The chairman is responsible for
all the ratings on each dog and grades them as
"pass" or "fail".

The Versatility Test consists of three
categories: Field, Obedience, and Conformation. In order to receive a Versatility Certificate, an eligible Vizsla must pass all three category tests three times under three different
judges.

Any registered Vizsla over 6 months of age may be entered in the Field or Obedience category. However, he must be 12 months old to be entered in the Conformation test. Your dog may be entered in as many Field and Obedience tests as it takes to earn a pass, but there is a limit of three failures in the conformation class, after which a dog is no longer eligible for entry.

Field Test Requirements

This test consists of at least ten minutes, but not more than fifteen, in the backcourse, and at least five minutes, but not more than eight, in the birdfield in which two game birds have been planted.

The Vizsla must show a natural desire to hunt and must locate, point, and retrieve. He must show a keen willingness and desire to find game, hunt with intelligence, and show an aggressive style of running. He also must be obedient and respond to commands.

In the birdfield he must locate the bird and then point with style (with his head and tail high). After the bird is shot he must be willing to retrieve it without mauling or mouthing the bird.

Any Vizsla that is a Field Champion, an Amateur Field Champion, the holder of Senior or Master Hunter titles, or has had placements in three field–trial retrieving stakes or Senior or Master hunting tests, may receive his Field certificate without testing, upon providing proof of proper performance.

DCh. and AFCh. Bo Sassy Delibab
Sire: Ch. Pilgrim's Pride
Dam: Heide of Highland Falls
Owner: E. Antenberg
Photo courtesy of C. Smith.

Ch. Csisckas of Golcoltanya, owned by Charles and Joan Hunt, shows excellent form in the field.

Conformation Requirements

Any Vizsla that is already a Breed Champion and is over 18 months of age need only be measured and found within the breed standard to be able to apply for a Conformation Certificate.

If he is not already a Breed Champion, three major wins under three different judges in any class but puppy will suffice in applying for the certificate, along with the age and measurement requirements. All measurements must be conducted by a Versatility Test committee or test judge at a test site.

Obedience Test Requirements

Any Vizsla that has already earned any obedience title (CD, CDX, UD, UDX, or OTCH) is eligible for his Obedience Certificate simply by applying to the Versatility Chairman. A Vizsla taking the Obedience test must score at least fifty percent of the points required for each of the following exercises.

Heel on lead (20 points). Your Vizsla will have the same commands that are used in the Novice Obedience ring, but you may choose to have your dog stand instead of sit at your left side at the end of heeling simply by stating your choice before the exercise begins. The heeling pattern will be an "L" shape, with no figure–eight exercise.

Heel free (20 points). Same as above except off leash.

Stand for examination (30 points). Your Vizsla will be judged the same as in the regular Novice Obedience exercise.

Recall (30 points). This exercise will be the same as in the regular Novice Obedience test with the exception that your dog may stand rather than sit, and upon reaching you, may stand instead of sitting, provided you state that option before starting the exercise.

Stay exercise (30 points). Your Vizsla will be judged in a group for this exercise, with a minimum of three dogs, using the AKC novice routine, with the exception that your dog can be left standing, sitting, or in a down position. You must state your choice of position before the exercise starts, and your dog must remain in that position for a full three minutes.

Qualifying dogs receive a Certificate of Versatility from the VCOA and the letters VD may be used after their registered names.

DUAL CHAMPIONSHIPS

Numerous Vizsla owners have added the titles of Dual Champion and also Amateur Field Champion to their dogs' lists of accomplishments. An amateur is a person who, during the period of two years preceding a trial, has not accepted remuneration in any form for the training or handling of a dog. Amateur stakes have done a lot to encourage novice

DCh. and AFCh. FK's Rivendell Reaghan, CDX
Sire: DCh. and AFCh. Bratt's FK Gippen
Dam: Ch. Firebrand's Witchy Woman, CD
Owner: Chauncey Smith

Dual Champions

Dual Ch. Futaki Darocz	1965
Dual Ch. Weedy Creek Lobo	1969
Dual Ch. Bobo Buck Selle	1970
Dual Ch. Szekeres Kis Szereto	1970
Dual Ch./AFC Brook's Amber Mist	1971
Dual Ch. Behi's Csinos Csiny, CD	1971
Dual Ch./AFC Sir Lancelot	1972
Dual Ch./AFC Amber's Windy Autumn	1972
Dual Ch./AFC Pirolin	1973
Dual Ch. Chip Odsseus	1973
Dual Ch. Rippi of Webster Woodlands	1974
Dual Ch. Rebel Rouser Duke	1974
Dual Ch. Sir Amber Sam	1975
Dual Ch./AFC Jodi's Jump N Bing Bang Bucz	1975
Dual Ch./AFC Csibesz Rotkopf	1975
Dual Ch./AFC Arco's Arco	1976
Dual Ch./AFC Rothan's Rozsda Kisany, CD	1976
Dual Ch. AFC Brook's Willie Whompum	1976
Dual Ch./AFC Janos VW Come Lately	1977
Dual Ch./AFC Victor of Holzworth Farm	1978
Dual Ch./AFC Mehagian's Peppy Paloma	1979
Dual Ch. Cline's Olympia Blitz	1979
Dual Ch. W D Regina	1979
Dual Ch./AFC Valhi's Liberty Valence	1979
Dual Ch./AFC Behi Csecse Gyors Lab	1980
Dual Ch./AFC Fieldstone's Hey Duke	1980
Dual Ch./AFC Bratt's FK Gippen	1980
Dual Ch. Bry-Lynn's Golden Taurus	1982
Dual Ch./AFC Fieldstone's Tip Top Timmy	1982
Dual Ch. Rotkopf's Minor Miracle	1982
Dual Ch./AFC El Cazador's Ripp Van Winkle	1982
Dual Ch./AFC Sage Richards	1983
Dual Ch. Cody's Dark Star	1983
Dual Ch. Redef's Hella Poppin	1983
Dual Ch. Fieldstone's Tip Top Chester	1983
Dual Ch./AFC Bo Sassy Delibab	1984
Dual Ch./AFC FK's Rivendell Reaghan CDX	1984
Dual Ch. Pride's Joy	1984
Dual Ch./AFC Willie's Cedar Chip, CD	1984
Dual Ch. My T Hi Thunder Storm	1984
Dual Ch. Popple Dungeon Super Star	1985
Dual Ch./AFC Boyd's J R of Futaki	1985
Dual Ch./AFC Papago Samsson, CD, MH	1985
Dual Ch./AFC Ceasar's Image Barging Buck	1985
Dual Ch./AFC Upwind Selkie	1986
Dual Ch./AFC Askim	1986
Dual Ch./AFC Popple Dungeon Trillium	1986
Dual Ch./AFC Camarily Sandman	1986
Dual Ch./AFC Randy Bee's Rambling Man, MH	1986
Dual Ch. Futaki Marci	1986
Dual Ch. Pleasant Run Gunner	1986
Dual Ch./AFC Popple Dungeon What A Dickens, CD	1986
Dual Ch. Paradox Title Chase of Behi	1987
Dual Ch. Golden Empire's Beauregard, CD	1987
Dual Ch. Behi's Gyors Vonat PD Carla	1987
Dual Ch./AFC Semper Fi Chesty Puller, MH	1987
Dual Ch. Rebel Rouser ET	1987
Dual Ch. Masha's Best Flash Dancer	1988
Dual Ch. Russet Leather Pretty Pawnee	1988
Dual Ch./AFC Berry's Mason Dixon Lover	1988
Dual Ch. Riverbend Deacon's Dandy	1989
Dual Ch./AFC Golden Empire's Doctor T	1989
Dual Ch. Viesoo's Prodigal Son	1989
Dual Ch./AFC Askim's Diamond Reo	1990
Dual Ch. Oakleaf's Screamin' Demon	1990
Dual Ch. Oakleaf's Whiskey Pete	1990

trainers and handlers to compete, with great success.

Many amateurs start out by way of the show ring. After gaining Championship titles for their Vizslas, and anxious to show the versatility of the breed, they enter the field arena. Some use professional help in training until their dogs have reached the stage where they are ready to compete and earn a Field Championship title.

The Dual Champion is one that has earned both a show and a Field Championship title. The Vizsla has many Dual Champions in comparison to other pointing breeds due to the constant desire to keep and promote the natural abilities that the breed is so well known for having.

TRIPLE CHAMPION CARIAD'S KUTYA KAI COSTA, VD

No book on the Vizsla breed would be complete without mentioning a dog that did it all — Cariad's Kutya Kai Costa. Kutya made history not only for Vizslas, but also for the AKC by becoming the first dog of any breed to finish titles in three categories. No other dog has done so much to exemplify the versatility of the Vizsla.

Kutya was owned by Robert and Marianne Costa of Staten Island, New York. An amateur, Robert trained and handled Kutya throughout

Triple Champion Cariad's Kutya Kai Costa
Sire: Ch. Glen Cottage Loki Barat, CDX; **Dam:** Ch. Cariad's Gaybine, CD; **Owner:** Robert and Marianne Costa.

his career. Kutya completed the requirements for his Breed Championship in 1976 with four major wins to his credit. In the same year he also earned his CD in obedience, and was on the way to his Field Championship. The following year on 16 October, he completed his Field Championship making him a Dual Champion.

During the following two years, Kutya earned his CDX and his UD Obedience degrees while at the same time he was gaining points toward his amateur Field Championship. He was top Obedience Vizsla in 1978, 1979, and 1980, as well as the fifth best Sporting Dog in Obedience in 1979, the first Vizsla ever to place in this elite category.

In 1980 Kutya was in constant competition in the Obedience ring gaining points required for the Obedience Trial Championship (OTCh), placing High in Trial seven times, had seven High Combined scores and over seventy class placements, plus becoming the first Vizsla to place in the Superdog Competition at the Gaines Eastern Regional where he took sixth place.

Kutya gained the final point for his OTCh on 25 October 1980, becoming the first dog in history to earn the three titles: breed Champion, Field Champion, and Obedience Trial Champion.

A few days after gaining his new title, Kutya was the High Scoring Vizsla at the Vizsla Club of America's National Specialty, winning that honor for the second year running.

In the midst of all the shows, trials, and awards, Kutya and his owner still managed to find time to hold demonstrations for schools, civic associations and children's groups, proving that the Vizsla is a versatile, loyal and devoted family member.

AGILITY

In 1979 the Kennel Club of Great Britain designed agility tests as a form of competition where the animal's fitness and the handler's ability to train and direct his dog over and through obstacles are tested. It began as a special event at the International Horse Show in England, but the sport grew and different obstacles were introduced until regulation equipment was a requirement. As enthusiasm and interest grew, the sport developed in the U.S.

Agility training offers an opportunity to refine a dog's skills and have fun at the same time. Several Vizslas are presently in training as the trials become more popular. A very exciting activity, it is an excellent outlet for a Vizsla's natural exuberance and intelligence. It also offers an opportunity to the owner and his dog to interact as the dog needs to be well trained to heel (on and off leash), sit-stay, come when called, and obey instant commands with faith in his handler.

Essentially, an agility trial is one in which a dog is required to progress through a series of various types of obstacles. There are open and closed tunnels, raised walkways, teeter-totters, "A"-frames, hoops, a variety of hurdles to jump, and a sway-bridge. Each dog is scored on his performance and the time it takes to complete the course. The handler runs along with his dog, directing him in the correct sequence of jumps.

The two agility organizations in the U.S. are the United States Dog Agility Association (USDAA) and the National Committee for Dog Agility (NCDA). There are distinct differences in that the NCDA has smaller, portable obstacles with the jump height lower, and you compete in divisions according to breed rather than the size of your dog. USDAA is patterned after the agility clubs in England. The obstacles are larger, course lay-outs are longer and more difficult. Dogs compete in one of three divisions according to their height.

Agility is permitted at AKC shows as an exhibition sport only at this time, since mixed-breed dogs are allowed to compete. Currently the USDAA is awarding titles of Agility Dog (AD), Advanced Agility Dog (AAD) and Master Agility Dog (MAD) with prescribed requirements for each title. Throughout the year USDAA regional events are held all over the country and it has become a growing sport among enthusiasts interested in continued obedience diversions.

Brent Aronson's Vizsla, Vic, is being introduced to the new fun of Agility training.

Deacon's Starburst clearing the double-wide jump. The handler runs with the dog to direct the jumps.

Deacon's Starburst navigating the see-saw.

Deacon's Starburst weaving the poles in Agility.

Deacon's Starburst clearing the brush jump.

Deacon's Starburst coming through Agility tunnel.

Deacon's Starburst on the Agility A-frame. The hoop on the end is used in training to prevent the dog from jumping off prematurely.

Ch. Sandyacre Poquito Chili Bean, UD, SH, shown placing first in Agility competition.

The first Vizsla to receive an AD title was Deacon's Starburst, CDX, TDI, AD, owned by Marilyn Belli. "Jessie", as she is called, is also one of the first six dogs in the U.S. to receive an AD — another "first" for our breed to be proud of.

THERAPY DOGS

Virtually every major newspaper, news program, human interest magazine and article has featured a story about the therapeutic benefits of an animal. Dog clubs all over the country have enlisted their members who have friendly and obedient dogs to visit nursing homes and other institutionalized residents. Associating with an animal provides physical and emotional benefits, not only to healthy individuals, but also to those who are sick and emotionally ill. Pet–facilitated therapy refers to any treatment in which interaction with an animal is used as part of the healing process.

Although many pet owners had been visiting nursing care centers with dogs for years, it was not until 1980, when the organization Therapy Dogs International (TDI) was formed, to unite and increase the number of therapy dogs available, that they gained recognition and hospitals and other institutions were alerted to the importance of animals as therapy.

Dogs accepted by TDI wear "Registered Therapy Dog" tags on their collars, and their owners are issued with an identification card along with a list explaining the function of a TDI dog. The dog must have a current health certificate along with all shots, and a stool check, and heartworm test. Bitches must not be in season, and all dogs must be well groomed and clean. Dogs must be at least 1 year old, be a graduate from a training course or have an obedience title. Puppies are usually not allowed to go into a nursing care center because of their sharp teeth and nails which might inadvertently injure an older person's fragile skin.

Many unresponsive, older patients have taken a renewed lease on life after a visit from a TDI that they have related to. Perhaps they bring to mind pets from the past. Autistic children, unable to respond to anything else, have bonded immediately with friendly visiting TDIs.

Because of his gentle and sensitive nature, a Vizsla is able to communicate by showing love and trust to institutionalized people.

While most of the dogs registered are involved in obedience, many are also show and field dogs. Used to different people and different situations, these dogs offer many faces to therapy as they visit all kinds of day-care centers, VA hospitals, rehabilitation centers, and children's hospitals, bringing joy to a sometimes depressing situation.

Many Vizsla owners across the country have become interested in the program. Because of their gentle and sensitive nature, Vizslas are able to communicate with institutionalized people without speaking — simply by showing love and trust.

Any Vizsla owner interested in information on therapy dogs can contact The Delta Society, P.O. Box 1080, Renton, WA 98057 or TDI, Elaine Smith, 1536 Morris Place, Hillside, NJ 07205.

SERVICE DOG ORGANIZATIONS

The use of a trained dog often reduces a disabled person's need for human attendants. Most service organizations or schools depend on donations of puppies or dogs. These dogs must exhibit intelligence, sound temperament, physical soundness, and adaptability. Many schools are now geared to the needs of those with physical disabilities as well as blindness, with the emphasis on retrieving and support. These schools not only teach dogs to bring independence to disabled people, but also teach individuals leadership skills to master their dogs and gain the most from their use. Schools for training select dogs to assist hearing-impaired and physically challenged persons, and give extensive obedience training. Other schools train support dogs to help with balanced walking and wheelchair movement.

Guide Dogs for the Blind

The sole purpose of the Guiding Eyes for the Blind schools is to provide mobility and independence for blind people. They also provide dignity and purpose for dogs that are eager, anxious, and capable of working. The versatile Vizsla meets every criteria, and after years of focus on the Golden and Labrador Retrievers, the guide dog training associations are now taking a longer look at the Vizsla. Concerned over the inability of young and old blind people to groom or handle the larger, stronger retriever, the Vizsla fills the need for a smaller but robust, intelligent, and easy-care animal.

Hearing and Service Dogs

Hearing or service dogs allow deaf or disabled people to compensate for the loss of sound and mobility that plays an important role in everyday life. They provide a source of enthusiastic help, unconditional love, and a sense of freedom and independence. In training, the dog must display curiosity and no fear of loud noises, sudden movements, or unusual circumstances. The training of a hearing dog takes three to four months, and a service dog, six months to one year. During this time the dogs are taught house manners, basic obedience commands using both hand and voice signals, as well as sound response, retrieval and other specialized work.

Both guide dogs for the blind and the hearing and service dogs are socialized and trained to work and behave in public situations such as shopping malls, restaurants, public transportation, and around other dogs and animal species. Anyone interested in donating or raising a Vizsla for a service dog organization should research the organization well, and determine which type of training your dog would best be suited for. Those dogs that pass the training "graduate" and go on to provide years of happiness, independence, and support to their handicapped owners.

Penlee Southeast Scizzle in his working harness for his blind owner. *Photo courtesy of Betty Anderson.*

The Versatile Vizsla

At Home: Never underestimate the intelligence of a Vizsla. This one studies the Scrabble® board.

In the Field: Nine-month-old Victor's Hillary has the bird located and holds her point. Owned by Brent Aronson.

In Competition: Ch. Boelte's Manhattan Marquis
Sire: Ch. Cariad's Alydar Loki Santana
Dam: Ch. Boelte's Bronze Brea
Owner: Ron Hershberger
Photo by Harkins.

With the Kids: Always a loving companion who needs lots of attention and affection.

A Vizsla likes to have his own chair in which to rest while still happily watching family activities around him.

11

Preventive Health Care

PREVENTIVE health care is a wise investment since the prevention of viruses and diet problems costs substantially less than any treatment. Good health is the result of a simple program of exercise, training, vaccinations, dietary management, and regular veterinarian checkups.

Close association with your veterinarian is important. Select one who is willing to give the time to answer any questions regarding your Vizsla's general well-being, but do not wait until the annual checkup to present him with a list of problems. Learn which part of a preventive health program you can handle at home, and which needs a skilled professional.

NORMAL LIFE SIGNS

Unless you know what is normal for your dog, you will not be able to recognize a problem. The normal temperature for an adult dog is 100 to 102.5°F (rectal). Using a rectal thermometer, shake it down to below 97°F. Coat the tip with *Vaseline*® and insert almost half of it into the anus. Hold it there for three minutes, and do not let your dog sit.

A well dog breathes ten to thirty times a minute, but after any exercise or stress this rate will increase. Watch your Vizsla as he breathes through his nose while lying quietly and you can count the chest movements.

The average heart rate of an adult dog is 70 to 130 beats per minute with puppies having a faster rate. The beat, or pulse, should be firm and steady. With your dog lying down, take your index and middle finger and press on the inside of his thigh near at the point where the leg joins the body. You will be touching his femoral artery which reflects the heartbeat. Count the beats for one minute.

Your dog's urine should be a clear yellow color, and bloody or cloudy urine is indicative of a problem. The intensity of the color will increase if the quantity that he excretes decreases. A sudden increase in water intake along with the volume of urine produced may be an indication of disease.

Small blood vessels, or capillaries, carry the blood supply to the skin. Pressing a finger against your Vizsla's gums will cause the gum to grow pale. When you remove your finger that area should refill with blood and regain the normal pink color rapidly. A slow return to color could indicate shock or anemia.

By making a point of examining your puppy or adult dog every day, you can easily monitor his overall health at home and become aware of any signs of a low level of health, or impending problems.

EAR PROBLEMS

Vizslas can be prone to ear problems since their ears hang down and prevent good air circulation. The inside forms a warm incubation area for ear mites and infections. Check the inside of the ears daily.

A dog with an infected ear may hold a sore ear low and shake or scratch at it. The external ear will be inflamed and sore and will have a smelly, light-colored discharge. In extreme cases, the ear canal will harden, blocking the discharge and impairing hearing. An ear infection is difficult to treat as it is usually a com-

---

Table 11-1
How to Recognize A Healthy Versus A Sick Dog

Signs of a Healthy Dog	Signs of Illness
Normal temperature 101 to 101.5 F.	Temperature 102 F. or above, or under 100 F.
Normal pulse rate 70 to 130 beats per minute	Rapid or slow pulse when dog is resting
Normal respiration 10 to 30 per minute	Labored breathing
Eyes clear	Eyes dull, cloudy, red, watery, or filled with pus
Nose moist	Pale gums
Gums pink	Change in appetite
Appetite good	Dull coat
Glossy coat	Drinking increased amounts of water
Active and alert	Change in behavior; hyperactivity, listlessness
	Blood in stool, urine, or vomit
	Constipation or diarrhea
	Convulsions
	Dehydration
	Lameness
	Pain in abdomen, limbs, ears, etc.
	Pawing or scratching excessively at an area
	Strong odor from mouth or anus
	Stomach distended
	Straining to urinate
	Vomiting
	Weakness

bination of fungus, mites, and a bacterial invasion. Hot, humid weather is an inducer, promoting the problem, and not all ear infections respond to treatment no matter how hard you try.

Ear mites live on the surface of the ear canal and feed on it by piercing the skin and causing an irritation, infection, and discharge. A thick brownish-black paste in the ear canal can sometimes be a sign of ear mites. Clean the ears with a cotton swab. If you have an otoscope or a microscope, the mites can be seen as small white insects. Adding a few drops of warm mineral oil, or Betadine, in warm water, use a bulb syringe to flush the ear canal, while massaging to clean the ear and kill the mites.

Mites can possibly be controlled by constant supervision and treatment, and administering antibiotic ointments for the bacterial infection. However, you will have to be persistent in inspecting and cleaning the ears if you ever hope to resolve the problem.

EYE PROBLEMS

An inflamed eye may be caused by almost any kind of foreign object such as dirt, sand, pieces of bark, pollens, chemicals, and other infecting material. If you see your Vizsla squinting, look under the eyelids. If you find any foreign material in his eye, remove it by flushing it with warm water, or eye drops, or even by using the tip of a hankerchief. If the eye is red and irritated, your veterinarian can prescribe an eye ointment.

Due to a slack inverted lower eye margin in many Vizslas, a pale mucous discharge will often collect. A daily check and cleaning of your dog's eye may be necessary. If the discharge is yellow it may indicate an infection and use of antibiotic ointments may be indicated.

Letting your Vizsla hang his head out of a moving automobile can result in eye injuries from flying stones and debris. An injury to his eye can ulcerate the cornea, causing excessive pain, and ultimate sight loss.

A healthy Vizsla will have clear, clean, expressive eyes.

TEETH CARE AND GUM DISEASE

Gingivitis, or inflammation of the gums, is characterized by tender gums which bleed when probed. Pockets alongside the teeth retain food which causes bacterial infections that spread to the roots, destroying the support of the tooth within the jaw. Without treatment, extraction of the tooth may become necessary if the root becomes abscessed.

Examine your Vizsla's teeth periodically for any buildup of dental plaque, or tartar, which is an incrustation on the teeth consisting of salivary secretions, food residue, and various salts. Left uncleaned, it can cause severe gum inflammation. Blood on the gum line and a bad odor are the best indicators of trouble, since dogs often do not show any signs of pain or tenderness as they chew.

Weekly brushing of your Vizsla's teeth with a soft toothbrush and paste, or cleaner, will remove food particles and buildup of tartar. If your dog already has a layer of tartar, it will be necessary to use a dental scaling tool to remove it. Since Vizslas like to chew on sticks

Figure 11-1
Care of the Teeth

Figure 11-2
Cleaning the Anal Glands

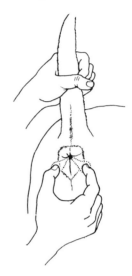

To clean the two anal glands, apply gentle pressure on each side of the anus.

and stones, check also for any broken or damaged teeth.

ANAL GLANDS

The two anal glands are located on each side of the anus. They are about the size of small cherries and can enlarge if they get overfilled with secretions. Normal bowel movements help to express the glands and keep them from becoming irritated, but soft stools caused by incorrect diet or parasites will lead to retention, impaction, and eventual infection of the glands.

Scooting on the rear may not always be a sign of worms. If your dog shows discomfort in sitting, and pain, or constant licking at the anus it could be from impacted anal glands. Continued impaction can cause abscesses.

These smelly secretions can be expressed with a little practice. Apply gentle pressure with a thumb and finger on each side, just below the anus. Milk each gland toward the anal opening. Be sure to cover the area with a

paper towel, as the secretions may come shooting out under the pressure.

FEET PROBLEMS

Occasionally too much running over wet ground, or even an eczema condition, will bring about an angry, sweating, redness between your Vizsla's toes. Feet trouble of this kind is aggravating and the first sign you may have of anything wrong is when your dog starts limping or licking at a particular foot.

For temporary relief, sprinkle a human foot powder between the toes to relieve the pain and redness. There are several good fungal foot powders on the market which will serve this purpose. If the condition persists, your veterinarian may have to take a culture to determine the exact cause in order to prescribe a treatment.

Little boots can be made or bought to protect the foot, keep it dry, and hasten healing, or clean socks can be kept on the foot to keep your dog from aggravating it with licking.

GASTRIC TORSION (BLOAT)

Bloat is an emergency situation. It has been linked to the feeding of dry food, large consumption of water, gas or swallowed air, and exercise too soon after eating.

Bloat is associated with all deep–chested breeds and can occur at any age. Signs are prostration, a severe abdominal distention, unsuccessful tries at vomiting, and difficulty in breathing. The distention of the stomach may cause it to rotate at the pylorus, the opening into the intestines. This torsion cuts off the blood flow, sending your dog into shock. Emergency treatment will be required to release the gasses trapped by the rotation and to counter the shock. Surgery may be necessary to reposition the stomach. Without immediate professional help, your dog will die.

Feeding two smaller meals a day, instead of one large one, may help to prevent bloat. Moisten the dry meal before feeding in order to prevent the large consumption of water after eating, and restrain your dog from strenuous exercise both before and after eating.

CANINE HIP DYSPLASIA

Hip dysplasia occurs in almost every breed that matures at over twenty–four pounds. Dysplasia is a term applied to any abnormality of a joint, and is a condition where the hip joint is malformed. Instead of fitting neatly between the top of the thighbone and the pelvis, the edges are rough and uneven, losing close contact and resulting in a looseness in the joint.

Hip dysplasia can be mostly controlled and prevented by only breeding Vizslas that have hips X-rayed and verified as sound. Besides being proven that the problem with dysplasia is usually inherited, there is also evidence to suggest that environment plays a big role in the development of bad hips.

The condition could start in a whelping box with a smooth surface, which presents a problem to the small puppy trying to get on his feet. Smooth, slippery tiles, or linoleum floors would compound the problem as the young puppy learns to run and play. Hip dysplasia could also be the result of poor nutrition — a lack of vitamin C causes weak ligaments and muscles around the joint.

Figure 11-3
Hip Dysplasia

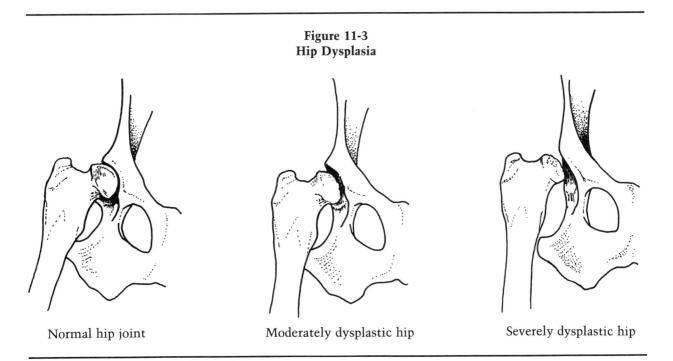

Normal hip joint   Moderately dysplastic hip   Severely dysplastic hip

It could also be a disease affecting the elasticity of the pectineus muscle. The pectineus is a small muscle on the inner surface of the thigh. It originates on the lower surface of the pelvis and has a broad body that tapers into a long tendon attached along the femur. The hip joint changes are not primary; they are secondary and are seen as secondary changes.

It has been shown that a degenerative lesion occurs in the spinal cord at the level of the fourth and fifth lumbar vertebrae and nerve (loin area.) This lesion in the spinal cord is in the neuropathway of the pectineus muscle. Once the nerve is destroyed at the spinal cord, changes occur in the pectineus muscle. This degeneration begins to appear in the muscle between the tenth and one hundred twenty-first day of age.

Once the pectineus muscle becomes diseased, as a result of the alternation of its blood supply, its growth stops. The muscle does not grow, but the shaft of the femur continues to grow and lengthen. Because of this, an upward pressure develops, with the femoral head resting against the rim of the acetabulum. As the pectineus muscle stops its growth and the shaft of the femur goes on in growth, the rim of the acetabulum begins to deflect upwards due to the contant pressure applied to the femoral head. This produces the shallow acetabular socket that is seen in radiographically evident hip dysplasia.

In extremely painful cases, surgery to sever the pectineous muscle can relieve both lameness and pain.

Whatever the cause, it is heartbreaking for the owner when his young Vizsla is suddenly unable to get up on his hind legs, or is reluctant to run, play, or climb stairs. Decreased activity may be the first indication of the problem, along with an uneven gait with the rear legs moving together under the dog because of the inability to extend them back. The rear legs will slant in a "cow-hocked" position from the weak muscles.

Another suspect is with the young adult that noticeably lacks rear angulation, and appears to have an extremely well developed front, because he must carry the weight of his body forward. He will stand with his hind legs close together and tucked under his body, thus shifting the weight forward.

The disease is a progressive one and, at times, even crippling, but many dogs build a muscle mass around the affected joint, holding it in place, and show no signs at all of the abnormality. As an affected dog grows older arthritis may present a problem, depending on the severity of the dysplasia.

Providing your Vizsla with a warm bed away from drafts, keeping his weight down, giving anti-inflammatory medication, and moderate exercise will ensure a comfortable life most of the time. Spaying or neutering is a necessity as no Vizsla diagnosed with any degree of hip dysplasia should ever be used for breeding.

Vizslas have a low incidence of dysplasia compared to many other breeds of the same size. The use of diagnostic X-rays and responsible breeding practices have kept the problem to a minimum.

The hip X-ray has to be performed by your veterinarian while your Vizsla is under anesthesia. Your veterinarian can give you his diagnosis, or the X-ray can be submitted to the Orthopedic Foundation for Animals (OFA) for evaluation. The OFA is a non-profit organization which collects information about orthopedic diseases and finances research into them. They will examine the X-ray of any age dog and give the verdict of his hip condition but will not issue a registry number for him unless he is over 2 years of age and has good hips.

VIRUSES AND VACCINATIONS

Vaccinations provide immunity from highly contagious diseases which can seriously jeopardize the life of your Vizsla. It is important that your dog get the complete series of vaccines needed to ensure his protection, right from puppyhood. The immunity he received from his dam diminishes as he gets older and the vaccines he is injected with will stimulate his immune system to produce his own anti-

Table 11-2
Your Dog's Medicine Chest

Include the following items:

A rectal thermometer
Liquid antiseptic soap such as *Betadine*®
Cotton swabs and cotton balls
Hydrogen peroxide
Gauze pads and bandage wrap
Clean towels
Blunt-nosed scissors
Styptic powder to control bleeding
Kaopectate® concentrate
Biosol M® or *Amforal*® for diarrhea
Rectal suppositories
Artificial tears or boric acid eyewash
Gauze or nylon stocking for muzzle
Dramamine® for motion sickness
Otocide® for ear mites
antiacid tablets
Panalog® neomycin sulfate wound ointment
antibiotic or sulfa tablets
Variton® cream for moist eczema
Bitter Apple® to prevent chewing
Activated charcoal as universal poison antidote

Conversion table for medications:

16 drops = 1 cc or 1/4 tsp.
 5 cc = 1 tsp.
15 cc = 1 tablespoon
 1 oz = 30 cc or 2 tablespoons
 I qt = I liter; 4 cups

Dosage by weight of dog:

Aspirin - one 5 grain tablet per 30 lbs. every
 six hours
Charcoal - one tablespoon in four ounces of
 water per 30 lbs.
Dramamine - 25 to 50 mg one-half hour before
 traveling
Kaopectate - one teaspoon regular strength
 per 5 lbs. every four hours
Milk of Magnesia - one teaspoon per 10 lbs.
 every six hours

---

bodies. They are a necessity, even if your dog never leaves the confines of his own yard. Many viruses are airborne or carried into the home on shoes or clothing.

Distemper

Distemper is an airborne virus, and droplet infection from secretions passed by an infected animal is the main source. The illness usually begins with an elevated temperature lasting one to three days, slowly subsiding, and recurring in a few days, along with purulent material in the eyes, diarrhea, listlessness, vomiting, cold-like symptoms of a runny nose and coughing, and in a severe case, convulsions and paralysis. Any chance for recovery is poor as intensive care is long and necessary.

Infectious Hepatitis

Hepatitis is a highly contagious disease with signs varying from a slight fever and congestion of the mucous membranes, to severe depression, vomiting, a lack of appetite, intense thirst, and a blue cloudiness over the cornea of the eye. There is a direct correlation between the severity of the disease and blood clotting time. Controlling a hemorrhage is difficult for that reason, and a long recovery period with antibiotics, vitamins, and close nursing care is required.

The main route of infection is from urine, feces, and saliva from an infected animal and the mortality rate is highest in young dogs that may have a low level of passive antibodies when exposed.

Leptospirosis

Leptospirosis is spread by a bacterial infection in the urine of a diseased animal, usually a rat. It can enter your Vizsla's system through a break in the skin, or if he drinks urine-contaminated water. The disease can have a sudden onset with weakness, vomiting, high fever, lack of appetite, jaundice, ulcers in the mouth, extreme weight loss, and mild conjunctivitis. In a few days the body temperature may drop as low as 97°F with breathing and swallowing becoming difficult. There is an increase in urination, thirst, bloody diarrhea, and vomiting.

Because of the serious damage to kidneys and liver, intensive care is necessary, along with antibiotics and control of vomiting and diarrhea. Rat control is important to reduce the chance of exposure to any rodents carrying the disease.

Kennel Cough

Canine cough is commonly called "kennel cough" because of its highly contagious spread among dogs kept together. It is evident by its harsh persistent cough accompanied by gagging. The slightest bit of exercise, or even a tug on a collar will set off the coughing reflex. Quiet and rest are necessary as the cough may hang on for as long as three weeks. While it is not usually serious in the adult Vizsla unless complicated by pneumonia, it is a potential danger to young puppies.

There is no vaccine for complete protection against infectious canine cough, as there are thirteen viruses and bacteria which are implicated as its cause. However, by vaccinating for two known components, Parainfluenza and Bordetella, part of the problem is eliminated.

Parvovirus

Every dog in the country, no matter where he lives, should be vaccinated for this disease. It is a highly contagious gastrointestinal virus which strikes without much warning and can cause death within twelve hours. It is especially dangerous, and most often fatal, in young puppies. It can easily be carried home on your shoes as the virus can persist in a kennel area, soil, or elsewhere for six months or longer.

Be able to identify each shrub or tree in your yard with which your Vizsla may come in contact.

Safe fencing will keep your Vizsla away from stray dogs that may carry infectious diseases.

The first sign is a high temperature accompanied by severe vomiting. Diarrhea starts with grayish or yellow-gray stools, often foul smelling and streaked with blood. There will be a loss of appetite, depression, and rapid dehydration with sunken eyes and dry, inelastic skin. Without immediate professional help the survival rate is low, with collapse occurring within a few hours. Due to this sudden onset it is probably the most serious gastrointestinal virus there is.

If you have had a Vizsla ill from Parvovirus, do not bring another dog into your home until he has had sufficient vaccinations against this disease. Vaccines are available in combination form with other canine vaccines, and as a separate dose. If your Vizsla is exposed to dog shows, field trials, or a boarding kennel, it is advisable to get boosters for Parvovirus every six months to give added protection.

Coronavirus

Although similar in some symptoms to the Parvovirus, Coronavirus is usually not as severe or deadly if the diarrhea is brought under control. Carried in the feces of an infected animal which may shed the virus for three weeks or more, Coronavirus may cause repeated illnesses. Fever is absent or mild, and the virus has a suddden onset of diarrhea, vomiting, and mental depression. The vomiting usually decreases in frequency after the first day or two, but the diarrhea may continue as an oozing of frothy yellow-orange, semi-solid material with an offensive odor. It may be projectile and often bloody.

Good supportive care is necessary to prevent any dehydration, especially in a puppy, and effective sanitation and hygiene are essential, as the virus is highly contagious.

Lyme Disease

It is now known that the tiny deer tick, no larger than a flea, is a carrier of an arthritic type of illness called Lyme Disease, named after the town of Olde Lyme, Connecticut where humans and animals both contracted the disease. This disease has been rapidly spreading throughout the country. The tiny tick can be carried by migratory birds, mice and squirrels.

Lyme Disease is not usually fatal, but it can be debilitating. Early signs in your dog may be fever, pain with lameness in more than one limb which involves the large joints, possible rash, and lethargy. If you have had your Vizsla in an area known to have ticks and observe a rash, illness, or limping, and you can eliminate joint trauma or stress as the reason for the lameness, ask your veterinarian to do a blood test for Lyme Disease. A course of antibiotic treatment is usually prescribed.

Rather than subjecting your Vizsla to the problem of treatment, vaccination as a preventative against the disease is recommended. The vaccine is available with two initial doses, three weeks apart, and a yearly booster.

Rabies

Rabies is a deadly viral disease that is transmitted in the saliva of an infected animal by way of a bite. Infection may not be evident for at least two weeks or up to six months, but when the symptoms show, death is usually within five days.

The virus travels to the spinal cord and then spreads to the brain, invades the salivary glands, and rapidly becomes infectious. It can be transmitted even though no obvious signs are showing. Symptoms are first evident in the way an animal starts behaving. He becomes excitable and aggressive, and from there, goes to being withdrawn and seeking solitude. Within three days he will show signs of becoming vicious and attack anything at the slightest move.

The disease rapidly progresses to the onset of paralysis causing the mouth to hang open and drool from the inability to swallow. The paralysis spreads rapidly and coma and death follow in a short time.

Rabies is a tragic disease. A Vizsla working in the field can be exposed to a rabid animal, but it can also happen in any suburban or rural yard. An unvaccinated dog bitten by a rabid animal has to be destroyed immediately.

Your puppy can receive his first vaccine as early as 4 months of age. I prefer not to give it in conjunction with other vaccines.

INTERNAL PARASITES

Continuous monitoring of your Vizsla for any intestinal parasites is vital for his health and well-being. Worms rob a puppy's growing body of the nutrition it needs and they are debilitating to the older dog. They drain the tissues of blood and moisture, cause diarrhea, appetite loss, and a dry dull coat. Since the cycle of most canine parasites causes reinfestation, your yard must have strict sanitation supervision, combined with a routine schedule of fecal checks.

Unnecessary or indiscriminatory worming can be detrimental to the health of your Vizsla since a positive identification of the parasite must be made first to determine the type of medication required. Stool samples should be checked by your veterinarian several times a year, especially if your dog has a history of worm infestation.

Roundworms

Roundworms are the most common of the parasites that a dog owner has to deal with. Once they have infested your yard, they are almost impossible to get rid of. Do not allow children to play barefooted in an area where dog feces lie, as children are susceptible to migrating larvae from the worms, which can cause lesions in the eyes, liver, and kidneys.

A litter of puppies can be born with roundworms due to transplacental passage of larvae from the infected dam, into the unborn fetus, where the larvae develop in the lungs. The larvae crawl into the trachea, are swallowed, and enter the small intestines where they ma-

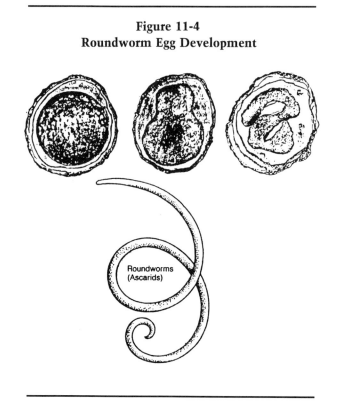

**Figure 11-4
Roundworm Egg Development**

Roundworms
(Ascarids)

ture. This method of infection is so common that most puppies are born with roundworms.

A Vizsla puppy so infected will be potbellied, thin, have a dull coat, diarrhea, vomiting, and look poor. The worms can cause anemia and interfere with the absorption of food. Roundworms in your older Vizsla will not cause much difficulty as only a few of the larvae return to the intestines, but encyst in the tissues and remain dormant.

Hookworms

Hookworms are tiny, thin, and threadlike, only getting as long as half an inch. Your Vizsla can become infected by larvae entering the skin or mouth, where they wander through the body tissues until they enter a blood vessel. The larvae travel to the lungs, crawl up the windpipe, and are then swallowed. When they reach the small intestines, they attach themselves to the wall of the intestines, suck blood, and lay up to 20,000 eggs per day.

The amount of blood loss in a day to a single hookworm has been estimated to be as much as a milliliter, which can cause chronic anemia, weakness, emaciation, and fatality in your small puppy. Because hookworm larvae cross the placenta wall, a puppy can display the infection as young as 10 days of age.

Typical symptoms in both a puppy and an adult dog are bloody and tarry diarrhea, pale gums, anemia, and impaired food absorption. A fecal check should be done several times a year if your Vizsla has a history of hookworm infections.

Whipworms

Although whipworms are the least common of the intestinal worms, they can be an obstinate problem if your Vizsla has them. Unless he is heavily infested, your dog may not show any external signs. With a heavy infestation he will have intermittent bloody and mucousy diarrhea, a dry coat, and be undernourished.

Since the female whipworms lay fewer eggs than other worms do, infestation is lighter and harder to detect in a single stool sample. Several samples may have to be taken before any diagnosis is reached.

Tapeworms

The least dangerous to your dog's health, tapeworms usually cause only a dry coat, occasional weight loss, and intermittent diarrhea. However, in the case of a heavy infestation, your Vizsla may seem nervous and hyper, with a loss of appetite, and he may drag his rear on the ground because of irritation from the worms.

Tapeworm eggs are passed through an infected dog's feces where they are ingested by flea larvae. Inside the flea, the egg segments soon develop into tapeworm larvae. The infected flea jumps onto a dog and the dog, in biting at the flea, ingests it. The tapeworm larvae then start to develop inside the dog's intestines.

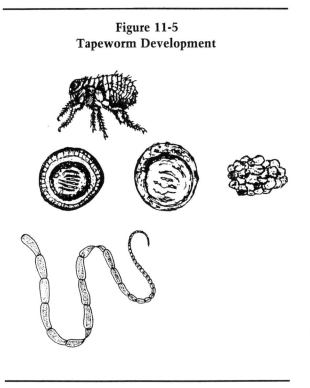

Figure 11-5
Tapeworm Development

Tapeworms can grow to a length of several feet and are divided into separate sections which break off and are passed in the stool. Easily visible, the segments are only a quarter of an inch in size and look like pale–colored grains of rice or cucumber seeds.

Special medication is needed to rid your dog of a tapeworm as the worm has a head, or scolex, which stays firmly attached to the lining of the small intestines. If this head is not removed during treatment, it will regrow another body.

You will have a never-ending battle against tapeworms unless your Vizsla's environment is treated for flea infestation.

Coccidia

Older dogs are mostly resistant to Coccidiosis but can be carriers, infecting a young puppy that has just been weaned and is possibly under stress.

The Coccidia parasite lives in feces of infected animals, reproducing rapidly and causing such severe illness in a young puppy as to be fatal if correct treatment is delayed. The first signs are a mild diarrhea which will soon show mucous and blood. This progresses to weight loss, anemia, dehydration, abdominal pain, weakness, and a loss of appetite. Further symptoms confuse the diagnosis as they are the same as those of distemper: eye discharge, cough, and a runny nose.

Good sanitation is a must and all feces should be cleaned up immediately to prevent possible contamination if your young dog walks through it. Medication must be started to relieve the diarrhea and dehydration, and also a drug treatment against the life cycle of the coccidia parasite. Known carriers of coccidia should be isolated and treated, or reinfection will be a problem.

Heartworm

Previously only found in the warm and moist areas with a mosquito problem, heartworm has now spread throughout most of the United States. Without preventive care, the infection rate would be many times greater than it is now. Being a "house dog" is no guarantee that your Vizsla will not become infected.

The heartworm parasite lives in the heart and pulmonary artery of an infected dog, and can grow as long as twelve inches. The female parasite produces microfilariae, or young ones, which are released into the bloodstream. These can remain active for as long as two years, and if during that time a mosquito ingests the infected blood through a bite, the baby heartworms will develop into infective larvae in that mosquito. The mosquito will go on to feed on a new dog, releasing the larvae to develop under the skin and then to migrate to the bloodstream. From the blood, the larvae go to the right ventricle of the dog's heart, arriving two to four months after being released by the mosquito. In the heart, the worms mature and reproduce, and the cycle starts again with another infected dog.

Symptoms of heartworm are a gradual weight loss, less tolerance for exercise, a

Good sanitation practices are an absolute necessity for a healthy dog. A pooper-scooper makes it easy.

cough, pale mucous membranes, lethargy, and collapse. The growth of the worms in the heart causes increased pulmonary blood pressure and impaired circulation. Your dog may cough up fresh blood, have difficulty breathing, consume more water, and have frequent bloody urination.

The treatment for heartworm disease is serious and not without risk. Injection of an arsenic-form drug is used over a period of two days and your dog must have complete rest for several weeks. As the adult worms die, they pass from the heart into the lungs and can lodge in the arteries where there is a chance of an embolism.

Several weeks after the treatment to rid your dog of the adult heartworms, treatment must be started to get the microfilariae out of the bloodstream. If the ten–day treatment is successful, your dog will be able to take a heartworm preventative drug.

A blood test can determine if a dog is clear of heartworm infestation. Prevention is accomplished by giving a heartworm preventative from a month before to a month after frost. A daily dose of Diethylcarbamazine Citrate should be given year round in warm areas. If you find it inconvenient to give your Vizsla a daily medication, using *Ivermectin®* in a once-a-month dose will kill any microfilariae that may be present in the bloodstream. Both preventive medications are available from your veterinarian and are given according to weight, so weighing your Vizsla as he grows is essential.

EXTERNAL PARASITES

Many a Vizsla's coat has been ruined by his scratching to get rid of fleas and ticks. They are a common problem in every part of the country and your dog does not even have to leave his own yard to be exposed to them.

Fleas

Fleas spend only ten percent of their lives on your dog. The other ninety percent is spent in carpeting, bedding, crevices and cracks of floors, furniture, and the yard. Ten producing female fleas will result in 1,800 new fleas in only one month so it is important to kill all the eggs before they hatch in your dog's environment.

Fleas not only carry the tapeworm egg to infest your Vizsla, but a great percentage of Vizslas are allergic to flea saliva, and break out in bumps and a rash. Constant biting, digging, and scratching breaks the coat and skin down into erupting sores and "hot spots" and your dog will look and feel miserable.

Cortisone medication prescribed by your veterinarian will alleviate a lot of discomfort caused by any severe allergic reaction. Going through your Vizsla's coat daily with a fine-toothed flea comb will bring any parasites to the surface to be killed by hand or with a flea spray. Do not use a flea collar. Not only are these ineffectual, but they are also extremely toxic, and can be dangerous to young children who may handle dogs and their collars.

Ticks

Ticks cling to bushes and trees, attach themselves firmly to a dog's skin as he runs through the woods, and feed on blood for several days before dropping off.

Increases in the deer population, along with home development closer to woodlands, have brought about an increase in Lyme Disease, carried by the tiny tick that feeds on the wild animals carrying the bacteria for this disease in their digestive tracts. White–footed mice and wild deer are the primary animals associated with transmitting the disease to ticks.

Checking your puppy each day for fleas and ticks also gives you a chance to teach him to behave on a grooming table.

Adult ticks feed and mate on deer, then drop off to look for a new host such as a dog, which can become lame and ill from the disease.

Any removal technique of a tick must be fast as it is important to get the tick off your dog before it has had time to inject the disease–carrying microbe under the skin. Since it is also possible for a person to contract the disease, care must be taken. A safe way to remove a tick is to pull it out with tweezers or small forceps. Grasp the tick as close as possible to its mouth (the part sticking into the skin), then, without jerking, pull it upward. Do not squeeze, crush or puncture the body of the tick, or handle it with bare hands. Dispose of it in alcohol, and disinfect your dog's skin with alcohol or iodine.

Another serious disease transmitted by a tick is Rocky Mountain Spotted Fever. Carried by the female wood tick in the west and American dog tick in the east, the disease comes to a head rapidly with a very high temperature of up to 105°F, depression, loss of appetite, lethargy, weakness, and hemorrhages under the skin.

The dog tick can also transmit a blood infection called Haemobartonellosis, which can cause anemia in your Vizsla. He may tire easily and have pale mucous membranes. The disease weakens the immune system to other illnesses.

Sprays and dips are usually effective for your Vizsla if you have a tick problem, but control over infestation in his environment is also essential. Labels on all pesticides now have to contain explicit information of their hazardous use around the house and yard. With a large and bewildering variety of products for use, make sure you read labels carefully for any toxicity to an animal. It is usually advisable to switch brands every other time you spray to achieve accepable parasite control.

Mites

Mites are any of the numerous small to minute arachnids that often infest animals. They are not only disease carriers, but cause irritation to the skin. They are smaller than ticks and are covered with a relatively soft, often translucent skin. Their legs are provided with clawlike hooks or suction cups to either draw fluid or adhere to the dog's skin. Depending on the species, the food of parasitic mites includes mainly blood, lymph, living and dead epithelial cells.

Cheyletiella mites — Diagnosis depends on the identification of these mites in dandruff or skin brushings. A scaling process occurs primarily on the back, head, and neck of a dog and causes extreme itching and scratching, possibly leading to secondary skin infections.

These mite infestations in your Vizsla are highly contagious and can extend to humans. Lesions similar to ringworm appear, but they lack the inflammatory border. Treatment is successful with dips and scrubs of insecticides for your dog, and the application of topical insecticides for you.

Sarcoptic mange mites — These mites are tiny spiderlike parasites which burrow in tunnels under the skin and lay eggs. Lesions appear within seventeen to twenty–one days and cause intense itching, which leads to skin inflammation and secondary infections in your dog.

Preferred areas for the mites are the base of the tail, the area around the eyes, ears, muzzle, legs and head. The skin becomes irritated by the chemicals produced by the salivary secretions of the mites, and breaks down into seeping sores from your dog chewing and scratching. The sores crust over and scab, and the skin becomes thick and dry with hair missing in patches.

Sarcoptic Mange is highly contagious and several treatments with an insecticide dip may be necessary over a period of several weeks for a complete cure, along with a cortisone medication to relieve the itching. It is very readily transmitted, by direct contact, to humans, although of a shorter duration.

Demodectic mites — These mites are normal inhabitants of the skin and probably at least ninety percent of all short–haired dogs harbor this tiny cigar-shaped mite. Few ever

Figure 11-6
Demodectic Mite

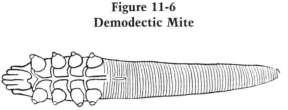

exhibit clinical signs and infestation will usually show up in a young Vizsla due to a stress factor.

There are two forms of Demodectic Mange. The benign form is the most common, seen as a localized condition with patches of hair loss on the face, and front and rear feet, and legs. Sometimes called a "childhood disease" it will evidence itself in a young puppy during the time he is cutting teeth, going to a new home, changing diets, in need of worming, or any other stress period which might lower his resistance. This localized condition is mild and will usually cure itself, without any problem, in just a short time.

The generalized form of Demodectic Mange is characterized by a vast multiplication of the mites in the hair follicles, with severe hair loss, and skin lesions oozing blood and serum caused by bacterial infections and giving off a bad odor. The skin becomes swollen and inflamed and the dog is in a miserable state due to intense itching.

The treatment for generalized Demodectic Mange can be long and frustrating as it often responds poorly to treatment. Antibiotics for secondary infections along with applications of a topical insecticide are used and it is important that your Vizsla be maintained on a good diet supplemented with vitamins, fatty acids and minerals. He must be free of any intestinal parasites or stressful conditions.

Both genetics and a depressed or altered immune system are blamed for the development of the generalized form of Demodectic Mange. Because of this critical factor, any Vizsla that has had the condition, even though recovered, should not be used for breeding.

PUPPY PROOFING YOUR YARD AND HOME

A Vizsla can be very much like a small child in the way he explores every place he can get into and tastes or chews everything with which his mouth comes in contact. Being a concerned owner means taking the time to examine your entire yard and home and remove potential dangers before your Vizsla gets into trouble.

Take a good look at the trees, bushes, and plants in your yard and be sure that you are able to identify each one. Many plants will be completely harmless and others will cause vomiting, abdominal pains, cramps, diarrhea, and sometimes heart and respiratory failure. Some plants may cause skin rash and indirect damage due to your dog constantly digging, chewing, scratching, and licking his feet or coat. Painful lesions of the mouth can result from him trying to remove the common burdock from his body.

The greatest safety factor for your Vizsla is going to be the fencing around his yard. It will protect him from roaming loose, possible injury by a car, theft, exposure to viruses, and attack from stray dogs.

First aid help given at home for toxic ingestion or poisoning from an insect bite or sting should only be undertaken after identifying the source of the problem and then getting your veterinarian's advice.

Your garage may hold some of the most toxic substances which present a danger to your Vizsla. Anti-freeze contains Ethylene Glycol, a poisonous liquid which can attract a puppy with its sweet taste and smell. It also contains Methyl Alcohol, a volatile, toxic liquid used as a paint and varnish remover. It is toxic if absorbed through the skin, or, if taken internally, will cause death from respiratory failure. Make sure there are no spills or leaks on the garage floor.

The same ingredients in anti-freeze are also found in windshield washer fluid, brake, and hydraulic fluid. An amount as little as two teaspoons can be fatal to a fifteen–pound puppy. Damage to the kidneys and the central

Table 11-3
You and Your Veterinarian

Selecting a Veterinarian
Select a veterinary clinician when you first get your puppy or dog. Some guidelines are:
      Is the location convenient to your home, with easy, quick access?
      Do clinic hours that fit your schedule?
      Is the clinic clean and well lighted?
      Have you obtained a good recommendation from several long-time clients?
      Do you like the veterinarian and his office personnel?
      If you prefer to be billed, can you make arrangements or must you pay cash?

When You Need A Veterinarian
      For a yearly physical examination and booster vaccinations.
      For periodic stool checks for worms.
      For any emergency.
      When you suspect internal problems or a possible broken bone.
      When your dog doesn't respond to routine home treatment.
      When your dog's temperature is 102 F. or greater, or lower than l00 F.
      When diarrhea or vomitimg continue more than 24 hours.

nervous system can result in death within twelve to thirty-six hours after ingestion.

Kerosene, gasoline, mineral spirits, paint thinners, insect and rat poison, weed killers, insecticides, old batteries, putty and solder materials should all be disposed of or placed in a locked closet.

An open cabinet door under the kitchen or laundry-room sink can attract a curious puppy and result in some very serious problems from the ingestion of steel wool pads, disinfectants, furniture polish, detergents, bleach, drain cleaners, soaps, and moth balls.

In the bathroom, not only deodorant soaps, bath oils, shampoo, shaving lotions, perfume, and health and beauty aids can result in toxic poisoning, but a sponge left carelessly on the side of the tub can be chewed and swallowed with disastrous results to your Vizsla's intestines.

Sleeping pills, tranquilizers, stimulants, aspirin, barbituates, antibiotics, decongestants, and narcotics must be kept out of reach.

Electric cords are used in almost every room in the house and provide an attractive nuisance to a young puppy. Be sure to unplug them if your puppy is going to be unsupervised, if only for a short period. A shock from a chewed cord will result in a burned and damaged mouth, circulatory collapse and difficulty in breathing.

Chocolate contains the alkaloid theobromine. At toxic doses it can cause vomiting, diarrhea, depression, muscle tremors, and even death. It is estimated that around four ounces of un-

Keeping your dog from roaming is the responsibility of every Vizsla owner.

Above, left: An uncovered garbage can is a temptation to a young Vizsla.

Above, right: Vizslas like to carry sticks and stones in their mouth. Check frequently for teeth that may have become damaged by your dog chewing on hard objects.

Left: Vizslas love to play in the snow, but care should be taken to wash any salt from their feet.

sweetened chocolate, or thirty-two ounces of milk chocolate is enough to kill a 45–pound dog. Your puppy could have a toxic reaction to a four–ounce candy bar.

The active ingredient of tobacco is nicotine, a poisonous alkaloid. Make sure that ashtrays are kept empty and that packs of cigarettes are kept out of your Vizsla's reach.

Garbage cans, both indoors and outside, should be securely covered. Spoiled foods can cause vomiting, abdominal pain, diarrhea, and prostration within four hours. While this condition may not be fatal, ingestion of pins and needles, splintered bones, fruit seeds, and corn cobs can cause complications in the digestive tract.

Windows without protective screening should never be left open. A puppy has no idea of what may present a danger to him and can not judge distance or depth.

House plants present the same danger as outdoor shrubs and bushes. The only way to keep a puppy from chewing on a dangerous plant or putting any strange substance in his mouth, is to completely remove them, especially those which are toxic.

Accident prevention is your responsibility. Keep your young Vizsla safe, happy, and healthy by heading off trouble before it happens. A puppy can, and does, get into problems even in the most secure home. Keep the telephone number of the Poison Control Center (217-333-3611) in a handy place and if you think your dog has chewed or swallowed a toxic substance, call them immediately.

Ch. Taunee's Loki Santana, CD, and his dam, Ch. Cariad's Gaybine, CD.

12

Breeding and Reproduction

THE dog of today is the product of evolution, that complex combination of forces which includes heredity and environment, with heredity being the inner and stronger influence and environment the outer and weaker. Between them they mold all life. Then there is the breeder. Not just someone who breeds dogs, but a *dog breeder* — the one who brings it all together and gives it balance; the one who has been using the Mendelian laws of dominance and inheritance for years by only knowing the basics. How much faster that breeder could have succeeded had he had possessed just a little better knowledge and understanding of those important laws.

UNDERSTANDING MENDEL'S THEORY OF INHERITANCE

Johann Gregor Mendel was a Morovian monk who studied inheritance in garden peas. He wished to establish one thing — height in his plants. In so doing he proved that when two individuals, each one pure for a pair of opposite traits or characteristics such as tallness or dwarfness were crossed, the first generation

183

the offspring would all look like the tall parent. He thus determined that tallness was a dominant characteristic, but that each of the hybrid offspring also carried the factor for dwarfness recessively.

When two of the hybrids were crossed the next generation produced an average of one tall, one short, each breeding pure for that trait, and two hybrids like the parents. These two hybrids appeared tall but carried the factor, or gene, for the dwarfness.

Mendel's work was not taken seriously until after his death when, in 1900, a Dutchman named DeVries read Mendel's papers and rediscovered the law of inheritance. He drew up what he considered the rules for dominant and recessive traits as this applied to both plants and animals.

Dominant traits do not skip a generation. Breeding only from individuals displaying desirable traits will mean there is less danger of continuing undesirable characteristics in a line.

Recessive traits may skip one or more generations. Only by breeding can it be ascertained whether any individual carries a certain determiner, or gene. To be expressed, it must be carried by both of the parents involved.

An individual in which like traits, or characteristics, are paired is known as a homozygous individual; the one in which unlike characteristics are paired is known as heterozygous. Recessive genes are always homozygous and always breed true to their own type, which is a test of their purity. An individual can be homozygous for one characteristic and heterozygous for others.

The breeder's task is to decide what kind of genes his Vizsla carries and how they will behave in combination with the genes of other individuals.

There are two kinds of cells in the body, reproduction, or germ cells, and body cells. We only have to be concerned with the germ cells, which develop into sperm and eggs in the process of reproduction. Each germ cell has within it a nucleus with chromosomes, and within the chromosomes are the genes that will determine the hereditary factors.

When a dog and bitch mate, the sperm cell of the male fuses with the egg cell of the female to form a new cell which in time develops into a puppy. One–half of the male's chromosomes, along with his genes, are shed in the ripening of the cell, as are one–half of the bitch's. Thus, when we do any breeding, we never know which genes are discarded by nature and which are used to determine the characteristics of the offspring. All we do know for sure is that one–half of each puppy's hereditary traits will be supplied by the sire, and the other half by the dam.

Each puppy in a litter is different because in the ripening of each sperm and egg to form a new cell, there will be a chance survival of genes different from those that go into the making of every other cell, or puppy. Not only is each puppy in a litter different,, but each puppy in every subsequent litter by the same sire and dam will be different.

That is one thing so many breeders fail to understand. After getting a beautiful first litter, they repeat the breeding with the same sire and dam, but they are never able to duplicate the first breeding. The germ cells have within their chromosomes thousands of genes. Some will be used, others discarded and lost for all time.

We have no control over the loss and preservation of the chromosomes or characteristics we wish to perpetuate. All we can do is use for breeding good parents possessed of all of the hereditary factors we want, and then trust to luck that they will be passed on.

If not passed on in the next litter, they may be passed on in the one after that, or never at all. The point is that you *must* use a dog and bitch that are endowed with the characteristics you consider desirable and even more so, a dog and bitch whose parents are also endowed with everything you want. Only in this manner can you ever hope to obtain the good traits in succeeding generations.

Probably the most valuable lesson taught by the study of heredity is that both faults and virtues will be passed on. This means that breeding good to poor will not result in something in between the two but rather in good specimens and poor specimens. In other words, breeding a big Vizsla to a small Vizsla does not give you a medium–sized Vizsla. If, when selecting two dogs for breeding, one of them possesses traits that you absolutely do not want in your puppies, do not use that dog. You should remember that the individual is as important as his pedigree. Do not join the army of breeders who never get anywhere.

Linebreeding

The object of linebreeding is to be able to keep all the good qualities that have been attributed to one very outstanding ancestor. It is the mating of two dogs that are closely related to that common ancestor, such as a granddaughter to a grandsire, or simply dogs that go

---

Figure 12-1
A Pedigree Showing Line Breeding

Parents	Grand Parents	Great Grand Parents	Great Gr. Grand Parents
		CH. Glen Cottage Loki Barat	CH. Puerco Pete Barat CH. Glen Cottage Diva
	CH. Taunee's Loki Santana **Grand Sire**		
		CH. Cariad's Gaybine	CH. Golden Rust's Kernel CH. Balatoni Sassy Olca
CH. Dorratz Diamond Jim **SIRE**			
		CH. Copper Cannon's Red Cloud	CH. Johnson's Titian Charger Tunde Von Copper Cannon
	CH Dorratz Diamond Tiara **Grand Dam**		
		CH. Rotkopf's Spicy Nutmeg	CH. Jado's Copper Cannon CH. Rotkopf's Gyemont
		CH. Glen Cottage Loki Barat	CH. Puerco Pete Barat CH. Glen Cottage Diva
	CH. Taunee's Loki Santana **Grand Sire**		
		CH. Cariad's Gaybine	CH. Golden Rust's Kernel CH. Balatoni Sassy Olca
CH. Cariad's Pride N Joy **DAM**			
		CH. Brance N Carob's Solo's Son	CH. Chestry & Carob's Solo Sun CH. Brance N Carob's Shenandoah
	Cariad's Casandra Baratam **Grand Dam**		
		CH. Cariad's Gay Leanyka	Cariad's Tallisen von Wold CH. Cariad's Gaybine

---

Above: Ch. Yorsla's Cinnamon Sassy and her son, Ch. Kitron's Buster Bayleaf, a lovely example of thoughtful line breeding in Canada. Breeder-owner, Kit Browne.

Left:
Best in Show Ch. Boelte's Brant of Penlee is from a close line breeding of top producers and top winners. Owner/handler Pat Boelte.

back to a common ancestor several times in the last four generations. This joining of the related individuals narrows down the number of ancestors, and thus intensifies whatever hereditary tendencies are present.

By breeding together related individuals the breeder is concentrating on only one line. It should not be persisted in for too long without recourse to outcrosses, and should not be done at all unless the breeder knows a lot of the Vizslas involved.

Inbreeding

Inbreeding is the fastest way of fixing type but should never be used by inexperienced breeders since it requires complete, personal knowledge of each Vizsla involved, even more so than for linebreeding. Inbreeding does not create new or different traits — it brings out

what is already there in the genetic structure, the good and the bad.

Inbreeding, in a true sense, is mating brother to sister, father to daughter, son to mother. For such a program, it is essential that you use two Vizslas with the least possible number of common faults and whose common ancestor is likewise almost faultless.

Outcrossing

Outcrossing is considered the safest procedure for the amateur and will result in satisfactory puppies provided that all of the ancestors are credible specimens. You will, however, have to accept the fact that even if a dog with this genetic background became a champion, he may never prove to be a really prepotent breeding specimen.

Outcrossing is usually considered to be the mating of two individual dogs that have nothing in common for four generations. The breeder who outcrosses can introduce many unwanted qualities into his line since he is dealing with so many different genes.

You can successfully outcross if your bitch has been closely linebred or inbred. Look for a stud dog that has also been closely bred, and although both dog and bitch have no common ancestor, you will be cutting down on the number of unrelated ancestors in their combined pedigrees. This will help to eliminate a tremendous number of unknowns.

HEREDITARY PROBLEMS IN VIZSLAS

The best way to develop a line of dogs with sound genetic composition is to do your homework. Exhaustive research through the pedigrees of the dog and bitch should be the foundation for your decision to breed or not. Simply looking up the number of champions in the pedigrees is not enough; you will require much more data to ensure genetic soundness.

Make phone calls and write letters. Ask owners of dogs in the line you are considering

Figure 12-2
A Pedigree Showing Outcrossing

Parents	Grand Parents	Great Grand Parents	Great Gr. Grand Parents
		Herzog Schloss Loosdorf	Kurtzschwanz Babette Povazia
	CH. Debreceny Dezso **Grand Sire**		
		CH. Besa Von Debretsin	CH Sandor Von Debretsin Lady Ria Olca
Debrecene Amber Rotkopf **SIRE**			
		CH. Napkelte Vadasz Dalos	Janora's Pawlane Suntan Bakony Csikcsicsoi Boske
	CH Totton's Fenyes Vadasz **Grand Dam**		
		Totton's Princess Tutu	CH. Warhorse Sammy Nefico's Golden Zsazsa
		CH. Glen Cottage Loki Barat	CH. Puerco Pete Barat CH. Glen Cottage Diva
	CH. Taunee's Loki Santana **Grand Sire**		
		CH. Cariad's Gaybine	CH. Golden Rust's Kernel CH. Balatoni Sassy Olca
CH. Cariad's Egyke Barat **DAM**			
		CH. Glen Cottage Loki Barat	CH. Puerco Pete Barat CH. Glen Cottage Diva
	Cariad's Gay Nyala **Grand Dam**		
		CH. Balatoni Sassy Olca	CH. Glen Cottage Charlie Sunshine Tanya

Three generations of Best in Show winners. Ch. Penlee's CLutter UD, with his dam, Ch. Firebrand's Constant Comment and his son, Ch. Lyons's Brewster of Harann, CDX.

if they have had any health problems with their dogs. Some breeders may be reluctant to discuss problems or admit there even is a problem so some cooperation is necessary. Explain that your reasons for researching the line are to better determine the potential qualities of your own proposed breeding stock, and that the ultimate goal is to enhance the genetic soundness and quality of the breed.

Keeping in mind that birth defects can be classified as inherited, induced, or spontaneous, it will be up to you to research fully individual dogs, littermates, and offspring before reaching a conclusion.

Hereditary factors are those programmed to happen because of the genetic material from both the male and female. At the moment the egg is fertilized the final genetic outcome is determined as long as no mutations occur. Many congenital deformities occur in the developing fetus, caused by genetic mutations. These are totally unpredictable chance deviations from the normal genetic pattern. Such a mutation is assumed to be induced or spontaneous if a careful check of the lineage reveals no tendency toward the problem and you know of a probable inducer, such as the use of vaccines or insecticides during the bitch's preg-

nancy. In that instance the same bitch and dog can be bred again.

This is why it is so important to get an honest and complete accounting of all the individuals. It is as necessary for the welfare of the Vizsla breed to know who is begetting the defects as it is to exhalt those producing the breed and field champions. Do your research and do not listen or depend on gossip. If a similar defect keeps showing up in a careful search of lines, the answer is that it is an inherited problem and the individual and parents should not be used for breeding.

There are very few hereditary defects in the Vizsla breed because of conscientious breeders. Canine hip dysplasia is the leading problem, and with the use of X-ray diagnosis and published OFA certifications, the breeder can determine by careful study of different lines which ones are the cleanest. Unfortunately, the dogs which are not certified are not listed so there is little way of knowing if a top–producing sire or dam had a littermate with dysplasia. If so, the genetic disposition will be in every breeding combination in the next generations.

The first litters of Vizslas in the U.S. brought numerous problems such as dysplasia, bad temperaments, and eye faults. Luckily, those that showed problems were put down and future faults were kept to a minimum with careful selective breeding. However, there have been reports of ideopathic epilepsy coming down from one of the early lines. To establish a diagnosis of hereditary epilepsy the attacks, or seizures, must be recurrent and similar. Other things can be confused with epilepsy and the novice should not believe what could be misdiagnosis or gossip. Check reports carefully.

Several isolated cases of Von Willebrand's disease have been reported in the Vizsla. This is a hereditary blood disease which is characterized by excessive bleeding and slow clotting of blood. Bloody diarrhea, prolonged and excessive bleeding during estrus and whelping, dangerous hemorrhaging during surgery, and occasions of bloody urine are some of the symptoms.

Von Willebrand's disease has been reported in 49 breeds of purebred dogs. Since many drugs can interfere with normal platelet function, and certain clotting factors can be depressed by agents in dog food, or by various diseases, diagnosis is often incorrect and misleading. The collection and processing of blood samples is critical, along with a complete history of physical and physiological stresses, as well as any concomitant disease such as parvovirus, hypothyroidism or auto-immune disease.

Other hereditary problems which show up frequently are cryptorchidism (neither testicle descended), or monorchidism, involving one undescended testicle. A male with one testicle can still produce but should never be used for breeding, and neutering is recommended.

Other inherited problems in the breed include incorrect bite, eye problems such as entropion and ectropion, skull defects, and allergies. None of these are classified as being major problems, but they exist and should be eliminated by careful breeding.

Certain characteristics are not a problem but are also inherited: yellow eyes, light-colored coat, and hare-feet. These faults can be eliminated from the gene pool very easily with selective breeding. The one problem which every breeder is concerned about, however, has to do with the amounts of white on their dogs' chest and feet. Even with careful, thoughtful breeding, the white cannot be completely eliminated. The spots will probably always be with us since the early Vizslas imported into America had large amounts of white on their chest and feet. When only a limited number of dogs were available for breeding, the white was not a consideration, but the problem remains with us in the form of recessive genes.

THE BROOD BITCH

The decision to breed your Vizsla bitch and raise a litter of puppies is not one to be taken lightly. It involves time, money, energy, and a commitment to raising healthy, happy puppies able to adapt to whatever their new owners desire.

If you want to produce show specimens, and you feel that your bitch has something to contribute to the breed by way of her puppies, see how she compares to other Vizslas by entering her in the show ring. The dog show ring is a testing ground for breeders. If she is a champion she should be good enough to breed, but that is not necessarily the case. Since many Vizslas hold Dual titles, it is important to keep in mind that you will want her puppies to adhere closely to the Vizsla Standard in order to be able to compete in both field and show competition.

The brood bitch is actually a lot more important than the stud dog you will be using. She is the fixture of the strain. She will be contributing one of the two sets of chromosomes which determine the characteristics of each puppy. The stud dog is finished with the puppies at the end of the tie, but the bitch is not. Her overall health and condition can affect the puppies. So will her parasites, diet, and temperament.

Bad temperament is a genetic as well as an environmental problem, but the temperament of the puppies, from the beginning, is more dependent on the bitch than on the stud dog.

Ch. Boelte's Brant of Penlee, two-time Best in Show winner, with his dam Ch. Firebrand's Constant Comment, the first Vizsla bitch to have a Best in Show.

Triple Ch. Cariad's Kutya Kai Costa with son Tomas and daughter Anya.

Her temperament greatly affects the puppies even while she carries and nurses them, and in the early weeks of their development and training will have a lasting effect.

The ideal brood bitch comes from a closely linebred family with few faults. She must not have serious faults. Her coat, eye color, body, angulation, bite, and size should be near perfect. She should have substance while still being feminine, with a lovely head and expression. She must be sound in body and mind and be everything that you would like to duplicate in your litter of Vizsla puppies.

A Vizsla bitch should not be bred before her second birthday, at which time she becomes physically and mentally mature. Before that time even though her body has developed fairly rapidly, her brain has not developed enough to take on the responsibilities of maternity and she may lack common sense when caring for her puppies.

Weeks before she is due to be in season, take the time to take a good look at her physical condition. An overweight bitch is unlikely to conceive and, if she does, may have a hard time whelping her litter. If she is underweight, she should be started on extra nourishment and supplements which will need to be continued after breeding, since the need to nourish the fetuses will be a drain on her body.

Stool samples must be checked early enough to carry out worming if needed. Worming your bitch does not always guarantee that her puppies will be born worm-free but it does put your bitch in better condition for the job ahead.

Every Vizsla bitch or male being used for breeding should be X-rayed for hip dysplasia and no Vizsla should be bred unless their hips have been certified free from any degree of canine hip dysplasia.

Your bitch should also have a heartworm test and all her vaccinations updated. A booster

Ch. Brance N Carob's Shenandoah, and Ch. Chestry & Carob's Solo Sun, foundation of the Brance Kountry Kennels. Owner, Barbara Watt.

given several weeks before breeding will raise her titer level and give passive immunity to her babies. She should not have any vaccinations or worming medications after she has been bred.

A blood test for Brucellosis should be done on both the bitch and the stud dog before breeding. Brucellosis is a highly contagious disease and breeding stock can be infected through sexual contact. It can cause abortions and stillborn puppies in the bitch and possible sterility in the male.

PICKING A STUD DOG

The stud dog should always be a good representative of the breed. Once you have established that, you can get into the finer points of what will make him a good mate for *your* bitch. The most prestigious winner in the show ring is no credit to the breed if he can not pass along his excellence. Furthermore, a big winner may not be an exceptional specimen. Some judges do the breed a great disservice by putting up dogs with major faults while playing a political game.

A big string of wins sets the stamp of approval on the head of a dog and does much to bring him to the attention of the breeders. But a show or field record does not assure that the holder of all those laurels can pass on his own good merits, if he has any. Only the best of the best among the males should be used at stud. It is a painful truth for enthusiastic owners of new champion males, but most males should *never* be used at stud.

If you are interested in using a certain male for breeding to your bitch, try to see as many of his offspring as possible. Evaluate what he

Ch. Glen Cottage Loki Barat, CDX, a member of the VCOA Hall of Fame and the sire of 32 champions, including the first Triple Champion, and also the record-winning 7 Best in Show Vizsla.

has produced from different bitches to see if any dominant trait comes through which you would not like to see in your litter.

From a breeding standpoint, it is far better to use an average, but good, male that is from top breeding stock than a top–winning dog from only an average or below-average line.

After thinking, and looking at stud dogs for your bitch, go back and study Vizsla pedigrees, because that is what is going to be most important in the final decision. Study the quality of the grandsires and granddams because your litter will be inheriting their traits or characteristics.

Make your arrangements with the stud dog owner well in advance, with an approximate date for breeding, so that you are certain he will be available. Make sure that you understand, and are in agreement with, the terms the dog's owner will want for his stud fee. Most stud fees are based on what the stud dog may have already produced or perhaps his show and field record. While there may be a difference in some areas of the country based on whatever price breeders are getting for their puppies, be prepared to pay from $350 to $500 for a stud fee. Most stud fees are paid with half down at the time of breeding and the other half when the puppies are born.

A stud dog owner will usually guarantee a certain number of live puppies or a return service will be offered the next time your bitch is in season. Get a written agreement on a stud contract to avoid any hard feelings over a misunderstanding at a future date.

RESPONSIBILITIES OF THE STUD DOG OWNER

As the owner of a new field or show champion it will be flattering to be approached about using him for stud. There are many good, proven, Vizsla studs. Think about what your dog has to offer. Is he potentially a better stud than the others?

As the owner of a stud dog you will have the sole responsibility to breed him only to the best bitches presented. You cannot consider the possibility that if you turn a bitch down, her owner will only go to another stud. You have to refuse service and be able to give a cogent reason for it. If the bitch being presented is in poor health or condition, or if she is too old or young for breeding, or if you have any doubts at all about what care and attention her puppies will receive, you have the responsibility to refuse stud service. It is your dog's reputation that will be ruined if the puppies do not amount to anything. If you want to safeguard that reputation, then save him for the best. Do not let the temptation of a stud fee influence your better judgement.

Right: Ch. Taunee's Loki Santana, CD with his sire, Ch. Glenn Cottage Loki Barat, CDX.

Below, left: Ch. Taunee's Loki Santana and his son, Ch. Trisha's Bogart by Loki.

Below, right: Ch. Csisckas of Goncoltanya and his daughter, Gellert Csintalan. Breeder and owner Joan Hunt.

That a dog offered at stud should be free from any disease is self-evident, but this also means free from any hereditary defects such as poorly shaped head, yellow eyes, a bad bite, and bad temperament. Your Vizsla stud must not only be in good condition, which means lean and hard, but also free from worms, skin ailments, and parasites. He should have OFA certification of good hips and a clean bill of health with a Brucellosis test, and a sperm check.

If your Vizsla is going to stand at stud, you must be prepared to cope with visiting bitches whether it is a convenient time for you or not. If a bitch is coming by air travel, you will have to drop all your plans, drive to the airport to get her, and several days later, drive back to the airport for her return trip. Her safety while she is under your care means extreme caution at all times to see that she does not panic in a strange area and escape from your home or yard.

Your basic responsibility of course, is that your dog knows what to do. Just because he is a male does not necessarily mean that he knows what the process is all about or how to

Figure 12-3
Kennel Stud Service Contract

The _____ stud dog, _____
            BREED   NAME

Registration # _____ owned by _____ kennels

was bred on _____ to the bitch _____

owned by _____ of _____.

_____ kennels guarantees two living puppies to the age of eight weeks.

If less than that number result the owners of the bitch are entitled to a free return service to a male owned by _____

_____ kennels subject to the availability of the dog requested. Stud fees are payable at the time of service and will not be refunded. A culture may be required at the owner's expense to protect both dogs if an infection is suspected.

The owner of the bitch agrees that no puppies from the resultant litter will be sold to pet shops or other whole-sale outlets.

Stud fee for this animal: $_____. Paid in full ☐ yes   ☐ no

Special Provisions:

Signed _____
                                    owner of bitch

Signed _____
                                    owner of stud

Address _____

---

handle it. If your Vizsla was continually scolded or punished for any abnormal sexual behavior as a puppy, such as riding your leg, you may find him reluctant to breed his first bitch since he will be expecting you to reprimand him. He may even refuse to breed her if you are nearby. However, a stud dog should be taught from the first service that you will be holding his bitches for him.

If you are offering an inexperienced, young male for stud, it is always helpful for his first mating to be with an experienced bitch, known to be flirtatious and easy to mate. The worse thing that can happen to a beginning stud dog is for him to fail to mate his first bitch. Give him a lot of encouragement and reassurance.

Whether it is in your garage, home, yard or kennel, take your Vizsla stud dog to the same place each time you use him for breeding. In this way he will associate that area with the act and know that he has your permission to go ahead and mate. An area used in the house can be washed afterwards with a vinegar solution.

Once your Vizsla male has been used for breeding, it is in your best interest to know the quality of the puppies he is producing. Be realistic and objective, not "kennel blind." Do not encourage owners to put his offspring in the field or show ring if you have to make excuses for obvious faults.

And finally, be absolutely sure that there is no misunderstanding about stud fee, whether it be cash or a pick puppy. Protect everyone's interest by putting the agreement in writing and having it signed by both parties involved.

REPRODUCTIVE ORGANS

The Dog

The most important of the male's sexual organs are the two testicles which produce sperm in a fluid called semen. Actually, the semen stays in ducts that run on the side of each testicle. The testicles are located outside the abdomen as sperm require a lower than body temperature. Since sperm can tolerate cold better than heat, you may want to avoid letting your dog lie on a hot surface prior to breeding. It could lower his sperm count. However, since thousands of sperm are released and only a fraction used, smaller litters do not usually occur with a normally fertile male.

The external sex organ for the male is called the penis, and its function is to deliver the semen into the bitch's vagina during the mating process. The penis is enclosed, and protected, by a sheath of skin called the prepuce. The prepuce pushes back out of the way as the penis enlarges. A small amount of yellow discharge is normally seen leaking from the prepuce, but an excessive purulent amount of discharge may indicate an infection.

Most of the area of the penis is a very elaborate system of blood sinuses surrounded by a lot of connective tissue. During sexual excitement these tissues fill with blood and the penis enlarges.

During mating a ball at the base of the penis, called the bulbus glandis, enlarges and keeps the two dogs joined until the blood recedes and the penis returns to normal size. A bone called the os penis gives the penis support.

The Bitch

In the female, cell division and growth take place within the ovaries. A bitch has two ovaries which lie behind the kidneys and close to the body wall. The ovaries contain a great many ova, or eggs, each of which is contained in a small sac called a follicle. The follicle enlarges as it approaches the surface of the ovary, bursts, and releases the egg. Rupture of this follicle and release of the egg constitutes ovulation.

The empty follicles then become a new gland, the corpus luteum, which contains a hormone — progesterone. It is this hormone which is directly connected to the physiological changes in the bitch which indicate when it is time for her to be bred. As soon as the follicle bursts and releases the egg, the sac then fills up rapidly with another mass of cells called luteal bodies. These bodies secrete a hormone, progesterone, and it is this hormone which signifies ovulation, end of the mating cycle and maintains pregnancy.

When an egg is released from the ovaries, it goes into the oviduct, a long, thin tubular organ that extends from the ovary to the uterus. There are two ovaries, so there are two tubes, each of which leads into a horn of the uterus. The eggs move along these tubes for a couple of days before they reach the uterus.

Fertilization is the uniting of a sperm and an egg. When sperm are present in the oviduct of the bitch, one will penetrate the outer covering of an egg. This covering immediately grows thicker to prevent penetration by any other sperm. The egg and sperm join and a new life is created.

Figure 12-4
Male Reproductive System

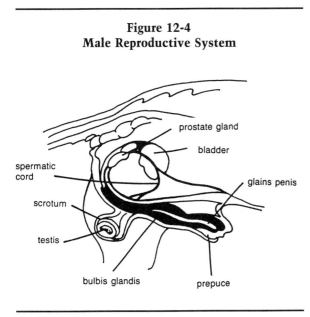

prostate gland

bladder

spermatic cord

glains penis

scrotum

testis

bulbis glandis   prepuce

Figure 12-5
Female Reproductive System

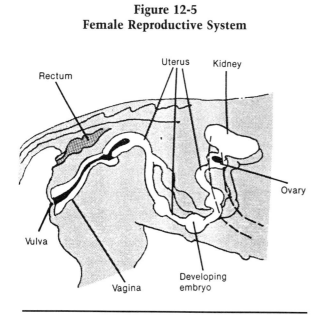

This new life, called a zygote, or embryo, moves into the uterus to develop into a fetus during pregnancy. The uterus is a hollow, muscular "Y"–shaped organ consisting of the two long horns, which form the upper parts of the "Y", and a shorter horn, which is the stem, going into the cervix. The cervix, a fibrous and muscular structure, is the opening connecting the uterus to the vagina, or birth canal. The vagina extends from the cervix to the vulva, the external genital organ of the bitch.

THE MATING

The perfect time for mating is, of course, as close to ovulation as possible. By approximately the tenth or eleventh day in season, your bitch's vulva will begin to swell and soften; her discharge will lighten in color and change odor. She will mount another bitch playfully but will snap and growl at a male if he attempts to mount her.

Behavior, more than anything else, is a good indication of readiness. She will become more restless and readily swing her tail to one side if you touch her rear. She will usually accept a male within two days of displaying this behavior.

Many Vizsla breeders try to determine the right time to breed with the use of vaginal smears. Your veterinarian will use a microscopic examination, staining the cells which line the uterus and are sloughed off in the vaginal discharge. Several smears should be taken over a period of several days in order to observe the changes.

A more exact method of pinpointing the time of ovulation is a simple blood test measuring the LH (luteinizing hormone) surge which actually causes ovulation. This new progesterone test is usually done by a veterinarian who specializes in reproduction problems. It is an advantage when performing artificial inseminations with either fresh or frozen semen, or with a bitch who has a history of problems conceiving.

The surest way is to depend on the male, especially an experienced stud dog. He will only sniff at her rear until she is ready, walking away if the odor is not there. As the bitch gets closer to ovulation, the male may refuse to eat. He will moan and howl, and he may attempt to chew his way through a door to get to the bitch in his desire to mate. It is almost impossible at this time to console him.

When the bitch is ready, she will let the male mount her. An inexperienced male may try to mount her head, but the bitch will usually swing her body around and present her rear to him until he gets the idea. Both dogs may spend several minutes going through a time of "courtship." If this continues to the point of tiring either of them they should be separated for a short time to rest.

When the male mounts the female he will grab her around her body and feel around with his penis for her vulva. Upon penetration he will thrust intensely until the penis becomes engorged and the bulbus glandis swells and locks, or "ties", the two of them together.

A short time later you will see the male's body relax. At this point he can be helped to dismount by placing both his front feet on the ground and lifting a rear leg over the back of the bitch so that he can turn, putting both dogs in a tail-to-tail position.

The male and female are both introduced to each other on leash and the courtship begins.

The bitch is at the right time in her cycle for breeding and is being the aggressor in this case.

The female has her tail to one side (flagging) to indicate that she is ready for breeding.

The play period will last for several minutes, but if the dogs get tired, separate them for a short rest.

It is always helpful if a young male is used with an experienced bitch for his first time.

The male will feel around with his penis for the female's vulva.

The dogs are "tied" and will remain that way until the blood recedes from the tissue surrounding the penis and the penis and bulb shrink.

Figure 12-6
Estrus Cycle in the Bitch

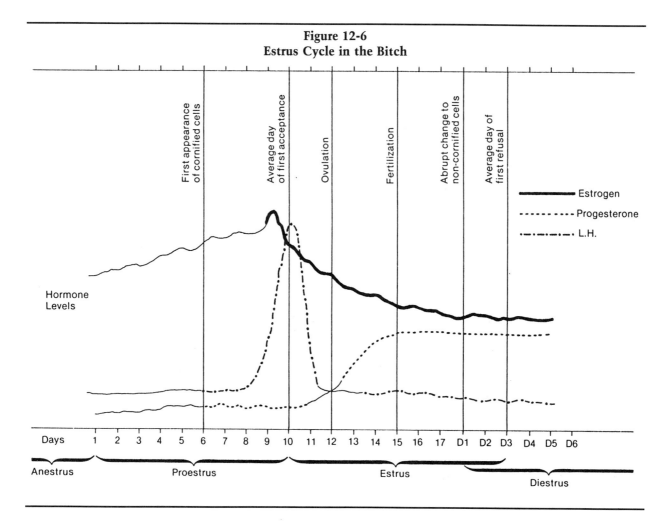

If there are two people assisting in the mating, each one can kneel on one knee beside a dog and place the other knee under that dog to give support. If only one person is supervising the mating, either sit on a chair, or kneel alongside the dogs. Encircle both dogs completely under their flanks, join hands and hold both Vizslas in place.

It is important that dogs being mated are supervised to prevent injury to either one. Even if it is hard on your back, do not allow a dog to sit or lie down. Most Vizslas are easy breeders, but if you have one that is restless, you can use a leash tied to a stationary object as a restraint.

There is no way of estimating how long a tie will last. It could last fifteen minutes or an hour. When the blood recedes from the tissues, the bulb and penis will shrink and the dogs will part. Place the bitch in a crate to rest quietly. Do not let her urinate.

Regardless of when the breeding takes place, the sperm will not join the egg until it is the right time for the egg to be fertilized. Nourished by secretions from uterine glands in the bitch, the sperm can live forty-eight hours waiting for fertilization. Rather than miss the right timing, a second and even third mating should be completed two or three days apart if both dogs are receptive.

THE PREGNANT BITCH

From the moment your bitch is mated, until you definitely know otherwise, consider her

Figure 12-7
Whelping Chart

In each column pair: left = **Date bred**, right = **Date due to whelp**.

Bred Jan	Due Mar	Bred Feb	Due Apr	Bred Mar	Due May	Bred Apr	Due Jun	Bred May	Due Jul	Bred Jun	Due Aug	Bred Jul	Due Sep	Bred Aug	Due Oct	Bred Sep	Due Nov	Bred Oct	Due Dec	Bred Nov	Due Jan	Bred Dec	Due Feb
1	5	1	5	1	3	1	3	1	3	1	3	1	2	1	3	1	3	1	3	1	3	1	2
2	6	2	6	2	4	2	4	2	4	2	4	2	3	2	4	2	4	2	4	2	4	2	3
3	7	3	7	3	5	3	5	3	5	3	5	3	4	3	5	3	5	3	5	3	5	3	4
4	8	4	8	4	6	4	6	4	6	4	6	4	5	4	6	4	6	4	6	4	6	4	5
5	9	5	9	5	7	5	7	5	7	5	7	5	6	5	7	5	7	5	7	5	7	5	6
6	10	6	10	6	8	6	8	6	8	6	8	6	7	6	8	6	8	6	8	6	8	6	7
7	11	7	11	7	9	7	9	7	9	7	9	7	8	7	9	7	9	7	9	7	9	7	8
8	12	8	12	8	10	8	10	8	10	8	10	8	9	8	10	8	10	8	10	8	10	8	9
9	13	9	13	9	11	9	11	9	11	9	11	9	10	9	11	9	11	9	11	9	11	9	10
10	14	10	14	10	12	10	12	10	12	10	12	10	11	10	12	10	12	10	12	10	12	10	11
11	15	11	15	11	13	11	13	11	13	11	13	11	12	11	13	11	13	11	13	11	13	11	12
12	16	12	16	12	14	12	14	12	14	12	14	12	13	12	14	12	14	12	14	12	14	12	13
13	17	13	17	13	15	13	15	13	15	13	15	13	14	13	15	13	15	13	15	13	15	13	14
14	18	14	18	14	16	14	16	14	16	14	16	14	15	14	16	14	16	14	16	14	16	14	15
15	19	15	19	15	17	15	17	15	17	15	17	15	16	15	17	15	17	15	17	15	17	15	16
16	20	16	20	16	18	16	18	16	18	16	18	16	17	16	18	16	18	16	18	16	18	16	17
17	21	17	21	17	19	17	19	17	19	17	19	17	18	17	19	17	19	17	19	17	19	17	18
18	22	18	22	18	20	18	20	18	20	18	20	18	19	18	20	18	20	18	20	18	20	18	19
19	23	19	23	19	21	19	21	19	21	19	21	19	20	19	21	19	21	19	21	19	21	19	20
20	24	20	24	20	22	20	22	20	22	20	22	20	21	20	22	20	22	20	22	20	22	20	21
21	25	21	25	21	23	21	23	21	23	21	23	21	22	21	23	21	23	21	23	21	23	21	22
22	26	22	26	22	24	22	24	22	24	22	24	22	23	22	24	22	24	22	24	22	24	22	23
23	27	23	27	23	25	23	25	23	25	23	25	23	24	23	25	23	25	23	25	23	25	23	24
24	28	24	28	24	26	24	26	24	26	24	26	24	25	24	26	24	26	24	26	24	26	24	25
25	29	25	29	25	27	25	27	25	27	25	27	25	26	25	27	25	27	25	27	25	27	25	26
26	30	26	30	26	28	26	28	26	28	26	28	26	27	26	28	26	28	26	28	26	28	26	27
27	31	27	May 1	27	29	27	29	27	29	27	29	27	28	27	29	27	29	27	29	27	29	27	28
28	Apr. 1	28	2	28	30	28	30	28	30	28	30	28	29	28	30	28	30	28	Dec. 1	28	30	28	Mar. 1
29	2			29	31	29	July 1	29	31	29	31	29	30	29	31	29	Dec. 1	29	31	29	31	29	2
30	3			30	June 1	30	2	30	Aug. 1	30	Sep. 1	30	Oct. 1	30	Nov. 1	30	2	30	Jan. 1	30	Feb. 1	30	3
31	4			31	2			31	2			31	2	31	2			31	2			31	4

Courtesy of Gaines.

pregnant. This means that, from that first day, she should not receive any wormings, medications, or vaccinations, unless prescribed by your veterinarian.

For the first four weeks of pregnancy she will have no extra needs. If she has been on a well-balanced diet and is in good condition there will be no need to increase her food supply or give supplements, and she can continue with normal exercising as long as there is no danger of injury. However, if she is being trained in advanced obedience work which requires jumping, it is advisable to delay that exercise. Use one board for retrieving over jumps.

Your bitch may experience some "morning sickness" or mild vomiting in her third week as the embryos attach themselves to the uterus and placentas are formed around them. Some enlargements of her breasts and nipples may also be evident at this time.

If you are not sure that your bitch is actually pregnant, your veterinarian can palpate her abdomen between twenty-eight and thirty-two days after breeding. By this time the fetuses are about the size of walnuts and can be felt by an experienced person.

A safe and sure method of diagnosis is with the use of ultrasound. It is available at schools of veterinary medicine at large universities, or at specialized veterinarians' offices. It is an easy and interesting procedure which shows density on a screen at a very early stage in the development of the fetuses. It also enables a fairly accurate count of the fetuses.

X-rays are not recommended during the early stages of fetal development as their use can result in deformities. If an X-ray is desired or necessary, it can be done after the forty-eighth day when the skeleton of the fetus has been formed.

Your Vizsla bitch will sometimes show changes in her personality very early into her pregnancy by becoming very affectionate and clingy, seeming to need more reassurance that you are near. If she is around other dogs she will try to stay apart so as not to be jostled or bumped by them. She will also be less inclined to exercise, but it is important to keep her from gaining too much weight and to maintain good muscle tone.

The last couple of weeks of her pregnancy will see her rib cage expanding and if she is carrying a large litter, she will want to exercise even less. Take her for slow walks on a lead but avoid over–exertion. Go only as far as she can go without returning home tired and panting. As her girth increases, the walks must be taken more slowly, and as the eighth week ends, do away with them.

If she is unable to finish her regular amounts of food as her stomach is pushed out of position by the growing fetuses, do not try to tempt her with table foods. You will only end up with a fussy eater. Instead, divide her regular two meals into several smaller meals. Vegetables or cottage cheese can be given in between.

During the last half of her gestation period your Vizsla may have a clear, thick string of mucous discharge from her vagina, especially if she is carrying a large litter. If at any time there are signs of pus or blood in this discharge, have her examined by your veterinarian immediately.

Ch. Topian's Foxsea Kelly, one week before whelping. Note the sagging topline and swollen breasts. Owned by Hilda Bosien.

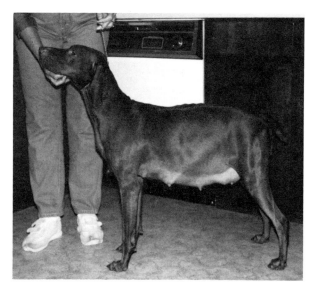

When the litter has reached its maximum development as far as size is concerned, your bitch will probably appear very fat, though a certain percentage of that will actually be water. In her final week of pregnancy, the carried litter will begin to settle down leaving her hipbones gaunt where before they appeared well padded with flesh. Her abdomen will sag with the weight and her backbone may look bent with the strain. Her eyes may look haggard and worn and she is continually trying tofind some way to get comfortable.

This is the time to introduce your Vizsla to the place where she will have her puppies. Be sure that her whelping box is in a quiet, draft-free area that will give her and her puppies the privacy and warmth they need.

Show the box to her often and try to convince her that she is having her babies in her own place — not in the middle of your bed, which is where she would rather have them.

Advise your veterinarian as to the due date and stay in close touch with him to make sure you will be able to contact him for assistance if needed. It will also be easier for the novice breeder if a friend, who has had experience in whelping a litter, is available to offer advice and a helping hand. Once whelping starts, someone has to be with the bitch every minute rather than take the chance of losing her from complications, or losing a puppy from an injury.

Table 12-1
Supplies for the Whelping Box

The following supplies should be handy to the whelping box:

- Clean, dry cloths (cotton diapers are the perfect size and weight)
- A clean, medium-size cardboard box with a covered heating pad
- Rectal thermometer
- Clock
- Baby scales
- Hemostat (s)
- Sharp scissors with blunt ends
- Paper and pencil to chart weights and times of births
- Rubber gloves
- KY Jelly®
- Dental floss or heavy thread
- Room thermometer
- Electric space heater with temperature control
- Water bowl for the bitch
- Blankets or flannel sheets for whelping box
- Clean newspapers
- Alcohol or Merthiolate for naval cords
- Garbage bag
- Flashlight and leash for taking bitch out at night

Figure 12-8
Building A Whelping Box

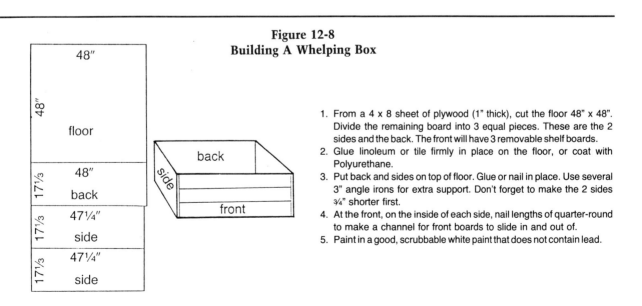

1. From a 4 x 8 sheet of plywood (1" thick), cut the floor 48" x 48". Divide the remaining board into 3 equal pieces. These are the 2 sides and the back. The front will have 3 removable shelf boards.
2. Glue linoleum or tile firmly in place on the floor, or coat with Polyurethane.
3. Put back and sides on top of floor. Glue or nail in place. Use several 3" angle irons for extra support. Don't forget to make the 2 sides ¾" shorter first.
4. At the front, on the inside of each side, nail lengths of quarter-round to make a channel for front boards to slide in and out of.
5. Paint in a good, scrubbable white paint that does not contain lead.

Ch. Cariad's Coppertone First Ed watches over her first litter. Owned by Mark and Bonnie Goodwein.

13

Whelping

AN average gestation period is sixty-three days but puppies can be born as early as the fifty-ninth or sixtieth day from the first breeding and as late as sixty-six days. Be prepared.

Start taking your Vizsla's temperature (rectally) on her fifty-eighth day to establish what is a normal temperature for her. Take it morning, noon, and night and keep a record of it. When it drops from a normal 101.5°F to almost 98.4°F, you can be sure of labor starting within the next eight hours. That is not to say that a temperature always drops; some bitches will whelp without that warning.

As her time gets closer she will become restless. She may even try to hide behind a chair or in a closet. She may refuse her food or eat very little; go from digging a nest to sleeping deeply. She will want to go out to eliminate more often because of the increasing pressure on her bladder. Do not let her go outside alone. If it is nighttime, use a flashlight and keep her on a leash. Watch her closely. You may see her roaching her back and think she is only having a bowel movement while in reality she is starting to whelp a puppy.

As the restlessness continues there will be excessive panting accompanied by quivering legs or a trembling body. In between she may stand or sit with glassy eyes. During this time raise the room temperature to 80°F, turn the heating pad in the cardboard box to low, gather all the necessary articles close to hand and prepare to spend the next few hours at her side with a pot of coffee if you are afraid of falling asleep.

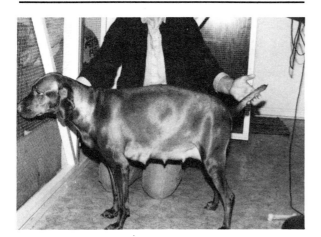

Two hours before whelping. Note the roached back as the first light contractions start.

Keep assuring your bitch that you are by her side and that you will help her through it. You have to remember that this is a frightening time for her, but do not overdo and smother her. Nature has provided for her to take care of this situation but it is up to you to help ensure the safe arrival of her puppies.

LABOR AND DELIVERY

Labor starts with pressure from within that forces the puppy down toward the pelvis. Abdominal contractions can be observed at this time and your bitch will roach her back as she pushes to get the puppy down the horn-shaped passage to the vulva.

Before the first puppy is expelled, a plug of mucous will precede him, along with a lot of fluid. Soon you will see the bulge over the vulva indicating that a puppy is pressing against it and is ready to be pushed out with the next contraction. Keep your bitch calm by talking to her constantly. You may have to hold her forcibly in the whelping box.

The puppy will be enclosed in a membranous sac which is attached to the placenta, or afterbirth, by the umbilical cord. When a puppy begins the whelping process, in his sac and protected by the surrounding amniotic fluid, there is enough oxygen left in his life–support system to see him through the journey down the birth canal. However, since each puppy can take a varying length of time to make this passage it is important that the newborn is removed from his sac as soon as possi-

Figure 13-1
Normal Versus Breech Birth

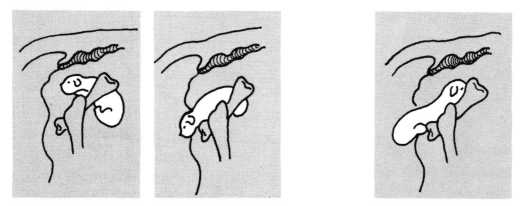

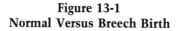

Left: A normal birth; the puppy is head first. Note the way the birth canal curves over the pelvic bone. If you need to assist, always pull down, toward the bitch's stomach.
Far Right: A breech birth. The puppy's rear is first. Breech births are sometimes more difficult. If possible, keep the bitch from breaking the sac until the puppy's head is out.

ble. Most breeders will help the bitch in this process instead of risking the chance that an overzealous, anxious, bitch might unintentionally injure her puppy.

As the puppy is being expelled from the birth canal, you may have to help him by gently grasping him with a cloth and easing him out. Gentle pulls might be timed with the contractions. Most of the time it is only the first puppy that will give the bitch a problem. Immediately stick your finger in the sac by the puppy's head and tear the sac. It will peel back exposing the newborn and releasing the fluids surrounding him. If the afterbirth is still connected, pinch it tightly about two inches from the stomach pushing the blood supply in it towards the puppy. Quickly cut the cord, leaving at least 1½ inches on the puppy.

Take the puppy up in a dry cloth with his head facing downward and wipe the nostrils and mouth clear of fluid. Then rub gently, but briskly, up and down his back with a cloth to stimulate his circulation. When you hear him give his first strong yelp, quickly weigh him, note the sex, time of delivery, and if the afterbirth was expelled. Then give him to his mother (dam) to be cleaned and fed.

If the afterbirth was expelled, scoop it up in a newspaper and dispose of it. There are different opinions on whether you should allow the bitch to eat it, and sometimes it can be a race to see if she or you get it first. It is unlikely that it has any nutritional value and it may give her messy stools for several days.

It is, however, imperative that a count of the afterbirths be made, to make sure that one arrives with each puppy. Quite often the afterbirth breaks away from the puppy and is retained. If it does not come out with subsequent births, make sure your veterinarian is told how many were retained when the whelping is over. A retained afterbirth can result in a serious infection and even the loss of puppies or your bitch.

The dam will get busy cleaning her new puppy and if she seems a little rough as she flips him upside down do not be alarmed. She is actually stimulating his circulation and respiration. Check that she is also licking his rear to encourage the passage of his first stool.

This will be dark in color and is called the meconium. Until it is passed the puppy may suffer from constipation and may not nurse.

Guard that the dam does not chew on the umbilical cord that is left on the newborn. If the cord is bleeding even slightly, clamp it with the hemostat for a few seconds and then tie a length of thread around it a good inch from the puppy's body. If the cord is still ragged and too long, trim it with scissors and put a drop of iodine on it.

If the cord was accidentally torn or cut too short, and if you have enough length left, tie it with thread as far to the end as possible, but never against the body of the puppy. If the dam licks it off again, and there is seepage, you will have to retie it. The umbilical cord will shrivel up and drop off within three days.

Most puppies are born with a tremendous instinct of where to go and how to suckle. A healthy, strong newborn with a will to live, will nurse quickly. This nursing action will aid in stimulating uterine contractions and help in the delivery of subsequent puppies. If the newborn needs assistance, express a little milk from a nipple for him to smell, then gently and carefully open his mouth with a finger, and insert the nipple into it while holding his body in place.

Your bitch may lie calmly feeding a puppy while having contractions or pushing a newborn out for you to take care of. She may become restless with another birth imminent and try to deliver it from a sitting or crouching position. If this is the case and you see the bulge over the vulva, quickly place all of the previously born puppies in the cardboard box with the heating pad on low, so that they do not get accidentally injured by her.

You may be able to tell when your bitch has whelped her last puppy if she gives a contented sigh once the contractions are over, and calmly settles down to either take a nap or concentrate completely on her newborns.

Now will be the time to offer her a small bowl of food. That old standby of chicken soup is usually accepted. If there have been several hours of labor, you might find her willing to go out to eliminate, especially if you take her puppies from her and place them in the heated

As birth appears imminent, the bitch's face takes on a worried look. *Photos by Paul Ratzlaff.*

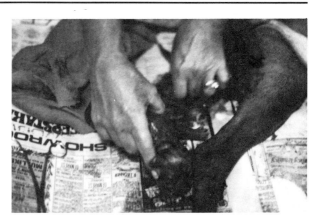

The newborn has been released from his sac so that he can breathe, and the afterbirth is gently being helped out.

The newborn is given to his dam to be cleaned.

Active cleaning of the newborn by his dam will stimulate breathing and circulation.

The dam turns her attention to consuming the afterbirth. It is doubtful that it offers any benefit and will give her messy stools.

The dam will stimulate the newborn's urination by licking and washing him.

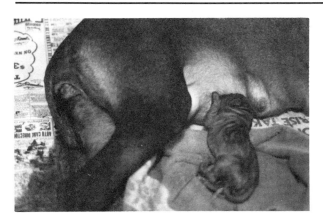

The first puppy nurses contentedly by himself.

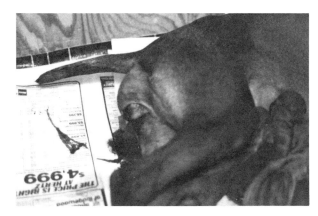

Note the bulge over the vulva, indicating that another puppy is being presented.

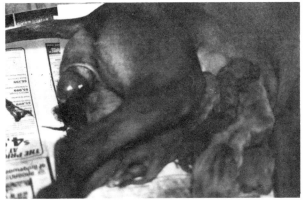

A large bubble appears first, indicating the sac with fluids.

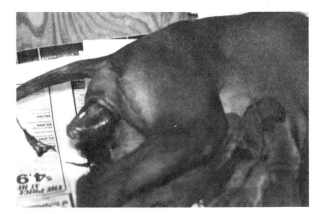

Assist the birth, but do not pull the puppy out. Work with the contractions.

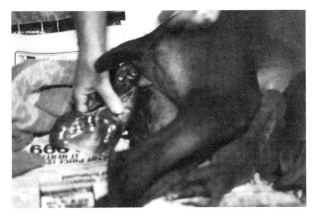

A normal delivery, with the newborn enclosed in the sac.

Keep the dam's rear and underside of tail cleaned of any discharge.

box. For the first few days, you may find it necesssary to put a leash on her and force her to go out and leave the puppies as she will be reluctant to go on her own. Taking her outside will also give you a chance to see if she can pass any retained afterbirths, and to feel her abdomen for any puppies still not born.

Take the time to clean the whelping box before letting her back in it. Remove the wet, soiled newspapers and put down a clean blanket making sure that it fits the bottom of the box and does not leave any places where a puppy can crawl under. The puppies need the rough blanket surface to push against as they nurse.

Return the new mother to her clean bed and give her babies back to her, making sure that each one is able to nurse. It is important that the newborn puppies are able to receive their dam's first milk which is called colostrum, and contains antibodies which will protect the pup from disease during the first several weeks of life. Since this milk will change in composition after the first twenty-four hours, the puppies must start nursing soon after birth. This nursing action will also help to stimulate an increase in the milk supply.

Even if the whelping was without complications and all the afterbirths are passed, it is still wise to have your bitch checked over by a veterinarian within twelve hours.

PROBLEM DELIVERIES

The time between each puppy may vary from five minutes to an hour in a normal whelping. Puppies are usually delivered head first enclosed in their sac but other types of delivery, which give some difficulty, are always a possibility. If left unaided, they may result in the loss of the newborn and even your Vizsla bitch.

Any delivery where a puppy is being presented rear-end or back first is going to be more difficult. As you check the puppy in the vulva, you will be able to feel or see if he is still in the sac or if the sac has already broken under the pressure of delivery. This is a dry delivery, and is quite common. If this is the case, it is imperative that you get the puppy into the world as quickly as possible before he asphyxiates. You must also do any delivery without injury to the puppy or your bitch.

Sometimes just standing your bitch on her feet and changing her position will force the puppy from her without any problems. In some cases the puppy may have a leg or two stuck inside the passaage, or he may be turned sideways so that neither end is presented. In those instances the dam can not pass the puppy without it first being turned. If you are dealing with a dry delivery and the puppy is out of the sac as you are attempting to turn him, he will be in danger of drowning or suffocating so you must work fast, but calmly.

Put lubricant on your surgical gloves or scrubbed finger and carefully lubricate the inside opening of the vulva and as much of the puppy as you can reach. Determine if it is the back, rear, or stomach that is being presented. The puppy may be jammed against the vulva and if that is so, push it very gently a small way up so that you are then able to reposition the legs or the total body. At no time should you attempt to pull the puppy out.

After turning the puppy, the dam should be able to expel it. As you help in the delivery, and if the puppy is arriving rear-end first, you will have to remember to keep that end towards the dam's feet as he is being delivered. If the puppy is coming out head first, it should be brought out in the direction of the dam's stomach.

If contractions are strong and visible but no puppy is being presented in the vulva after two hours, there is a chance that a puppy could be stuck further up in the birth canal. Puppies are carried in both horns of the uterus and if one is coming down into each horn at the same time they can become jammed at the lower stem of the "Y."

If you are unable to feel anything within reach of your fingers, you are going to need veterinarian's assistance. Do not let this condition go beyond two hours.

Your veterinarian will be able to determine the exact problem with an X-ray. A caesarean section may be necessary to prevent the bitch's uterus from rupturing.

Uterine Inertia

Primary inertia is the name given to the condition in which contractions and whelping do not start at all, even though early signs of whelping were present. The uterus is unable to contract, due perhaps to a large litter and the muscular wall of the uterus lacking either the room or the strength to contract. It could be that the bitch is overweight with poor muscle tone, or she may even have a hormonal problem.

Whatever the reason, if your bitch's temperature has dropped to below 99°F and stayed there without fluctuating for twenty-four hours without any signs of the hard contractions of the second stage of labor, take her to your veterinarian.

Secondary inertia may be the reason for a long drawn-out whelping where your bitch does not have strong enough contractions to keep pushing the puppies down the birth canal. She may be able to whelp only part of her litter before the uterus loses strength and elasticity.

Your veterinarian may decide to give an injection of the hormone oxytocin, to stimulate the uterine contractions, if the inertia is due to a fatigued uterus.

Caesarean Section

Surgical delivery of the litter is the only solution in some cases, and the chances of saving both the puppies and their dam are good if the surgery is performed before your Vizsla becomes exhausted.

If she has already whelped some puppies, leave them in the whelping box on a warm, not hot, heating pad. Take the cardboard box, lined with cloths and another heating pad, with you to the veterinarian's. In fact, it might be wise to take along a stack of clean cloths as the veterinarian may not have anything except paper towels with which to dry newborns.

Your veterinarian will probably be glad of an extra hand to help in getting each newborn rubbed down and breathing as he removes it from the bitch. If you are able to help, it will be an interesting experience for you.

The newborn puppy may be limp, blue, and slow to breathe, and you will not have very much time to stimulate one before the next one is handed to you. Try to get that first strong cry before placing each one in the warm box. As your veterinarian is completing the surgery, keep working with the puppies if they are still limp and weak. Do not give up on them too soon.

When the veterinarian is finished, he will give your bitch a shot to reverse the narcotic analgesic, and she should be able to walk out of his door for the trip home. However, once back in the whelping box, it is possible that she will go into a deep sleep, leaving you to care for the newborns. It will be up to you to encourage their urination and passing of the meconium and to get them nursing to stimulate milk production.

Stroke each puppy's stomach, genital and anal area gently with a warm, wet cotton ball to stimulate urination and defecation. This will need to be repeated after each feeding until their dam takes over.

If the puppies are still weak and without a healthy pink color to their skin and feet, it may be necessary to tube-feed them to get them over the trauma of their birth. Each puppy should receive almost 2cc of formula for their first feeding. It may be that this one time will be all they need to give them the strength to nurse from their dam or a bottle. Your veterinarian can show you how to do this and provide the proper equipment and formula.

Your bitch may wake from sleep and not even recognize the newborns as being hers. She may need reassuring to accept them, but gradually the maternal instinct will win.

Take your bitch's temperature twice a day for a week following surgery and watch the incision carefully for any signs of infection. Use small manicure scissors or a nail clipper to keep the puppy's nails short, so that they will not injure the incision.

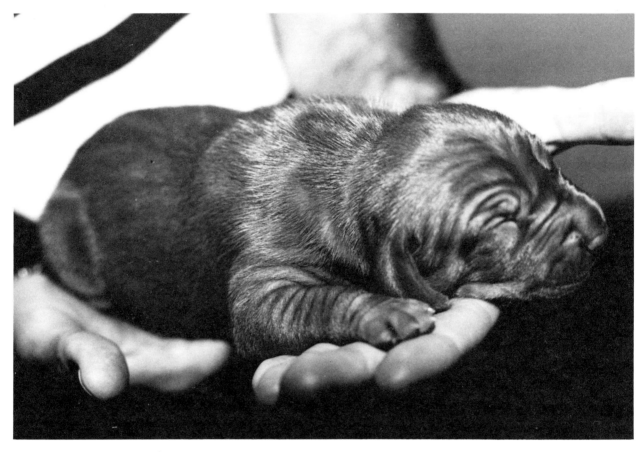

Daily checks should be made for any injury or illness.

14

Care of the
Newborn Puppy

MANY times an exceptionally good puppy has been saved by the extra attention given at the time when he really needed it. The inconvenience of almost constant supervision of the litter is more than worthwhile.

For the first week of the newborn's life he will look as though he is nursing incessantly, and although it looks like the dam does not have very much milk, the nursing action at her breasts will stimulate milk production. However, while a newborn may be able to exist for several hours without that milk, he can not live long without warmth. Make sure that a weaker puppy is not being pushed away from the warmth of his dam's body.

THE HEALTHY NEWBORN VIZSLA

The newborn puppy arrives with the instinct to seek warmth and food. You will be amazed at the strength and energy shown as, barely out of the sac, he struggles so much it will be hard to get an accurate reading of his weight. Place him anywhere in the whelping box and he will rapidly propel himself to the warmth of the dam's mammary glands. He will react immediately to touch by looking for a nipple to suck.

Marking each puppy for identification with a different-colored ribbon on the neck will enable you to monitor any problem.

While you may think that each puppy is constantly nursing, one may just be lying there with the nipple in his mouth. Check often to make sure the smallest or weakest one is not being pushed out of the way while the strongest are getting all the milk. Hold a puppy in place at a nipple if necessary.

For careful monitoring each puppy should be weighed daily until a week old, then every three days until 3 weeks of age, and from then on only once a week. Making a mark on different feet or ears with a marking pencil will help to keep an identification system for each puppy. Keep an accurate weight chart for each puppy.

Normal Vizsla puppies will gain weight steadily, although there is an initial loss of up to ten percent during the first two days of life. They should double their birth weight by seven to nine days and from then on, steadily gain a pound a week. The average birth weight of a Vizsla is about fourteen ounces and, gaining steadily, he will probably weigh around five pounds at 4 weeks of age. A puppy weighing only eight ounces at birth will gain weight at a slower pace for the first three weeks, and will need extra attention to make sure he is getting a place on a nipple without being pushed aside by larger littermates. He may also benefit from supplemental bottle feeding.

A healthy, happy puppy is generally quiet but sometimes makes a singing sound as he nurses. He may fuss and get angry if his nipple is out of milk, but you will learn to tell by the tone of his voice what is wrong. While sleeping, his body will twitch and jerk. This pattern is called activated sleep, and is necessary in the development of the neuromuscular system. A puppy that is ill will not show this movement, so watch your litter carefully. A puppy lying by himself is not necessarily ill as long as he shows this activity. Even tiny pups will crawl away from their heat source if too warm. If all the puppies cry and heap together in a pile, it is usually because they are cold.

A puppy that is thin, weak, does not nurse or that is continually found pushed off into a corner needs attention. Puppies quickly dehydrate if they aren't nursing. You can check on a puppy's condition by lifting the skin on the neck. In a healthy animal, the skin will rapidly fall back into place; the skin of a dehydrated pup will remain away from the body for several seconds or a minute. Dehydrated pups need immediate veterinary attention and will probably require supplementary feeding by tube or bottle.

Do not be overly concerned if a puppy shuffles around and cries a little. He might have some gas or, in the case of a large litter, the

Table 14-1
Average Weight Chart

	Bitches				Dogs		
	1	2	3	4	1	2	3
	dark no/w	dark no/w	lighter color	small w/on/rt rear	lighter color	dark w/on chest	dark sm. w/ on chest
Birth	.15	.15	.14	.13	1.	1.	1.2
3 Days	1.2	1.3	1.2	1.	1.4	1.3	1.6
Gain	.3	.4	.4	.3	.4	.3	.4
5 Days	1.6	1.8	1.6	1.1	1.6	1.8	1.8
Gain	.4	.5	.4	.1	.2	.5	.2
7 Days	1.14	1.14	1.10	1.4	1.12	1.14	2.2
Gain	.8	.6	.4	.3	.6	.6	.10
10 Days	2.2	2.8	2.4	2.	2.14	2.6	2.6
Gain	.4	.10	.10	.12	1.2	1.8	.4
2 Weeks	3.	3.	3.	2.10	3.14	3.	3.4
Wkly Gain	1.2	1.2	1.6	1.6	2.2	1.2	1.2
2½ Weeks	3.4	3.14	3.4	3.	4.8	3.14	3.8
Wkly Gain	1.2	1.6	1.	1.	1.10	1.8	1.2
3 Weeks	4.	4.2	4.4	3.12	5.4	4.4	4.4
Wkly Gain	1.	1.2	1.4	1.2	1.6	1.4	1.
4 Weeks	5.10	5.10	5.12	4.8	7.	5.14	6.
Wkly Gain	1.10	1.8	1.8	.12	1.12	1.10	1.12
5 Weeks	7.2	7.2	7.	5.14	8.4	7.6	7.2
Wkly Gain	1.8	1.8	1.4	1.6	1.4	1.8	1.2
6 Weeks	8.8	9.	8.6	6.14	10.8	9.6	9.6
Wkly Gain	1.6	1.14	1.6	1.	2.4	2.	2.4
7 Weeks	10.4	11.6	10.6	8.6	13.4	11.6	11.6
Wkly Gain	1.12	2.6	2.	1.8	2.12	2.	2.
8 Weeks	12.8	13.6	12.4	10.	14.8	13.12	13.14
Wkly Gain	2.4	2.	1.14	1.10	1.4	2.6	2.8
Total Gain	11.7	12.9	11.6	9.3	13.8	12.12	12.12

Puppies that are too warm will spread out in the box instead of heaping together in a pile.

dam may not have stimulated him to urinate or defecate. Pick him up to massage or burp him, stroking the stomach with a warm, wet cotton ball to stimulate elimination. You should then be able to return a relaxed, happy puppy back to his mother.

Dewclaw Removal and Tail Docking

If the puppies are all born healthy and in good weight, the tails and dewclaws should be cut by their second day. Dewclaws are what the Hungarian Standard calls "bastard toes." Located on the inner part of the pastern area on front feet they are removed from most sporting dogs to keep them from being torn when working in the fields.

The dam will fret and tear her bed apart if left behind, so take her along on the trip to the veterinarian. Do leave her in the car, however.

Make sure that your veterinarian understands that the Vizsla Standard calls for two-thirds of the tail *to be left on*. Eyeball or measure each puppy individually before he cuts so as to be satisfied with the decision.

There are several methods used for docking, and your veterinarian will usually go along with your choice. A single suture can be put across the cut of both the tail and the dewclaw area, or the areas can be cauterized after cutting, with medication designed to stop any bleeding. Either way leaves a satisfactory result after healing.

Until healed, check the sites daily for any sign of infection. Vizsla puppies are very determined as they climb over littermates on the way to a nipple. They can easily tear the scabs off dewclaw areas with their sharp nails. If one does become infected, clean the area with hydrogen peroxide and put a drop of iodine on it.

This two-day-old litter is due to have their tails docked and dewclaws removed.

ORPHAN PUPPIES

In a case where the dam is unable to feed her litter because of surgery or illness, or when a dam is lost through death, the entire job of raising orphan puppies will take over your life for several weeks. There is nothing difficult about hand-rearing a litter, but it is very time consuming.

You must keep the puppies warm, clean and fed. A smaller size than normal whelping box should be used for the first couple of weeks as the puppies will not have the warmth of their dam's body to lie against and they will want to stay bunched up close together. It is important that the box is in a draft-free area where you can control the temperature. Place a thermometer on the floor to get the correct reading at the level of the puppies.

Since a newborn is unable to control his body temperature for the first couple of weeks of life, the area should be maintained at a constant 85°F. Humidity is very important and, if too low, the puppies will tend to dehydrate. A pan of water near the heat source will help balance the environment.

Cleanliness is essential since the pups have not received colostrum from the dam to protect them from viruses. Bedding must be changed daily and all feeding utensils, nipples, and bottle, should be sterilized. Be aware that your clothes and shoes can carry infectious diseases. Do not allow visitors.

The easiest way to bottle feed a puppy is to place him, stomach down, on your lap with a rolled towel in front of him. A pup will push and knead at his dam's breast as he nurses and the towel will enable him to simulate his normal behavior.

If you squeeze a drop of milk from the nipple first to give him a smell, a hungry pup will wrap his tongue around the nipple with a strong sucking action. The formula *must be the right temperature*. Too hot or too cold and he will refuse it. Squeeze a little onto the back of your hand first to test it — if it is uncomfortably hot or cold for you, do not attempt to feed it to the puppy. Feed enough that his stomach becomes just slightly distended, and keep a slight pull on the bottle to encourage strong sucking.

For the first two weeks of life a young puppy relies on being stimulated in order to urinate or pass a stool. In the case of the orphan, these functions will have to be aided by you. Gently rub his rear and the abdominal area with a warm, wet cotton ball.

After you feed and clean the pups, burp each one as you would a baby. Hold him against your shoulder and rub his back. This will relieve him of any air taken in from the bottle. This entire process will need to be repeated every four hours. Start with an ounce of formula per puppy each feeding and gradually increase as needed.

A puppy with a loose stool could either be overfed or ill. At the first signs of diarrhea, dilute your feeding formula with some additional sterile water. If the condition persists, have your veterinarian check for any bacterial infection. A healthy puppy fed six times a day will have from six to seven bowel movements.

At 2 weeks of age the puppies will be able to eliminate on their own and maintain their own body temperature. If your puppies are gaining weight daily and seem reasonably happy and quiet, you can be sure that they are adequately fed. They should actually be at the same stage in their development as a normal litter, so by 18 days of age you should consider feeding them more solid food from a pan. Do not eliminate the bottle completely for several days until you are sure that each puppy is eating well and still gaining weight.

Puppies raised without their dam will associate you with the food supply within a couple of days after birth and will have a very close attachment to you, so continue to give them a lot of attention even when the bottle feeding has been discontinued.

ILLNESS IN NEWBORNS

The most frequent time of death for a newborn is between twenty-four and forty-eight hours after birth. General signs of illness include poor reflexes when stimulated; puppy straying from the dam and not nursing; weight loss; high-pitched screaming; crying and restlessness even in a warm environment (a healthy puppy does little crying and will sleep relaxed with occasional muscle twitching); diarrhea; labored breathing accompanied by blue coloration of pads and membranes.

Above: At five days of age, a contented litter.

Left: Inspect each puppy every day for illness or injury. He will benefit from the handling.

Fading Puppies

"Fading puppy" is a term used to describe a prenatal death that occurs in the first few days of life, not including death caused by birth defects or any anatomical malformations. Changes in newborns can occur suddenly. Where just a few hours ago you had a happy, healthy puppy, you suddenly have one that is quiet, listless, cold, and lying away from the rest of the litter.

The normal temperature of a newborn is 94 to 97°F during the first week of life. Born soaking wet from his dam, his body temperature is 101°F, but within minutes it will drop to 94°F. By the time he is 24 hours old his temperature will stabilize if he is getting heat from his mother's body.

By the end of the first week of his life, his body temperature will rise to 99°F and by the end of the fourth week, the puppy will maintain a temperature of 101°F.

If, at any time, his rectal temperature falls below 94°F his digestive system becomes paralyzed and nursing becomes ineffectual. The puppy will die unless he quickly receives help for his low energy.

At this point, dehydration is a very serious development but giving any milk formula may be the surest way to guarantee the puppy's death. It is essential that the puppy be warmed gradually and this may take two to three hours. Mix a solution of one teaspoon of *Karo® syrup* or honey to one ounce of warm water. Give it to the puppy by dropper every half–hour until he is warm and responsive. It will be absorbed immediately into the stomach, raising his blood sugar and halting the hypoglycemic condition.

Try to keep him close to his dam's body for extra warmth, *never* on a hot heating pad. Examine him closely as he is being warmed, as his condition may warrant a specific treatment.

Toxic Milk

If there are any toxins in the dam's system, symptoms will appear in the puppies around the end of their first week of life. These toxins usually result from debris or a retained placenta in the dam's uterus breaking down into toxic substances that are excreted in her milk.

After the first stools, (which will be dark), have been passed, the dam will be cleaning up after the puppies so fast that it will be hard to

Table 14-2
The Healthy Versus the Sick Puppy: What To Look For

The Healthy Puppy	The Sick Puppy
gains weight	doesn't gain weight
sleek, smooth coat	rough, dull coat
cries infrequently	cries frequently
good muscle and skin tone	limp, wrinkled skin
round, plump, firm body	flat, tucked up appearance
pink mucous membranes	pot-bellied
activated sleep	reddish-purple or blue mucous membranes
yawns frequently	scattered around the nest
nurses strongly	cries or mews
	diarrhea
	can't or won't suck

Careful observation will warn you of any complication. If your bitch seems abnormally depressed, anxious, or upset, it would be wise to have her checked. It is in whelping and caring for puppies and their mother, more than at any other time, that you and your vet will need to work as a team. Be sure to have a veterinarian you can trust and work with; then consult him regularly.

find any evidence of their condition. However, there may be signs of fecal material left on the bedding when diarrhea is present.

The color of a normal bowel movement should be brownish yellow and the consistency fairly firm. If a case of diarrhea shows up as only a temporary problem it may be a result of overeating. If the color progresses to a dark green stool and you have a puppy with a red, sore anus the problem may have been caused by toxic milk.

The entire litter will have to be bottle or tube fed a formula and treated with both an antibiotic and an anti-diarrhea medication while the dam is also under treatment. Puppies may possibly be able to return to their nursing after twenty–four hours.

It is wise to give puppies yogurt or lactobacillus acidophilus any time they are under treatment for diarrhea in order to restore the normal bacteria level to their intestines. Two teaspoons every twelve hours should be sufficient.

Septicemia

Septicemia is a bacterial infection in a puppy's bloodstream which either enters the body through infected milk or from the site of an infected umbilical cord. It is essential to find the cause as one puppy can infect the entire litter and death may occur.

Inspect the umbilical cord for any pus, redness or swelling. If such is the case, clean the area with hydrogen peroxide and swab it with iodine. Antibiotic therapy must be started immediately. A clean whelping box is a necessity. Blankets must be changed several times a day and any infected puppy must be isolated. Check the site of tail docking and dewclaw removal daily.

Another site of contamination that can rapidly spread bacterial infection through the entire litter may be the dam's mammary glands. It may be necessary to remove the puppies from her and hand feed them.

Contented and well-fed at ten days of age.

These five-week-old puppies are now able to climb out of their whelping box.

Neighborhood children get called in to help socialize this litter of five-and-a-half-week-old pups.

At twelve weeks of age, a Vizsla puppy can climb up on a bed but should not be left unsupervised.

At six and a half weeks of age, this puppy is ready for his first series of protective vaccines.

Herpes

Herpes is a virus that may be acquired by the newborns as they pass through an infected vaginal tract at birth. The symptoms appear suddenly in previously healthy puppies. Starting with constant crying from abdominal swelling and pain, the puppies soon refuse to nurse and become chilled. Their stools are soft, green diarrhea. Hemorrhages of the liver and kidneys follow and it is almost impossible to save a puppy at this stage. Death could occur within twenty–four hours of the first signs.

Herpes usually affects a puppy under the age of 3 weeks while his body temperature is still at a low level. The virus will reproduce rapidly at body temperatures of 95°F. If a puppy's temperature can be maintained closer to 100°F by increasing the temperature and humidity in the box, plus treating him with antibiotics and fluids, there is a slight chance of saving him providing the treatment is started early.

The natural place to sit is always on a lap.

Vizslas adore children and naturally gravitate to them.

A child will always have a playmate if there is a Vizsla in the home.

This six-week-old puppy explores a life-size chess set on the floor. At this age, puppies show tremendous curiosity and intelligence.

15

The Growing Vizsla Puppy

PUPPIES are living, breathing creatures that require more than just their clean bed, food, and medical care. They do not, like Topsy, "just grow." After the whelping is over and the puppies are nursing on their own do not make the mistake of spending less time with them, depriving them of the individual attention which each one needs to assure him of accepting a human relationship. Socialization is the responsibility of the breeder from the minute the puppies are born.

SOCIALIZATION AND CARE

During the neonatal period, or the first 2 weeks of life, the dam will provide optimal care for her puppies, and your attention should be concentrated upon making sure the mother is well nourished and allowed to care for the litter quietly, undisturbed by strangers or commotion.

Inspect each puppy once a day for possible illness or injury, and put down clean bedding for them. Even puppies that young will benefit from handling. They will react very strongly to touch and will fuss and struggle. If picked up suddenly they may give a yelp of sudden fear as if in pain. Hold them close to your body so that they can get used to your smell. Their nails should be cut regularly to keep them from scratching littermates and their dam as they climb and scramble for a nipple.

As your Vizsla puppies go into their second week of life, they will have less activated sleep and go into deeper sleeps until their ears open around 13–15 days,when sudden noises will startle them.

Eyes should start to open at 11–15 days of age. That is, with puppies born at approxi-

From now on their development will be rapid. Handle and talk to them often so that they get used to the sound of your voice along with your smell.

At 17 days the puppies will be more active on their legs, mouth each other, and growl. They will be very aware of their surroundings, and they will no longer need the stimulus from their dam to urinate or defecate, although she will still clean up after them.

The eruption of their first teeth through the gums can be felt at approximately 18 days, and soon mother is glad to be away from them,

At two weeks of age, this puppy's eyes are still not completely opened.

At sixteen days of age, the eyes and ears are now opened.

mately the full term of sixty-three days. It will usually be found that puppies born early rarely open their eyes before their sixteenth day, while puppies born late may start to open their eyes as early as 10 days of age. Watch their eyes carefully during this time for any swelling or pus from irritation or infection.

During this time you should also keep direct sunlight out of the puppy's eyes and reduce the constant glare of overhead lighting until the eyes are completely opened. Eye color will be bluish for several weeks, but should darken by the time the pups are 8 weeks old.

At 12 days of age the puppies will be making awkward, comical efforts to get on their feet, and will stand for a few seconds at a time.

returning only when she knows they have to be fed. Normal room temperature should be maintained now, without drafts. The dam's body will keep the puppies warm at night if it gets cool. Make sure their bedding is clean and dry.

Suddenly at 21 days of age it may seem like a light bulb going on inside your Vizsla puppies' heads as they start to put it all together. Every day becomes a new experience. This is called the "socialization period" and the puppies become very much aware of any changes in their environment. They may not start to explore or relax outside their whelping box until they have been out several times. The bolder ones will be the most inquisitive and

This litter of three-week-old puppies is now at a period of emotional and physical development that will determine the pattern of their adult life.

the others will follow. They will generally react as a group and even a timid pup will not want to be left behind.

This period is the most critical time of their development. How you handle them will determine the emotional sensitivity, and pattern, of their adult life. Your Vizsla puppies have started to become independent of their dam, capable of knowing different people and voices. They should exhibit no fear of people as long as care is taken to prevent them from being injured or unnecessarily frightened.

Only daily observation, talking, playing and personal contact with your puppies can prevent fear behavior. The things that a Vizsla breeder should offer to each buyer of his puppies are dependability and a well–adjusted, happy dog that will readily accept the new owner as his leader.

Between the third and fourth week there is an amazingly rapid development in their senses. This is the time to give them safe toys to play with and encourage their natural retrieving instinct. Soft, washable stuffed animals, which are safe for small children, are the most fun for them to carry and will also encourage a soft bite.

Do not allow strangers to hold a struggling puppy. He may jump out of their arms and be injured. Ask them, especially children, to sit on the floor and allow the puppies to approach them on their own.

During this socialization period your puppies will start to go to one side of their whelping box to eliminate instead of soiling their sleeping area. Put a blanket on only one–half of the box and newspapers on the other half. The dam will clean up after her puppies only until they have meat in their diet. Even so, you will find that the box will stay clean except for urination once you have started to let them out on the floor to play. Cover an area on the floor with papers and wait until each puppy has a bowel movement before placing him back in his bed. Do this early in the morning and after each meal and there will be very little soiling in the whelping box.

The puppies can start to eat out of a pan as early as 18 days of age if they are fairly steady on their legs. Keep them away from their dam for several hours so that they are hungry and they will be eager to eat their first meal of baby cereal mixed with a milk formula.

The formula can be a prepared mix, made especially for puppies by a company specializing in animal care, or you can mix your own. To one can of evaporated milk, add equal water, one egg yolk, one tablespoon of *Karo®* *syrup*, and pediatric multiple vitamin drops. Keep the formula refrigerated and use only

Table 15-1
Developmental Stages of A Puppy

Age	Basic Needs	Behavior and Training
1-14 days (1st & 2nd week)	Warmth • Food Sleep • Mother	Not responsive to humans • Sleeps 90% of time Needs stimulation for urination & defecation
15-21 days (3rd & 4th week)	Warmth • Food Sleep • Mother	Eyes open • Begins to walk Should be handled carefully • Needs mother and littermates • First worming
22-35 days (4th & 5th week)	Socialization with canines and humans • Rest • Play	Begins to eat, bark, and play • Begins to respond to human voice Needs play and socialization outside the puppy pen
36-49 days (6th & 7th week)	Weaning • Separation from littermates • Human socialization	Strong dominant/subordinate relationships are developing • Motor skills improved • Temporary immunizations given • Capable of learning simple commands and being leash broken • May go to new home during seventh week
49-56 days (8th week)	Security • Love	Often termed the "fear period" • Puppy should not be frightened or unnecessarily stressed during this period
50-63 days (9-12 weeks)	Bonds to human • Learns to accept human as pack leader Socialization	Totally removed from dam and littermates • Capable of learning Come-Sit-Stay Needs confidence instilled • Begin housebreaking • Exposure to variety of environments important
64-112 days (12-16 weeks)	Security • Discipline Socialization • Attention	Learns by association • Goes through "avoidance period" Needs continued low-key socialization and exposure
113-168 days (16-24 weeks)	Socialization • Love • Consistent Discipline • Basic Training	Fully developed mentally; needs experience • Will attempt to establish dominance • Adapts a negative or positive attitude toward training at this time Praise lavishly for correct behavior
25-32 weeks (6-8 months)	Basic Training • Consistent discipline • Continued attention and socialization	Ready for beginning show or obedience classes • Attention span is lengthening • Needs continuing exposure to new situations • Males begin to assert dominance
33-56 weeks (8-12 months)	Continued socialization, reassurance and training • Affection and reassurance necessary	Show pups often in "puppy bloom" but should not be pushed too fast • Teething period ends • Puberty (period of sexual maturation) begins • May go through a second avoidance period • Neutering can be performed.

what is needed for each meal. It must be warmed first or the puppies will refuse it.

Their first meals will be messy as the puppies plaster themselves with the sticky cereal, standing with their feet in the dish or even laying on their stomach in it.

After they have mastered eating the soft sloppy gruel, gradually change their diet to a high protein puppy meal and get them started on what will become an established feeding program for them. Soak the meal in warm water until it has softened and then mash it well and add it to the cereal and formula for several days, still keeping it very sloppy. Feed three meals a day with their dam still spending time with them between meals and at nights.

By the time the puppies are 4 weeks of age, start adding boiled hamburger and the broth from it to the meal, eliminating the cereal and milk. Once a day add a little cottage cheese and the baby vitamin drops to the food.

By 5½ weeks of age, the puppies should be completely weaned from their dam. They will need four meals a day, with the last one given in the late evening. Their teeth will be stronger and they will be a great deal rougher. As a

At four weeks of age, these puppies will soon be eating only their puppy kibble and no longer nursing at all.

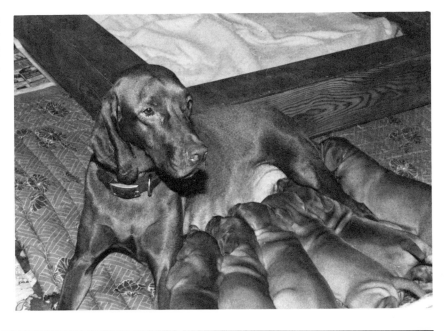

result, there will be a rapid change in their relationship with the dam. She may return to them only to regurgitate her food for them to eat. The puppies will have become completely independent of her. They will be active and happy. They will chew on everything they come into contact with, and show a rapid development of intelligence.

They may growl and fight among themselves, establishing a dominance pattern. In a litter with both sexes the most dominant puppy is usually a very active, outgoing female. Give special attention to any puppy which is not joining in the play group.

By 6½ weeks of age your Vizsla puppies will be ready for their first vaccinations. The new

Still closely watched over by their dam is this tired litter of five-week-old puppies.

vaccines include in combination form, distemper, hepatitis, leptospirosis, parainfluenza, parvovirus and coronavirus is a single dose. Vaccinations will carry the puppies from their passive immunity provided by their dam to their own active immunity against those diseases.

PROBLEMS WITH GROWING PUPPIES

Swimmers

This condition is not hereditary but environmental, and can possibly be controlled or prevented by realizing what is happening to an overweight puppy.

It usually occurs in a small litter of two or three puppies with a dam who has an abundant supply of rich milk. The "swimmer" puppy will lie and eat, getting a constantly filled stomach until, when he is about 2 weeks of age and should be learning to walk, he is too heavy to pull himself up on his feet.

He will lie sprawled on his stomach with the weight flattening his rib cage as he grows sideways instead of upwards. His rear legs will spread out behind him with the feet turned inward so that he looks deformed. He will try to propel himself by pulling with his front feet and using his head and neck as leverage.

The immediate problem can be helped by always keeping a blanket in the whelping box, instead of newspapers, in order to give good footing to the puppy. He needs a rough surface to provide traction. The puppy's rib cage, at this age, is very soft and pliable. If the swimmer can be taught to use his rear legs and walk normally, his rib cage will eventually round out and be normal.

Several times a day take him to a carpeted area. Place a hand under the rear and the other hand under his chest with the feet barely touching the carpet. Gradually let the weight come down on the feet until he learns to move all four legs. Keep your hand under his rear to support most of the weight.

It will take several days of following this procedure before he learns to straighten his rear legs enough to support himself, but from then on the progress will be rapid. While you teach him to walk, you can also control his weight gain by keeping him away from his dam for longer periods of time so that he is not constantly nursing.

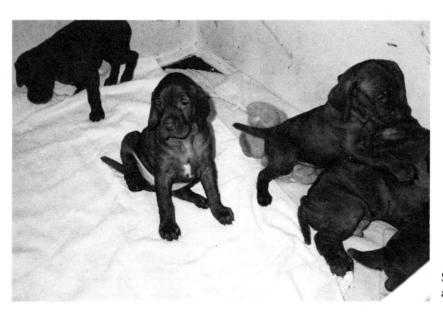

Six-week-old puppies are active and rough.

A cardboard box will give many hours of play to young puppies.

These six-week-old puppies have a basket of stuffed animals to play with.

Do not be discouraged by this condition. If you keep at it during the early stage, by 10 weeks of age the rib cage and legs will be normal.

Incorrect Bite

A puppy's first teeth begin to come through the gums around 18 days and become as sharp and pointed as needles. Puppy teeth have shallow roots and the puppy will start to lose them at 16 weeks of age, when a full set of permanent teeth will start to come in.

The Vizsla should have a "scissors bite." If he has an incorrect bite with his baby teeth, he will probably have it with his permanent set also. If he has an even bite, meeting edge to edge, the bite could go either way.

An "underbite" is when the lower teeth project in front of the upper set; the jaw locks in place as it grows and seldom corrects. In the case of an "overbite" the upper teeth project out in front of the lower set and there is usually a large space between them when the mouth is closed. This condition stands a good chance of improvement as the puppy's head and jaw grows.

Umbilical Hernia

If there is a great deal of strain and pulling on the umbilical cord as a puppy is whelped, there is the possibility that a tear can develop in the abdominal wall, allowing a portion of the skin to protrude, hindering the normal closing of the umbilical ring. Quite often this hernia, or protrusion, can be pushed into the opening and tape to hold it in place. However, most hernias have to be corrected with surgery when the puppy gets older, especially on a female puppy that may eventually be used for breeding. On rare occasions a hernia will get smaller and disappear by the time a puppy is 6 months old without any treatment.

Conjunctivitis

The eyes of Vizsla puppies usually start to open about eleven days after birth, but will stay as mere slits for a couple of days until fully opened. During this time of being only partially open they must be examined daily for any swelling or pus.

As young puppies push and scramble for a nipple, a toenail can scratch an eyelid and

These seven-week-old puppies are being very closely supervised while in a pool.

Litters growing up in a household where there are children will be socialized easily.

cause a bacterial infection which could rapidly multiply behind the eyelid.

Untreated, this can cause permanent damage. Pus must be drained out by gently opening the eyelid a little and pressing carefully to express the pus. Obtain antibiotic ointment or drops from your veterinarian and keep the eyelid from sealing over.

Skin Problems

Even under the cleanest conditions there will be problems, especially skin conditions that will require an expert diagnosis. These conditions can be caused by staphylococcus, fungus, or even allergies.

The dam's discharge after whelping may contain the microorganisms responsible for a staphylococcus infection erupting on the face and feet of puppies coming into contact with it. Sores erupt rapidly when the Vizslas are around 5 weeks of age, with the symptoms starting as inflamed, swollen areas of the feet, then opening up into sores, and finally infecting the muzzle area as the puppy lays his head down on his feet to sleep.

The affected area will have to be treated locally with a shampoo and internally with an antibiotic. It will take at least three weeks of consistent care to bring a staphylococcus infection under control. There will be hair loss in the affected areas, but this should start to fill in as soon as the sores heal.

In the case of a fungal infection, the sores may not be as penetrating and only show up as red areas with hair loss. A veterinarian may prescribe a good iodine shampoo combined with an antiobiotic treatment. In cases that do not respond, he may decide to do a scraping and culture.

One problem that can be readily identified is Juvenile Pyoderma (strangles). Along with pus–filled sores, the lymph glands in the neck are enlarged, the face and lips are swollen, the temperature is elevated and the puppy becomes very ill. The lesions must be handled very gently as they will be painful. They must be cleaned with a mild antiseptic solution. As they crust, mineral oil can be used to soften them so that the crusts can be removed without leaving any scars. In the case of a very young puppy, an antibiotic can be given with a medicine dropper.

Another skin problem among very young puppies has been called "Vizsla rash" although it is common in many breeds. Small pimples or pustules appear on the puppy's head and sometimes his entire body. These pustules break and scab over, leaving a very scruffy look to the coat.

There seems to be no clear evidence that attributes the condition to a dirty whelping box, but rather to the dam's tongue infecting the puppy after she has cleaned her vaginal discharge. Whatever the cause, the condition should be brought to the attention of your veterinarian and treatment started immediately with scrubs and medication. Blankets and newspapers in the whelping box must be kept clean at all times.

Internal Parasites

Keeping a litter of puppies worm-free is a primary concern for every breeder. Even worming your bitch before breeding does not guarantee that her puppies will not be born already infested. If at any time in her life your bitch harbored hookworms or roundworms, the parasites can live in a dormant stage until she became pregnant. At that point they migrate through the placenta and into the puppy *in utero*.

As early as 2 weeks of age the puppies may start having a dark stool with a mucous coating. You will have to monitor the box fairly closely in order to get a stool sample before the dam cleans it away. You can identify roundworms passed in the stool — as they are visible as small, skinny, spaghetti–shaped worms, usually wound into a coil. Hookworms must be identified under a microscope. These are the most debilitating of the parasites. The worm attaches itself to the lining of the small intestines and nourishes itself by sucking the puppy's blood. If left untreated hookworm can cause anemia and prove fatal to your puppy. Hookworm eggs can be seen in the stool as early as ten days after your litter's birth and early diagnosis and treatment is necessary. A puppy with hookworm infestation will have a dark, tarry stool and fail to gain weight.

Several liquid worming medications can be used safely on puppies even as young as 2–3 weeks of age. One worming treatment will not rid a puppy of the worms completely and a second treatment will be necessary two weeks later. Continue having stool checks done at two– or three–week intervals.

Russet Leather Kachina Doll

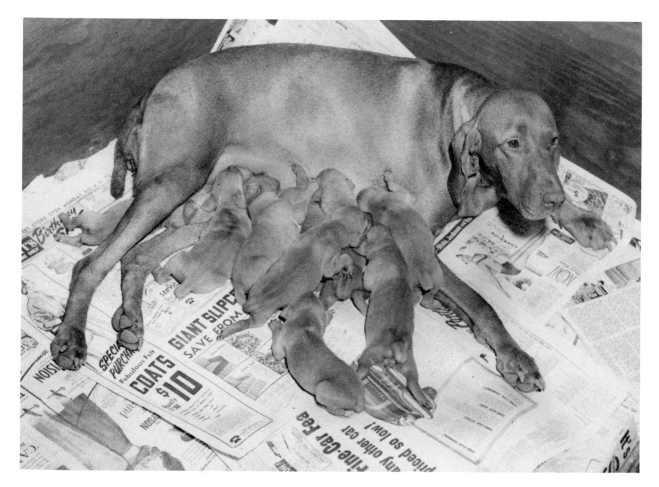

A photo taken in 1959 shows Asta Z Povazia with her week-old litter of nine. *Photo courtesy of Joan Hunt.*

16

Care of the Vizsla Dam

A Vizsla bitch is usually a very good mother. Even the one which you are so sure still acts like a puppy most of the time and will never know how to care for her litter, will surprise you with "instant motherhood." She will constantly push, clean, and count her puppies. She will be reluctant to leave them for the first few days and you will have to put her on a leash and forcibly make her go out to eliminate.

A new mother will be possessive and overprotective of her newborns. It is best not to allow any visitors for at least two weeks as an emotional upset in your bitch could cause her to step or lie on a small puppy.

PROBLEMS AFTER WHELPING

Soon after your bitch has had some rest and fed her newborns, you should take her to your veterinarian to be checked over for any retained afterbirths or even a dead puppy. Make sure you have kept an accurate count of any afterbirths missing and inform him of the problem.

Your veterinarian will administer a shot of oxytocin which will cause the uterus to contract and expel any debris left, perhaps saving your puppies from a serious case of Toxic Milk Syndrome. A shot of this hormone will also help to increase the milk supply if it is slow "coming down."

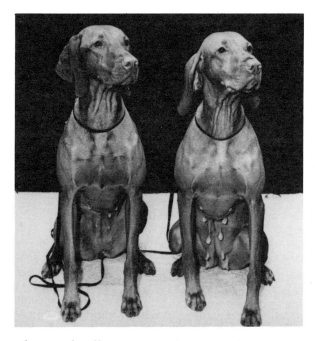

Ch. Cariad's Elkenyeztetett, foundation brood bitch for the Boelte's Vizslas, and her daughter, Ch. Boelte's Bronze Beauty, JH. As a brace they earned a Best in Show. Owned by Pat Boelte.

Ch. Cariad's Gaybine, CD, dam of 16 champions that include the record show winner for the breed, as well as the first Triple Champion on record.

It was formerly considered the routine procedure to include an antibiotic along with the oxytocin after whelping. The antibiotic shot is now thought to be the cause of "fading puppies" since it is transmitted through the dam's milk to the newborns, destroying the normal friendly microbial inhabitants of their intestinal tracts. Thus, it should never be given unless imperative.

If used, the dam and her puppies should receive daily doses of lactobacillus acidophilus to restore the natural flora. You can buy this from a pharmacy. The package of granules will need refrigeration and will require mixing — use one envelope in two tablespoons of sterile water.

The dosage for each puppy should be 300 milligrams (two teaspoons) every twelve hours, and can be given by eyedropper. Yogurt also contains the same ingredients and your bitch will enjoy it cold. Warm it for the pups.

Acute Metritus

Your bitch will have a discharge for as long as five or six weeks following whelping. A normal color is reddish-brown, starting with blood clots in it, or it could be a greenish-black discharge for the first few days as the uterus continues its cleaning–out process. It will change to a light–brown, mucoid discharge by the third week. Any foul odor, yellowish discharge, vomiting, fever, loss of appetite, listlessness with no interest in her puppies, could be a sign of an infection of the uterus called acute metritus.

The infection may run its course in less than a week with the uterus becoming swollen and the abdomen tender and painful. If the problem is diagnosed early, the prognosis for your bitch's recovery is good, but if she is not given immediate professional care, she may have to be spayed to save her life. The infection must be brought under control with antibiotics, but unfortunately, if there is no immediate response, a hysterectomy may have to be performed.

Either way, her puppies must be raised as orphans because her milk will be toxic. If your bitch has a history that includes any abnormal vaginal discharges, pyometra, vaginitis, or has been given mismating shots, all these should be taken into account as contributing causes in a case of acute metritis.

Eclampsia

Eclampsia is a critical condition that can occur at any stage of lactation. It is caused by the calcium level of the blood being lowered. Symptoms include nervousness, excessive panting, extremely high temperature, stiffening of the leg muscles, tensing and quivering, and staring wildly. Saliva will accumulate in her mouth, clogging her throat and causing a rattling sound. Finally, she will have convulsions.

Even supplemental calcium given daily may not eliminate this metabolic upset and it is important that you recognize the signs and realize that the condition can come on rapidly.

Call your veterinarian immediately. Your Vizsla's life will depend on your fast action.

Treatment is an intravenous solution of calcium given slowly until the normal blood level is re–established.

Mastitis

Mastitis is an acute inflammation of, or abscess formation in, the dam's breast. The breast will be very swollen, reddish blue, and extremely painful. The milk may have some streaks of blood or pus in it and your bitch will run a high temperature, have a loss of appetite, and appear very ill and listless.

Inflammation may be caused by an overproduction of milk combined with the puppies not draining each breast adequately, resulting in the milk glands becoming caked. In that case, if caught early before an abscess forms, the breast can be squeezed by hand and if the milk looks normal, the condition may possibly be halted.

However, if the inflammation has been caused by a bacterial infection into the glands, resulting in an abscess, surgery may be necessary if antibiotic treatment fails.

The puppies must be prevented from getting any of the infected milk. If only one breast is

Ch. Topian's Foxsea Kelly settles down for a rest after whelping her final puppy just a few hours earlier.

affected and needs treatment it may be possible to cover the sore one and still allow the puppies to nurse from the remainder. However, there is a chance that all the milk may become infected and toxic and it is wiser and safer to put the entire litter on bottle feeding if they are still too young to be weaned to solid food.

Mastitis can possibly be prevented by keeping puppies' nails cut short to avoid them scratching the dam's breasts and introducing bacteria into the scratches. Also, you should

a good supply of milk. This is only possible if she is being fed a well-balanced, adequate diet.

Your new mother may be fussy about eating for a few days following the whelping which may contribute to a slow supply of milk in her breasts. Make sure that she is at least getting a lot of liquids. Use soup, broths, and cottage cheese to tempt her. Within a couple of days the natural demand for her body to supply food for her babies will take over and she will be eating her regular meals.

The new mother must be allowed to care for her litter in peace and quiet.

Careful monitoring of the new dam will prevent swollen and infected breasts.

make sure that your bitch changes position often so that her puppies can use all of the nipples and keep each breast drained. If you have a small litter that can not keep all the breasts drained, reduce your bitch's food intake to slow her milk production.

FEEDING AND CARE OF THE DAM

If you expect to have healthy Vizsla puppies, then you must have a bitch that can give them

As her puppies grow, they will require more nourishment and you will have to increase her meals to keep up with the demand for a larger milk supply.

If she had an average–sized litter of eight, then three large meals a day of at least two cups of meal plus meat should be sufficient for the first ten days, with a fourth meal added if necessary. But more and more Vizsla bitches are having large litters of ten or more puppies, and if that is the case, by the time her puppies are 7 days old your bitch should be eating a minimum of four large meals a day, with smaller snacks in between.

As her puppies get into their fourth week of life and are eating solid food from a pan, start decreasing the dam's food intake in preparation for completely weaning the litter.

By the puppy's fifth week, your bitch should receive only two meals a day. Decrease the amount of food considerably with each meal in order to stop her milk supply. Watch her carefully during this period for any congestion of the breasts. If she is uncomfortable, with swollen breasts, you will have to put her with her puppies in order for them to drain each breast. Otherwise, keep her completely away from her puppies as their continued nursing will stimulate her glands to keep producing milk.

During weaning remember that her food intake will help to produce milk so you must not allow her any snacks, treats, or extra food, no matter how hard she begs, and she must not be allowed to play with her puppies until she is no longer producing milk.

From the time her puppies are 3 weeks old your bitch will probably be willing to spend time away from them, returning to the box several times a day to feed and clean them. She should have only controlled exercise and

not be allowed to run and play, the reason for that being that her breasts may get damaged while they are engorged with milk. Even as the weaning process is going on, the breasts will still be hanging down until the muscles surrounding the glands have regained their elasticity. It will usually take only a few weeks for all the muscles to tighten up, but until then the breasts will be flapping in the breeze every time she moves, and she must be restrained from hard running and jumping.

While it is not advisable to give the dam a complete bath while she is a nursing mother, keep her rear cleaned to get rid of the discharge after whelping. A clean cloth with warm water and a mild soap should be used several times a day. Pay particular attention to the underside of her tail and include that area in the washing.

Because of the higher temperature in the whelping room, combined with the hormonal changes in her body, the dam will have shed most of her coat by the time the puppies are 8 weeks old. Brush it out daily and the new coat will soon grow in. Until it does, she will look a little moth-eaten.

This Vizsla dam owned by Doris Ratzlaff is confident enough to allow the sire of her puppies to share the whelping box.

FIRST
VETERAN
WESTCHESTER
KENNEL CLUB
1982

Eleven-year-old Ch. Taunee's Loki Santana still shows the elegance and style that made him the top winning Vizsla on record.

17

The Aging Process

THERE is a nobility in the aging Vizsla that is unequaled at any other stage of his life. Getting old is not a disease, nor should a dog that has shown nothing but love and devotion to his owners be treated like a pariah just because he is well into an advanced age.

The Vizsla is a healthy, long-lived breed that is able to enjoy life well into old age. The foundation brood bitch for the Cariad line, Ch. Balatoni Sassy Olca, lived to 17½ years with fairly good eyesight and health to the very end.

A dog may be considered "old" when he has trouble functioning with dimmer eyesight, steps that begin to falter and slow, not as continent as he was as an adult in his prime, and when his hearing starts to go and you have to speak louder or use hand signals. Physiological aging is just a part of the natural order of things and neither man nor beast dies merely from "old age." Aging is a generalized condition, or multiple conditions, where one or more organs start to malfunction, and fail.

CARE FOR THE AGING DOG

A continued preventive health care program can increase the quality and length of your Vizsla's life and is also a wise investment since it will cost less in the long run than treatment for a problem.

It is extremely important that your veterinarian do a urinalysis and also a blood analysis at least once a year as your dog advances in age. If your Vizsla increases his water intake and the frequency of urination, do not try to cut back on his water supply so that he will urinate less frequently. Instead, bring it to the attention of your veterinarian.

The skin glands and hair go through a number of changes in old age, the most noticable of these being graying of the hair. Brush your dog weekly to remove the dead hairs and stimulate the skin. This will also give you the chance to let him know that you still care and love giving him all the little attentions.

Ears and eyes go through drastic changes and quite often deafness and cataracts, which must be accepted as a normal part of the aging process, occur.

Check the eyes daily since they tend to need mucous collections cleaned from them. Do not neglect his nails or ears just because he gets cranky about being handled. Nails that are kept too long will give added strain to weakened legs and poor traction on smooth floors.

Never should any vaccinations be delayed or neglected just because your Vizsla is growing older and never leaves his yard. Any virus in an older dog can have devastating results since he is without the strength and vitality of youth to pull him through. Keep him on an annual schedule of booster shots. It is also important not to neglect an annual blood test for heartworm, and regular fecal tests.

One of the most important concerns with your older Vizsla will be his weight. A dog that has a tendency to thinness in his advanced

Ch. Balatoni Sassy Olca at seventeen years of age.

Keeping your aging dog from gaining excess weight will help give him a healthier old age.

Table 17-1
Lifespan of the Dog

Dog Age	Human Equivalent
1 year	15 years
3 years	30 years
6 years	40 years
9 years	55 years
12 years	65 years
15 years	80 years

Eleven-year-old Ruffian shares a quiet time with his young owners as he grows older and is not as active.

years will be far healthier than an obese one. Obesity in a dog is the direct result of him being fed more food than he can properly burn up over a period of time, so it is stored as fat, or fatty tissue, in his body. A pet is more inclined to become obese than a dog still working in the field, but obesity is a concern for every dog as he gets older or his exercise is curtailed.

The life span of an obese dog is decreased for several reasons. Excess weight puts undue stress on the heart as well as the joints, the dog becomes a poor anesthesia risk, and has less resistance to viral or bacterial infections.

An aging dog experiences metabolic changes, and as a result he will need less volume and less protein to prevent obesity. Although if you have been providing him with an adequate basic diet and he is in a moderately good physical condition, there may be no need to change. Rather than changing the total dietary aspect, corrections can be made to bring it into better balance by adding prescribed nutrients.

Due to advanced age most older dogs are a poor risk for surgery. Their systems do not have the ability to tolerate anesthesia and they have slower recuperative powers. For this reason, surgery should be avoided unless absolutely necessary. Treatment of any kind should only be undertaken with the most serious problems, as the older dog eliminates drugs a lot slower and, as such, they could have an accumulative effect.

The best form of preventive medicine is early detection so that as soon as a problem is seen, it can be controlled to a point where the

Make sure that your aged Vizsla still has a place of her own to rest.

The aging dog needs extra care and attention.

The first change to be noted in the aging dog is the graying of the hair on the muzzle and legs.

dog can be reasonably comfortable. Good care coupled with careful feeding and exercise, plus a happy and interesting existence can slow the wheels of time a bit and help keep your old friend with you for a while longer. When the elderly dog has given you years of love and devotion, it is important now, in the brief time he has left, that you give him comfort and security.

CHANGES WITH AGE

Since one of the systems subject to senile changes is the digestive system, which starts with bad teeth, have your veterinarian check for tartar accumulation which is not only unsightly but can lead to serious problems. Dirty teeth infect the gums, cause root decay, and can lead to heart problems and arthritis by releasing bacteria into the blood stream.

An older dog can also suffer a loss of muscle tone and secretion of the digestive juices of the stomach. Slow emptying of the stomach can possibly lead to bloat, and indigestion. A special diet may have to be given. He will experience constipation due to the weakness of the abdominal muscles which results in lessened bowel activity. Giving him his meal soaked and softened in water may help relieve this problem. Frequent cleaning of the teeth will be necessary.

Older dogs sleep a lot and, probably because of the hearing loss, sleep deeper. A safe and comfortable bed out of drafts is a must as an aged dog is not capable of keeping warm. Most older Vizslas do not adjust well to any change in their environment so keep his chair in the

Thirteen-year-old Cariad's Masterpiece is showing the white face of the aging dog.

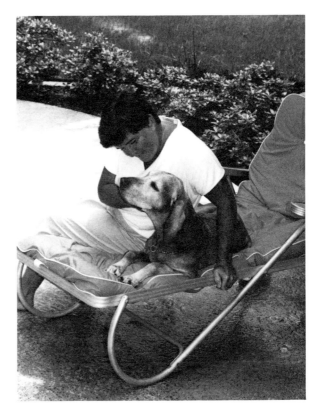

Triple Ch. Cariad's Kutya Kai Costa at eleven years of age.

same place, and if he has always slept on your bed there is no reason to exclude him now unless he has become incontinent. He may have to be helped onto the bed if he can no longer make the jump.

The nervous system undergoes changes as your Vizsla ages. Atrophy of the brain is manifested by a lessened response to, and decreased ability to obey commands. Irritability and, sadly, the forgetfulness of habits or training are also evident. Sometimes a dog can become so disoriented as to stand with his head in a corner, not knowing how to get out of it.

For these reasons, an aged Vizsla does not do well if he needs to be boarded at a kennel. However, if there is no way it can be avoided, duplicate his home surroundings by taking his favorite blanket and toys to help his mental outlook. Changes in environment or feeding routine will add stress to your older dog.

Probably the one sign of old age that every owner recognizes is changes that bones, joints and muscles undergo. The muscles suffer from atrophy and a reduction in their size. Joint lesions result in Spondylosis deformans, a degenerative condition that involves the spinal column and its discs. Most dogs do not reveal any clinical signs of this progressive, chronic disease until pain becomes evident and they become reluctant to move or are paralyzed.

ACTIVITIES AND EXERCISE

Very few Vizsla owners have attended a National Specialty and not had tears in their eyes watching the Veterans' class. This is the class where we honor the "retired" oldsters from the age of 7 and up. They may be champions, or not; they may be gray haired and slow moving, or still active and in their prime. But it gives each dog a chance to remember the companionship, fun, and applause as he is moved and judged in a Field, Conformation, or the Obedience veterans' class. It also gives the novice Vizsla owner a chance to see the dogs they might only have heard about and which influenced and shaped the generations behind the youngsters in competition now.

A Vizsla running in the bird field may keep going until he drops and a wise owner will curtail his older dog's activities to short sessions. Moderate exercise will keep the flexibility in his joints and your dog will make an excellent companion gundog as long as he is not arthritic or ill. It will also make life more interesting for him, especially if he has been put aside in favor of a younger, more active dog.

No older dog should be subjected to strenuous exercise if he invariably winds up appearing physically sore. It is only sensible to treat old age with some consideration, and the dog should not be exercised beyond his normal level of activity. With his failing eyesight and hearing, an older Vizsla may lack the self-confidence of his youth so it is essential that he get extra reassurance that his owner is nearby at all times. Getting the aged dog off the sofa and out for a slow, easy walk on leash will be beneficial to both the dog and his owner.

Swimming is the one exercise with the most beneficial effects, as it strengthens the body in the same way as running without putting any pressure on muscles or joints. If your dog tends to sink, hold him up by placing your arms under his body for support. A dog with partial paralysis from back problems will have to be handled gently, but the animal will benefit from massage of his back and legs, along with the passive movement of the limbs from swimming. Special care must be taken with an older dog to prevent chilling. When wet, he should be toweled dry and kept out of drafts.

An aging dog should never be placed in circumstances which are genuinely dangerous. That means that special treatment, consideration, patience, and thoughtfulness will demand more of the owner's time, and especially from family children. All should share the responsibility of their dog's exercise and health. Unless a dog is weak or has a bad heart, half an hour of activity at a time is a good rule of thumb.

An easy form of exercise for the aging dog is swimming.

PROBLEMS

Bladder problems are common in an older dog. The aging Vizsla that becomes incontinent and dribbles urine as he walks or sleeps may have a deficiency of sex hormones if he or she has been neutered or spayed. A female may have cystitis, a bacterial infection in the lining of the bladder. A urine culture will determine the problem and treatment.

Pain, a sudden suppression of urine with frequent attempts to urinate, depression, thirst, vomiting, and a weakness in the hindlegs,

Right: Ch. Csisckas of Goncoltanya still enjoying a day in the field at eleven years of age.

Below: Dual and AFCh. Rivendell Reaghan, CDX, at nine years of age, is still actively competing at field trials and is also still siring outstanding litters. *Photo courtesy of C. Smith.*

Ch. Cariad's Elkenyestetett, owned by Pat Boelte, enjoys a quiet rest in the warmth of the sun.

could be signs of a lesion called retroflexion, common to older males.

Your Vizsla may not show any obvious signs of kidney problems until he starts to consume a lot more water than usual combined with excessive and frequent urination. The kidneys are bean-shaped organs which are located behind and below the last ribs and near the spinal cord, and no dog can survive without at least one of them properly functioning because they eliminate metabolic wastes. If the kidneys are not working these poisonous wastes will accumulate in the body and death will result if the condition is not treated and arrested. In addition to treatment, your dog may need a special diet. It is highly important also to keep a fresh supply of water available.

Tumors

The incidence of tumors is greatest in dogs over 9 years of age and clinical signs may not be noticed if the tumors are small. Unfortunately, when they reach a large size they become an emergency. Vizslas are no more prone to cancer than any breed, it all just being a matter of chance, as it is with the human population.

A tumor of the kidneys has a greater tendency to develop in the older dog and this is frequently a renal carcinoma located at one of the kidney's poles. If it goes undetected it will metastasize into the lungs, glands, and liver. Blood in the urine, anemia, and a drastic weight loss may be associated with kidney tumors.

A common condition in an older male is senile atrophy of, and tumors in, the testes. In an advanced case his organs will become considerably smaller, and either hard, or soft and flabby. The effects are sterility and an endocrine imbalance. Castrating your older male will help to avoid some of these problems, and can possibly rejuvenate his life.

If your Vizsla bitch was never spayed, as an older dog her uterus can be subject to a number of ailments including metritis, pyometra, hyperplasia, cysts, and tumors. An ovariohysterectomy (spaying) while she is still young will prevent all these problems. Since mammary tumors are related to the ovarian functions the chance of their development would also be lessened. If your bitch does develop a mammary tumor it must be removed as soon as possible.

A large tumor in your Vizsla's spleen will produce an abdominal enlargement which can be felt on the left side behind the stomach. Symptoms will include weakness, weight loss, digestive problems and quite often, a disinclination to move. Your dog may have a tendency to keep sitting due to pressure from fluid in the abdominal cavity.

Sneezing, snorting, and breathing through the mouth can be a sign of a tumor in your dog's nasal cavity. Discharge or bleeding from the nose are also early signs.

Heart Problems

The chances of heart disease in an older Vizsla are quite high. Failure of the blood circulation in your dog's body due to the inability of his heart muscles to function adequately will affect his kidneys, lungs, and liver, causing a multiple organ problem.

Initially, rest and medication to increase urination are the prime requirements since the kidneys slow down their function and retain fluid.

Early symptoms of heart failure may be labored breathing, coughing, and a weak, irregular pulse. With early treatment, your dog can be put on a special salt-free diet, along with drugs to control and stabilize the condition. Limiting exercise will help reduce stress on the heart.

Pancreas

The pancreas is a vital organ, as it produces insulin and enzymes to help digest food in the small intestine. Insufficient output of these enzymes leads to an incomplete breakdown of food. As a result, the food passes through the intestines in a relatively undigested state. Since the dog does not receive nourishment from that food, he loses weight and becomes malnourished and skinny.

Usually the diminishing output of enzymes and loss of function of the pancreas will occur from atrophy as any dog gets older, more inactive, and obese from too much fat in his diet. The pancreas becomes inflamed and in a severe case a dog will have vomiting and intense abdominal pain, followed sometimes by shock and death.

Immediate diagnosis can be made from blood and urine tests, with long-term therapy including daily doses of enzymes to improve the digestive process, along with a sensible diet. If the pancreas does not return to normal, your dog may acquire diabetes.

Diabetes Mellitus

Sugar diabetes results from inadequate insulin production by the pancreas, causing faulty metabolism of sugars and starches. This results in an abnormal rise in the amount of sugar in the dog's urine and blood.

A diabetic dog will eat and drink a lot but still lose weight. His breath may have an odor of acetone due to the formation of acids in the blood. Ulcerations of the cornea, or cataracts, are common. In extreme cases, diabetic coma may occur. Overweight, older bitches are usually those affected and a strict high-fiber diet is necessary to control the blood glucose levels. Diabetes can not be cured, but it can be kept under control by routine urine testing, diet supervision and control, and daily injections of insulin if needed.

EUTHANASIA

We all wish that one day we could just find our beloved old Vizsla "asleep" without him ever having known any of the painful infirmities which advancing age can bring. We have a loving, incredible strong bond with our older dog, the strongest when near the end.

The pain of having to part with a beloved pet is the hardest thing for an owner to do. The death will not exist as an isolated occurrence because when his life comes to an end, so will a part of yours. It will not be just "old dog" that is buried; a very real part of you will go into the grave to keep him company.

Making a decision about euthanasia is the greatest act of love you can show your dog, and the most difficult. You will know when it is time. If your old dog is suffering, you have to accept death as being in his best interest. When the weight of time makes him weary he will be content to have it over. Give him peace for his tired old heart, head, and limbs.

Do not abandon him to strange hands in his last few minutes. No matter how bad your pain, hold him. It only takes a few seconds before his head grows heavy in your hand and his eyes close in sleep.

The pain over losing a "special" old Vizsla never really goes away. It is just that, with time, it is a little easier to bear.

Ch. Cottage Loki Barat CDX retrieves the dumbbell over the high jump.

Appendix I

VCOA Hall of Fame

IN 1978 the VCOA drew up the procedures and requirements for nominating a dog to their Hall of Fame in order to give recognition to Vizslas whose outstanding achievements have brought honor to the breed. The requirements for nomination were that the Vizsla was deemed to have made a significant contribution to the breed through exceptional merit in his own right. The Vizsla had to have been dead for two years before the nomination (this rule was later changed to five years). Two Vizslas are voted into the Hall of Fame each year.

1978
Dual Ch. FUTAKI DAROCZ
FCH and AFCH JODI OF CZUKI BARAT

1979
Dual Ch. BEHI CXINOS CSINY, CD
Dual Ch. WEEDY CREEK LOBO

1980
Ch. CSINOS V HUNT
Fld. Ch. WEEDY CREEK DUTCHESS

1981
Fld. Ch. RIPP BARAT
Dual and AFCH SIR LANCELOT

1982
Dual and AFCH BROOK'S AMBER MIST
Dual Ch. SZEKERES KIS SZERETO

1983
Ch. NIKKI'S ARCO
Dual Ch. REBEL ROUSER DUKE

1984
BROC OLCA
HAANS V SELLE

1985
Dual and AFCH AMBER'S WINDY AUTUMN
Dual and AFCH ROTHAN'S ROZSDA
KISANYA, CD

1986
Ch. GLEN COTTAGE LOKI BARAT, CDX
REBEL ROUSER BANDIETO

1987
Ch. JOHNSON'S TITIAN CHARGER
Ch. MIKLOS SCHLOSS LOOSDORF

1988
1977 and 1978 NFC, Fld., and AFCH
RANDY DUKE

1989
No nominations

1990
No nominations

Appendix II

Sources of Information

CLUBS AND ORGANIZATIONS

The American Kennel Club
51 Madison Ave.
New York, N.Y. 10010

The Canadian Kennel Club
2105 Bloor St. W.
Toronto, Ontario, Canada M6S 4V7

United Kennel Club
100 East Kilgore Rd.
Kalamazoo, MI 49001-5598

States Kennel Club
P.O. Box 389
Hattiesburg, MS 39403-0389

Orthopedic Foundation for Animals
2300 Nifong Blvd.
Columbia, MO 65201

National Dog Registry
Box 116, Dept. AK2
Woodstock, NY 12498-0116

North American Versatile
Hunting Dog Association
1700 N. Skyline Dr.
Burnsville, MN 55337

Vizsla Club of America Inc.
Marge Mehagian, Secretary
7043 N. Central Ave.
Phoenix, AZ 85020

Area Vizsla Clubs

Rio Salado Vizsla Club
Lynne Fickett
3438 E. Las Rocas Dr.
Phoenix, AZ 85028

Central California Vizsla Club
Kathi Parks
2752 Harmon Rd.
Bakersfield, CA 93307

Lone Cypress Vizsla Club
Arline Lovett
330 San Benancio Rd.
Salinas, CA 93908

South Coast Vizsla Club
Phyllis Bruckler
3373 Alma Ave.
Lynwood, CA 90262

Connecticut Valley Vizsla Club
Sandra Jacobus
44 Trails End Dr.
Canton, CT 06019

Tampa Bay Vizsla Club
Marlene Chumbook
405 Pelican Bend
Placida, FL 33946

Vizsla Club of E. Iowa
Steve Laughlin
110 Glen Dr.
Iowa City, IA 52240

Vizsla Club of Illinois
Gwen Tomlinson
513 Thomas Rd.
Bolingbrook, IL 60439

Vizsla Club of Greater New York
Doris Ratzlaff
30 Brandywine Pl.
Oakland, NJ 07436

Vizsla Club of Greater Cleveland
Myra Chudakoff
18265 Rolling Brook Dr.
Bainbridge, OH 44022

Texas Gulf Coast Vizsla Club
Robin Brumer
9238 Norton
Houston, TX 77080

Inland Vizsla Club
Mary DeLuca
W. 2840 Dell Dr.
Spokane, WA 99208

Osage Valley Vizsla Club
Kathy Riske
Rt.1, Box 75F
Edgerton, KS 66021

Trinity Valley Vizsla Club
Linda Lantz
905 Mission Dr.
Southlake, TX 76092

Vizsla Club of Utah
Verla Mortenson
417 E. E.12300 S.
Draper, UT 84020

Old Dominion Vizsla Club
Dave Pomfret
P.O. Box 1265
Orange, VA 22960

Puget Sound Vizsla Club
Jacqueline De Roo
1226 19th Ave. SW
Puyallup, WA 98371

Gateway Vizsla Club
Mary Reeg
13030 Woodley Lane
St. Louis, MO 63128

Vizsla Club of N. California
Nancy Jones
155A States St.
San Francisco, CA 94114

Vizsla Club of S. California
Linda Herz
33005 Barber Rd.
Agua Dulce, CA 91350

Hawkeye Vizsla Club
Paula Abbott
1505 Jackson
Ames, IA 50010

Nebraska Vizsla Club
Leona Dieter
Rt. 6
Lincoln, NE 68502

Vizsla Club of Central New England
Lisa DeForest
Upwind Farm, Pig Pen Corners
New Durham, NH 03855

Conestoga Vizsla Club
A.R. Seelye
7085 Rt.32, River Hill
Clarksville, MD 21029

Vizsla Club of Michigan
Sue Jagoda
1135 Eager Rd.
Howell, MI 48843

Twin Cities Vizsla Club
Debbie Hagen
1920 210th St. E.
Farmington NM 55024

Vizsla Club of N. New Jersey
Lois Smid
111 Hiawatha Blvd.
Oakland, NJ 07436

Miami Valley Vizsla Club
Clif Boggs
51 Cherry Dr.
Springfield, OH 48506

AKC Licensed Show Superintendents

William Antypas
P.O. Box 7131
Pasadena, CA 91109

Jack Bradshaw
P.O. Box 7303
Los Angeles, CA 90022

Norman Brown
P.O. Box 2566
Spokane, WA 99220

Thomas Crowe
P.O. Box 22107
Greensboro, NC 27420

Helen Houser
P.O. Box 420
Quakertown, PA 18951

Ace Matthews
P.O. Box 86130
Portland, OR 97286

Jack Onofrio
P.O. Box 25764
Oklahoma City, OK 73125

Bob Peters
P.O. Box 579
Wake Forest, NC 27587

James Rau
P.O. Box 6898
Reading, PA 19610

Jeannie Roberts
P.O. Box 4658
Federal Way, WA 98063

Kenneth Sleeper
P.O. Box 828
Auburn, IN 46706

Nancy Wilson
8307 E. Camelback Rd.
Scottsdale, AZ 85251

————————Appendix III————————

Recommended Reading

General Knowledge

American Kennel Club, The. *The Complete Dog Book*. New York: 1986.

Bergman, Goran. *Why Does Your Dog do That?* New York: Howell, 1973.

Fox, Michael. *Understanding Your Dog*. New York: Coward, McCann & Geoghegan, 1972.

Maxwell, C.Bede. *The Truth About Sporting Dogs*. New York: Howell, 1972.

Monks of New Skete, The. *How to be Your Dog's Best Friend*. Boston-Toronto: Little, Brown and Co., 1978.

Phaffenberger, Clarence. *The New Knowledge of Dog Behavior*. New York: Howell, 1963.

Smythe, R.H. *The Private Life of the Dog*. New York: Arco, 1965.

Spira, Harold. *Canine Terminology*. New York: Howell, 1982.

Field Training

Long, Paul. *About Training Pointing Dogs.* Slingerlands: Capitol Bird Dog Enterprises, 1974.
Mueller, Larry. *Speed Train Your Own Bird Dog.* Harrisburg: Stackpole, 1990.
Roebuch, Kenneth. *Gun Dog Training, Pointing Dogs.* Harrisburg: Stackpole, 1983.
Seminatore, Mike. *Your Bird Dog and You.* So. Brunswick: A.S.Barnes Publ., 1977.
Tarrant, Bill. *Best Way to Train Your Gun Dog, Delmar Smith Method.* New York: McKay, 1977.
Wolter, Richard. *Game Dog.* New York: E.P. Dutton, 1987.
     Gun Dog. New York: E.P. Dutton, 1961.

Obedience Training

Benjamin, Carol Lea. *Mother Knows Best.* New York: Howell, 1985.
Brunham, Patricia Gail. *Playtraining Your Dog.* New York: St. Martin's Press, 1980.
Pearsall, Milo. *The Pearsall Guide to Successful Dog Training.* New York: Howell, 1974.
Rutherford, Clarice & Neil, David. *How to Raise a Puppy You Can Live With.* Loveland: Alpine, 1989.
Saunders, Blanche. *The Story of Dog Obedience.* New York: Howell, 1974.
Volhard, Joachim & Fisher, Gail. *Training Your Dog, The Step-by-Step Manual.* New York: Howell, 1983.

Show Ring Training

Brown, M.H. & Mason, B. *The New Complete Junior Showmanship Handbook.* New York: Howell, 1980.
Forsythe, Robert & Jane. *Forsythe Guide to Successful Dog Showing.* New York: Howell, 1978.

Structure and Movement

Elliott, Page. *The New Dog Steps.* New York: Howell, 1983.
Lyon, McDowell. *The Dog in Action.* New York: Howell, 1966.

Breeding and Genetics

Holst, Phyllis D.V.M. *Canine Reproduction.* Loveland: Alpine, 1985.
Lee, Muriel. *Whelping and Rearing of Puppies.* Minneapolis: Plantin, 1988.
Scott, John Paul & Fuller, John. *Genetics and the Social Behavior of the Dog.* Chicago: Univ. of Chicago Press, 1965.
Serranne, Ann. *The Joy of Breeding Your Own Show Dog.* New York: Howell, 1980.

Nutritional and Medical Reference

Carlson, Delbert D.V.M. & Griffin, James M.D. *Dog Owner's Home Veterinary Handbook.* New York: Howell, 1980.
Collins, Donald. *The Collins Guide to Dog Nutrition.* New York: Howell, 1976.

Levy, Juliette de Bairacli. *The Complete Herbal Book for the Dog.* New York: Arco, 1973.
Merck Veterinary Manual, sixth edition. Rahway: Merck, 1986.
Pitcairne, Richard D.V.M. & Susan. *Natural Health for Dogs and Cats.* Emmaus: Rodale, 1982.

Breed Books

Boggs, B.C. *The Vizsla.* Ohio: Greenbrier, revised edition 1982.
Strauz, John & Cunningham, Joseph. *Your Vizsla,* Fairfax: Denlinger, 1973.

Ch. Taunee's Loki Santana, CD, top winning Vizsla on record with seven Best in Shows, shown with author Marion Coffman.

About the Author

MARION COFFMAN began her career with dogs in 1963 with a Golden Retriever which she trained in obedience. A year later she began instructing obedience classes, and went on to judge at matches.

Coffman obtained her first Vizsla in 1967, training him for both obedience and conformation ring. This dog, Glen Cottage Loki Barat, soon gained his championship title and went on to be accepted in the Vizsla Club of America Hall of Fame for his tremendous contribution to the breed.

Marion began breeding Vizslas in 1969, in limited numbers, and always with the betterment of the breed foremost in mind. Since then she has bred over 90 champion Vizslas under the Cariad name, including triple champion Cariad's Kutya Kai Costa. Cariad has provided foundation stock for numerous successful Vizsla breeders in the United States and Canada.

Coffman has also put a UDT and two CDX degrees on Vizslas, titled over 38 dogs, including a Top Winning American Foxhound and one Junior Hunter Title, and is currently training a dog for Senior Hunter.

She has been active in a number of kennel clubs as obedience and show handling instructor, board member, and other offices. She is a member of the Vizsla Club of America and the Magyar Vizsla Club, and the Greater Ocala Kennel Club, among others.

She has authored pamphlets on whelping, puppy rearing, showing, and other subjects, and continues to be active in the show ring. She resides in Ocala, Florida, with her husband.

Looking for more information to help you with your dog?

The following titles may be purchased at your local bookstore or pet supply outlet, or ordered direct.

How to Raise a Puppy You Can Live With
2nd edition
Rutherford and Neil

Skin and Haircoat Problems in Dogs
Ackerman

Owner's Guide to Better Behavior in Dogs
2nd edition
William Campbell

Beyond Basic Dog Training Workbook
Bauman, Santo, Zurburg

All Breed Dictionary of Unusual Names
Jarrett

Canine Reproduction, A Breeder's Guide
Holst

Positively Obedient
Handler

The Art and Business of Professional Grooming
Walin

For a Free Catalog
or information on other Alpine Dog Books, please write or call
our Customer Service Department.
Alpine Publications, P.O. Box 7027, Loveland, CO 80537
1-800-777-7257

Index